Gang Ranch
The Real Story

Judy Alsager

In Appreciation
Judy Alsager

Bluedoor
publishing

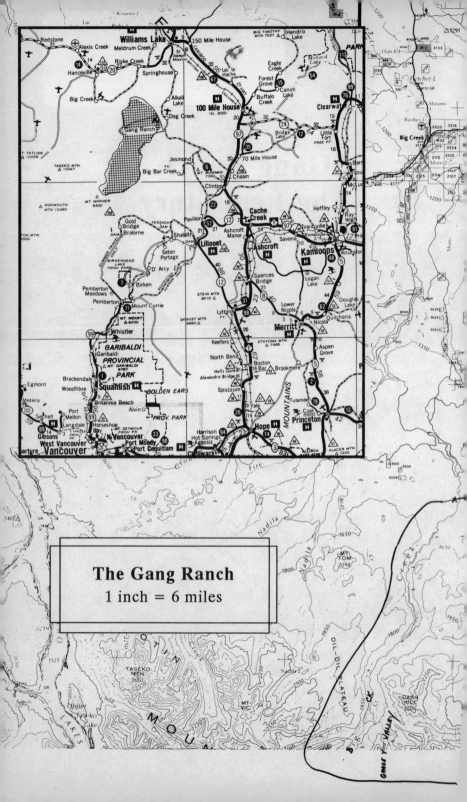

The Gang Ranch

1 inch = 6 miles

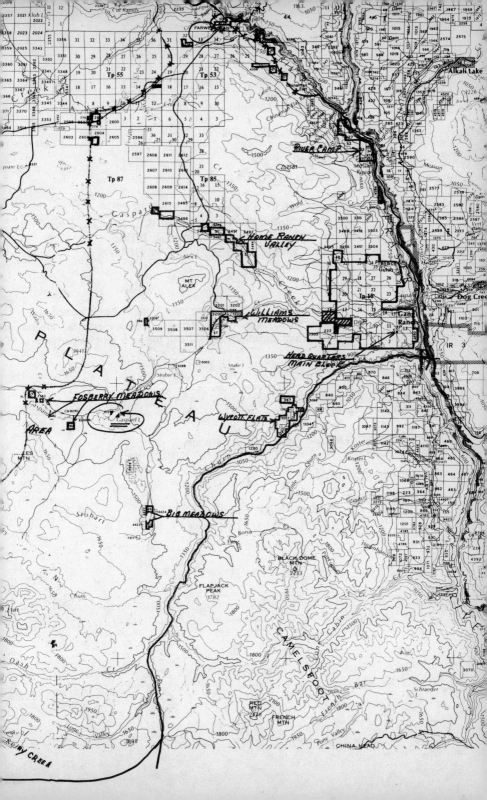

ISBN 0-9682283-0-8
Copyright © 1994 Judy Alsager

First Revised Edition 1997

Cataloging in Publication Data
Alsager, Judy, 1950
    Gang Ranch
    ISBN 0-9682283-0-8

1. Alsager, Judy, 1950 - Family. Gang Ranch (B.C.)
3. Ranch life - British Columbia - Cariboo (B.C.: Regional district)
4. Ranchers - British Columbia - Biography. I. Title
FC3845.C3Z49 1994 636.2'01'0971175 C94-910739-5
F1089.C3A47 1994

Edited: Carolyn Bateman
Illustrations: Leisa Dowler

Cover photo: Oren Alsager on Tall Timber

Published in Canada by
Bluedoor Box 4563
—*publishing*— Williams Lake, B.C.
    Fax: Phone: 250-747-8402

Contents

Ode to the Gang Ranch

It starts at Lorna Lake so deep,
High in the mountains, where the rocky sheep
Drink her green, green waters from the rocks
so steep
The headwaters of mighty Big Creek.

Big Creek flows so cold and clear,
Alpine meadows with grazing deer,
Grizzlies walk without any fear,
Graveyard cabin is a haven here.

Graveyard sleeps in the mountain sun,
Her doors are open to everyone,
Long live peace, and long live God,
And long live Graveyard with her roof of sod.
It leaves the valley and on it goes,
Down through the swamps to the lowlands it flows;
To Fish Lake where the trout jump high,
Wolves are howling to the sky.

Hungry Valley, so serene,
A lonely valley—deep and green,
Strawberries, mushrooms growing wild,
Feeding each lost and weary child.

On to Blue Door, over the pass,
I worship your silence, lying in the grass;
Fosberry Meadows welcoming me,
I'm feeling fine, so happy to be free.
Gaspard Dam, where old Chilco Choate
Keeps a watch; you can tell by the articles he wrote;
Trout, moose, and bear, he counts them everyday
To make sure the Gang Ranch isn't stealing them
away.

Up the China Freeway, you've got to be brave
Or the muck will pull you down till there's nothing
left to save,
On to Williams Meadow where the bluebells ring,
Showing you the way to Bear Springs.

Bear Springs sits above the clouds,
Coyotes are a-runnin' and the buffalo cows
Wander free while their calves are a-bouncin' around
Down through the trees to Broken Ground.

Bear Springs, Bear Springs, you set my soul free,
I've wandered on your hillsides,
I've talked to your trees,
Your sunsets have brought me to my knees,
Lord—don't you ever make me leave.

J. Alsager

Foreword

I thought it quite strange that I would be asked to write the foreword to Judy's book for, you see, I was the lawyer who was unsuccessful in defending the Alsager family (except Dale) against the claims of the Canadian Imperial Bank of Commerce (CIBC) under guarantees given to the CIBC by the Alsager family and their related companies.

The case against the Alsagers was based on guarantees (and security pledged for those guarantees) given in support of loans made by the CIBC to Alsager Holdings Ltd. Alsager Holdings Ltd. was owned by the family and was the purchaser and owner of all the lands, premises, equipment, and cattle commonly called the Gang Ranch.

As usual, going into the purchase, the Alsagers were excited and enthusiastic about becoming the owners of the "worlds largest ranch" especially since the deal that Dale had negotiated effectively allowed the family to lever the purchase almost 100 percent. Again, as usual, the enthusiasm of the family clouded the fact that in order to buy the Gang Ranch with little or no cash down the family would literally have to "bet the ranch." Each member of the family pledged all of their own personal real estate assets; assets which had taken each of them a lifetime to accumulate.

In all of the transactions leading to the purchase of the Gang Ranch and its administration afterward, the family placed their complete trust and confidence in Dale and relied on the CIBC to protect their interests as guarantors of Alsager Holdings' borrowings. The story you are about to read tells how this trust and reliance was misplaced and the consequences of same. For not only did the family lose all of their real estate assets to the CIBC, but a close and loving family was torn apart in such a manner that time will probably never heal the rift.

What follows is the true story of the Alsager's high times and low times at the Gang Ranch and afterward.

GEORGE DAVIS

Preface

This book had to be written.
There was no choice.

In 1990, Hancock House Publishers published a book called *The Incredible Gang Ranch*, written by Dale Alsager. For reasons unable to be established, I feel no research was undertaken regarding the authenticity of the material printed in the book, and no effort was made to verify the facts.

This book now sits in stores, service stations, resorts across more than one country and, worst of all, in the history section of public libraries and school libraries.

The book *The Incredible Gang Ranch* is not a true account of what happened on the famous Gang Ranch during the "Alsager Era." The following story *Gang Ranch: The Real Story* has been written to tell the truth.

The facts in this book *have* been researched.

JUDY ALSAGER

Acknowledgments

To my parents Ted and Irene Alsager, for allowing your strength and unfailing faith to carry yourselves and all of us through the toughest test of our lives.

To my brother Oren, who was my guiding influence in this book, with your memories, photos, and tapes. Thank you for leaving behind your laughter for us on a tape, and your wonderful and cherished paintings.

To my brother Rick, and his wife Suzanne, for being such survivors, and always being there when I needed you. Without your unselfish support, we would surely have starved. Thank you for the beautiful memories of our time together on the Gang.

To my four children Shan, Buffy, Dusty, and Lacey, for following me and supporting me unquestioningly down every chaotic path I have chosen. You were my strength. You have all grown up strong and honest and independent; I am proud of you. Thank you, Buffy, for your excellent job of proofreading and editing and constructive criticism. Thank you, Lacey, for possessing such unique artistic talents and ideas.

To Richard Keep for loving me, dancing with me, and surrounding me with your laughter and your fantastic sense of humor. Thank you for stabilizing my chaotic life, so that I could write this book.

To George Davis, for answering without hesitation my every call for help over the past twelve years. Without you, I surely would have been in jail long ago.

Posthumously, to Darly Germyn, for literally forcing me to write the first draft of this book.

To all the wonderful people whose paths crossed mine on the Gang Ranch—I will never forget you. Especially the people who were born there, lived their entire lives there, and now have had to leave. Special thanks to Old Jimmy for your invaluable and unspoken lessons on life.

To Stephanie and Beth, for your never-ending support, and your assistance in jogging my memory about dates and details for this book.

Introduction:
The Alsager Family

We were flatlanders—prairie oysters, gophers, hayseeds—born on the flat prairies of sturdy Scandinavian parents. My father, Ted Alsager, was Norwegian, and my mother, Irene, was Swedish. I am one of their five children. Some time after their marriage in 1941, my father bought the "Fulton Place" at Maidstone, Saskatchewan, and commenced to build up and expand a successful farming operation in the Idanell district south of town.

We spent our childhood doing prairie things—digging out from under the howling blizzards, making sure the firewood box was full to keep warm, battling grasshoppers and bertha army worms, picking wild saskatoons, pin cherries, chokecherries, and cranberries. We went to a country school and fought and toughed our way through the baseball games and the war games. We played kick-the-can, fox and goose, and auntie-I-over, and swung from ropes in the hayloft; we rode bicycles and horses all over the countryside. We went to the country dances and giggled in the cloakroom; we learned which kids would get too excited and throw up on the stage at the Christmas concert. We learned to go out and gorge ourselves on chokecherries the day before the traveling dentist came to town, so that we would be "sick" the next day. We circulated throughout the neighborhood in groups, the Donald kids, the Tuplin kids, the Wiltermuth kids, the Mitchell kids, the Alsager kids. The Mitchells were particular favorites of mine. Heather, Marcia, and Lorne Mitchell and I would flock across the field to Grandma Mitchell's for freshly baked shortbread. The path to Grandma Mitchell's was a mile-long sandy, winding trail with grass growing in the middle of it. Even today, I will travel many miles to find a trail that has grass growing in the middle—there aren't many left.

Our country school was called the Idanell School, named for two pioneer ladies of the community: Ida Pickle and Nell (Grandma) Mitchell. At the most, there were twelve or thirteen students in various grades. Mine was the largest class; there were three of us, and for some unknown reason this seemed to be of some elevating importance to us. Fights were always "east against west," the kids that lived east of the one-room schoolhouse would fight the kids that lived to the west. We Alsager kids were right on the dividing line, we lived beside the school. This put us in the prime position of being able to take whichever side had the best chance of coming out on top in any particular skirmish. The district kids were territorial. We fought each other until someone from another territory or, worse yet, a "town kid," would insult one of "ours." Then we would immediately band together against the intruder.

We grew up happy. In high school, we were all given aptitude tests to help steer us in the direction of our best abilities. Mine indicated that I should become a forest ranger. My face went crimson as the whole class, including the teacher, laughed at this seeming impossibility. In those days, girls were supposed to choose between three options: teacher, nurse, or secretary.

Upon graduating, most of us couldn't wait to get to the city with our great anticipations. Some, like myself, then spent the next years of our lives trying to figure out how to get back *out* of the city. I took a business course in Edmonton, but to this day, I am obsessed with the forest.

In the city, we country kids may as well have worn a stamp on our foreheads saying "country hick." The knitted Siwash sweaters gave us away, or maybe it was that faraway look in our eyes. I did not know what pizza was. I did not know that you had to step down onto the steps in the transit bus to make the doors open when you wanted to get off. I did not know what to say when the waiter in a fancy

14

restaurant asked me what kind of salad dressing I wanted. After thinking for a minute, I asked for "the kind that goes on lettuce." He tactfully asked, "Can I recommend Thousand Island?" to which I replied, "Where's that?" It was the same with the sour cream on the potatoes. I could not comprehend anyone wanting to put sour cream on their potatoes. I had visions of that lumpy, yellowish mass in the big milk jar at home that Mom allowed to sour, and which I had always carried as far away from my body as my arms would allow when I took it to feed to the chicks. By now the weary and stiff-faced waiter looked long and hard at my Siwash sweater and discreetly moved on to another table, where no one wore such a sweater.

My parents were happy people—happy with each other, their five children, their neighbors, their community, and their honest, hardworking country life. If we grew up a tad naive, it was the product of that simple life. Now that I am grown, I see people everywhere striving to recapture the sort of life we took for granted. We knew nothing else. These were the best of times, before the world seemingly lost its sense of innocence. We had it all—we just didn't know that we did.

The Alsager family was very close. There were no quarrels in the days of growing up on the Maidstone farm. My father, Ted, is one of those salt-of-the-earth, fiddle-playing prairie farmers who automatically acquires respect. I don't recall ever hearing my father so much as raise his voice. His heavy horse team stepped in time to his lively whistling and the jingling of the harness, as he hauled his hay out to feed his prize Herefords. He was a man who operated totally in an atmosphere of mutual respect—toward the animals he raised and the people he dealt with. Growing up as he did, in that era when a handshake between two people was adequate, sufficient, and sacred, he once bought an entire farm from his neighbor and not a single paper was signed; they shook hands, slapped each other on the back, and went away knowing they had a firm, fair deal.

15

My father raised purebred Hereford cattle, his pride and joy, but I can remember being involved with nearly every kind of animal on the farm: sheep, pigs, rabbits, horses, chickens, turkeys, ducks, geese. My brother Oren even had a tame fox that he never caged up. Sandy the fox followed Oren everywhere, even slept curled up around Oren's neck. He remained with us for a few years, enjoying full privileges as the family pet. Then came the day when he pricked up his ears, sniffed the air with a very interested twinkle in his black eyes, and moved out into the field where a pretty lady fox waited. No one denied him this decision, and periodically he came back near the yard, giving us the odd glimpse of some new little creations of his— playful reddish fox kits that fearlessly tumbled over each other in an effort to be first in line behind their strutting father.

My mother, Irene, was the perfect match for my father. She was quiet, strong, supportive, and totally capable in every aspect of the countless duties, expected and otherwise, of being the wife of a prairie farmer. She knew the best berry-picking places, and exactly which day to go before the birds got the just-ripened fruit. She knew when to step in and help, and when to stand back and keep quiet. When catastrophes happened, as they always will, her sense of humor would take over. My parents lived only for the good things in life, and this did not include money or power. What was important to them were the people in their lives. We did not know what a dishonest person was, there simply weren't any. I would not say we were rich people—not in the financial sense of the word—but we had all we needed or desired. My parents never spent money senselessly, but they saw to it that their children all had music lessons, that we all belonged to the 4-H club (my father was a 4-H leader for thirty-five years), and that we all were given the necessary ingredients to advance our growing interests. They saw to it that we each had a cow to milk, butter to churn, potatoes to plant, in other words enough chores to hopefully cram some sense of responsibility into us.

It amazes me now that through all my growing-up years, I don't think I ever heard my parents criticize or discredit anyone in any way. They never gossiped and were not interested in rumors, so no one bothered to tell them any. Entertainment was the old-time country dances held at the schoolhouse, where we learned to dance the polka, the two-step, the shauteese, and old-time waltzes. We gyrated, twirled, and hopped around the squeaky planked schoolhouse floor with grandfathers and grandmothers, babies, our brothers and sisters, the town drunk, the kid we beat up yesterday—anything that had legs that could move. Everyone knew better than to disturb the jumble of coats that were piled in the corners—there would undoubtedly be a sleeping baby or two tucked in there somewhere. Cracker boxes filled with egg salad sandwiches made with thick homemade bread, jars of homemade pickles, cardboard containers of cakes and goodies, jugs of Kool-aid and pots of hot coffee filled a stout-legged wooden table in the corner, and there was never anything left to take home.

I loved the tough beauty of the prairies: the crisp crackling of the harsh unforgiving winters; the way a heavy snow piled up on the fenceposts and branches; the blackness of the water beneath the ice when we chopped water holes for the horses to drink from; even the beauty and excitement of the prairie blizzards. Spring was so welcome afterward, when the sweet humus smell of new leaves in the willow thickets filled the countryside, and brave purple crocuses popped right up through the snow. There were long, soft, lingering sunsets in harvest-time, when the haze hung in the air over the grain fields, and you could actually smell the fat wheat kernels in their bulging hulls. There was the day the first birds came back in the spring. We would sit and watch carefully through the weeds for the "sump pump" bird—the gulping bittern who stood on one knobby-kneed leg with his pointed beak in the air just like another

17

slough weed. The only time you could spot him was when he "gulped" and his adam's apple bobbled up and down. I spent many hours sitting in my little refuge on top of the pigpen, chin resting on skinned knees, gazing at the line of blue hills in the distance; I don't know what I saw there, but I couldn't quit looking.

I had three brothers and one sister. Donna was the oldest and was out of school and away to nurse's training when I was only seven. She married Ken Smulan, a farmer from southern Saskatchewan. Ken was a wonderful person, but I spent their entire wedding day in tears because I sensed the inevitable changes in the family, and the distance she would be away from us. She and Ken proceeded to build up over the years a successful cattle operation at Wawota, Saskatchewan, and a family of five children. Donna was full of fun and full of music, and became very valuable and appreciated in her community and area as an accomplished music teacher and performer.

Dale was a year younger than Donna, so he too left home when I was quite young. My most vivid memories of him come from times when all of us sat around to shuck peas. He was the "clown" of the group. When we were sent out to the berry patches, he could pick his required pail of berries faster than anyone. We couldn't figure out how he would finish so quickly, until we discovered that he would fill the bottom half of his pail with leaves and just put a layer of berries on the top to cover them. He was a mastermind at figuring out ways to persuade the rest of us to milk his cow, as well as our own. Farming was definitely not for him, and he hit for the city as soon as he was out of school. He worked for a while at the Co-op Store, packing groceries, and eventually went to university in Edmonton. He worked at the *Edmonton Journal* and married a red-headed Edmonton girl named Betty Leard in her last year of high school. Dale and Betty had four children in the ensuing years.

Rick was six years younger than Dale, and a year older

18

than me. I spent my childhood tagging after him wherever he went. I got to haul the water to the gopher holes to flush the creatures out, and I would be the "fetcher" in duck and goose season for the unlucky ones that came tumbling out of the sky. Anyone who dared to hurt me must have really wanted to, because they knew they would get a licking from Rick afterward. Rick followed in his father's footsteps and grew up to be the totally capable farmer of the family. After high school, he attended the College of Agriculture in Vermilion, Alberta, and later married Suzanne Stoughton, who had grown up on her family's farm at Maidstone. They settled in at the Alsager farm and eventually had four children. Suzanne is one of those miracle women who can bake three batches of cookies, wallpaper two rooms, milk the cow, feed the animals, shoot a trophy deer, and have a six-course meal ready for supper—all done before breakfast. With Rick and Suzanne, and my parents at the helm, the ranch at Maidstone flourished and prospered.

My father was an orphan. Unlike others who inherit land and a start in farming, he began from scratch and, through sheer hard work and good management, he and Rick built up and expanded his original purchase to a well-respected and efficiently run purebred Hereford and grain operation. This operation later became Idanell Korner Ranch, set up with the original family members as shareholders: Ted, Irene, Donna, Dale, Rick, Judy, and Oren. The idea was that with this setup, Dad could eventually turn the farm over to Rick by having him purchase the shares, and avoid the inevitable tax situation that would occur with a sale.

I went away to Edmonton after graduating from high school, where I took a business course at the Northern Alberta Institute of Technology. After completing this, I got a job at the university in the department of mathematics, completed my Grade 9 in Conservatory Piano and worked during the day and taught music lessons at night at the ABC Music School. I lived in the city, and worked at various jobs over the next couple of years, but always with dreams of forested mountains somewhere in the back of my mind. Eventually, I met and married Denis Rivard, and we moved into his grandfather's big old-fashioned house on what became our 160-acre Laying R Poultry Farm south of Edmonton, near Leduc. His family farmed across the road, good, honest country people that I grew to love very much. Over the next five years, Denis and I brought four bundles home from the hospital—each one as cherished as the last. We applied for an egg quota and went into the business of producing eggs and growing feed. These were happy, busy times.

Oren was the youngest Alsager offspring, six years my junior, and grew up thoroughly loved and doted on by the rest of us. I think that's why he grew up to be so compassionate and personable. People and animals meant a great deal to him. Sensitive and caring, he remained that way throughout the short number of years he was allotted on this earth. He was one of those special people who put other people's needs and desires ahead of his own. His eternal sense of humor and personality opened doors for him that would be denied to more important people. Oren loved the bush and nature, and after he was out of school, he obtained his flying licence, which enabled him to join his good friend, Lloyd McMahon, on many and varied expeditions. One of their joint ventures was a hunting lodge in Alberta. Oren was an accomplished photographer, a talented artist, and an adventurer. His roving life took him from the Arctic Circle Lodge to the Gulf of Mexico. His quest was not for money or fame, but to simply be able to laugh, and to show his respect for the beauty of the world and the people around him. His philosophy of life was: "If you can't laugh about it, it's not worth it."

Ten years later, I still find it hard to believe it has all happened. I assess the damage: three generations of the Alsager family have lost everything they ever had and worked for, and my parents have had to watch helplessly as

20

their close-knit family became tragically unglued, caught up in an alien world of high finance and legal procedures. My husband and I lost everything we ever had and worked for, including our marriage; one brother is dead, another brother is lost to us; the remaining brother Rick is struggling to survive despite his crippling losses; all of us trying to recover from the stress of learning that our legal system and banking system are one and the same—corrupt beyond repair. We have had to change our way of thinking and living. We believed before in our country, our justice system, and the basic honesty of other human beings. We have learned that all we believed in was wrong.

The Canadian Imperial Bank of Commerce took it all—the Gang Ranch and its numerous properties, the Idanell Korner Ranch at Maidstone, Saskatchewan, our Laying R Poultry Farm at Leduc, Alberta, thriving operations that had no previous debt. While we struggled to stay on our feet from blow after reeling blow, Oren's short but glamorous twenty-six years were brought to a crushing halt in a tragic plane crash, and made our other problems seem insignificant. Shortly thereafter, still numbed by the tremendous void he left behind, we sat in stunned silence as we learned from an investigation into our operation that the financial end of our entire business was in a well-concealed, covered-up shambles. The local bank manager disappeared into thin air, receivers took over, we were thrown into bankruptcy, and Dale Alsager was arrested. The charge? Seventy-two counts of fraud, embezzlement, and cattle theft.

Ten years later, we are a lot more street-wise than we were back then. We have met every money-grabbing lawyer across three provinces, and have spent almost as much time in court fighting lawyers as we have fighting the bank. The court cases still go on today. I am the only woman I know of that has her own personal process server. He has served me so many summons, subpoenas, and court orders that I probably singlehandedly keep his business thriving. We

21

know every MLA, attorney general, minister, government official, inspector general of banks, and top brass of the Bank of Commerce from here to Toronto, and have concluded that our entire system is a circus of uselessness.

Out of the ashes, the seeds are regrouping and beginning to sprout again, stronger than ever. What happened, happened for a reason, and I believe it was a lesson to us to appreciate the finer things in life—the humorous incidents that are sprinkled along the paths of our lives, the good memories, the beauty of true friendships, and the people—especially the people.

The Gang Ranch

In 1977, the Alsager family was seriously contemplating purchasing the famed Gang Ranch in the Cariboo region of central British Columbia. Our family corporation of Idanell Korner Ranch was continuing to move along successfully. We had already branched out with the purchase of some buffalo and elk, even a pair of musk-oxen, and the need was felt for some investment and expansion. The Gang Ranch *sounded* like a good investment: an historic ranch bordering the west side of the Fraser River, with some 38,000 deeded acres, plus approximately 700,000 acres under lease.

The Gang Ranch was rich with history, dating back to the 1800s when Jerome and Thaddeus Harper, two handlebar mustachioed brothers fleeing from the law, rode from the States northward across the safety of the Canadian border, pushing into the interior grazing lands of British Columbia. They took over a vast empire of land to be known as the Gang Ranch. It acquired this name from a horse-drawn, land-breaking implement called the "gang plough" that was brought over from England and first used on the immense ranch. The Gang Ranch, at one time, encompassed some 4 million acres, all told, the majority of this area being lease land. The Kelly Lake Ranch and the presently operating Harper Ranch at Kamloops were once part of the Gang Ranch, as was the Perry Ranch right along the highway three miles out of Cache Creek. This 17,000-acre feedlot and haying operation was still an important part of the Gang Ranch. Still part of the Ranch when we purchased it were the 57 Mile properties, the Sullivan Pastures, and Meadow Lake properties, located along the road to Clinton, on the other side of the Fraser River from the main Ranch itself. Crows Bar was also part of the Gang Ranch on the other side of the river—a beautiful but not easily accessible 6,000 acre grazing area downriver from the main ranch in the Big Bar area. Crows Bar's mild climate allows for winter grazing for 700 head of cattle. These outlying properties of the Gang in those days were stopping-off places for the rugged cattle drives from the Gang Ranch to the Kamloops rail line.

Numerous Chinese people, who had drifted through the area following the building of the railway, inhabited the Gang Ranch area at that time. Their hand gold-panning operations and well-tended vegetable gardens dotted the banks of the Fraser River. They moved water from one area to another, sometimes miles and miles, in overhead "ditches"—wooden flumes, downhill chutes, built on top of periodic wooden supports, all hand labor. The flumes, although broken and rotted in places, still stand as a monument to their resourcefulness. Numerous Chinese utensils, such as deep round wooden spoons, metal soup ladles, and bowls, are still found along the Fraser River. What were mere necessities to them are now valuable artifacts to us.

Although the Chinese inhabited the Gang Ranch area first, the Harper brothers arrived to do business—establish a flourishing cattle empire. The story goes that when the time rolled around when it was possible to obtain proper paper land titles for the land that people were on, a race of sorts took place. The Chinese left on foot for the nearest land office (in the town of Clinton, some 100 kilometers from the Ranch area), but the Harpers definitely had the advantage on their saddlehorses. The Harpers filed for a

Crown Grant Application on 160 acres of land in the center of what is now known as the Home Ranch Valley on the Gang Ranch. Jerome Harper applied for the JH brand, which is now one of the most historic brands in the cattle industry. Animals on the Gang Ranch today still carry this famous brand. In their financial struggle to hang on to the growing giant, they took on English partners and formed the Western Canadian Ranching Co. Ltd. The Harpers had a struggle on the Gang Ranch, physically and financially. It did not help matters when Jerome was kicked in the head by a horse, and became generally disabled, leaving Thaddeus with the basic responsibility of holding things together. They were eventually taken over by the English company and, after their deaths, the Ranch remained in control of the Western Canadian Ranching Co. Ltd. The Chinese settled into the peaceful role of laborers on the Ranch, and farming the individual homestead areas. In retrospect, they were probably the lucky ones—able to enjoy the blissful beauty of the Ranch without the stress and constant struggle of trying to hang on to it. Historically, the mighty Gang Ranch has the reputation of virtually destroying everyone who has owned it. It makes me smile inside to think how the matriarch Gang Ranch has outsmarted her various ambitious and sometimes greedy owners over the years, even up to today. They could pluck the rose, but they couldn't make it bloom.

In 1947, the Gang Ranch changed hands again, this time to American owners Floyd Skelton and Bill Studdert from Idaho Falls. It was never smooth sailing for these two ranching partners, either. They slogged their way through rocky times: plummeting cattle prices, diseases, droughts that left them short of feed, and a myriad of management problems resulting from being absentee owners. In 1971, Bill Studdert passed away, leaving Floyd Skelton trying to run the Ranch from his home in the States. He put it up for sale. The Ranch now consisted of a million acres, including the lease lands.

It was a challenging enterprise. Dale learned that the Ranch could be purchased at that time for a "once-in-a-lifetime" deal. We were negotiating in the neighborhood of $4 million for the entire operation, including all land, livestock, and machinery. The Gang had been appraised at $15 million—$8,300,000; the Perry Ranch land and buildings at $2,500,000; the equipment at $1,118,000; feed and other Ranch supplies at $667,000; and the livestock at $2,500,000—(we were to discover later just how meaningless the word "appraisal" is) but it was in a rundown condition, with the surviving owner living across the line in the U.S. Our objective was to spend approximately five years uplifting and making improvements toward resale. If there were any problems within the family during that time, we all agreed the Gang Ranch would be put up for sale immediately. It wasn't worth risking any family rifts.

We all had lots to think about. Mom and Dad's Idanell Korner Ranch would be put up as collateral—everything they and Rick and Suzanne had ever worked for. Denis and I had lots to think about, too. Our 160-acre Laying R operation in Alberta was also being put up as collateral. It was appraised at $600,000, and we knew that by signing the personal guarantees required, we were essentially putting at stake everything we had.

Denis and I felt under incredible pressure. Although Mom and Dad were being very quiet and cautious, everyone else was excited and raring to go. Our refusal to put up our collateral would mean that the Gang Ranch deal would not go forward. It was a tough call: would we be saving ourselves from making a big mistake? Or would we be missing out on an adventurous chance of a lifetime? There seemed to be more pros than cons, and all the "worst scenario" situations had been contemplated, hashed, and rehashed. The projections looked good, we had comfortable appraisals, the buying price was a "deal," Dale and Rick would have joint signing authority on the company account. What was there to worry about? Life is full of

26

changes and chances. The hardest thing would be to leave behind our friends and Denis's family.

My first trip to the Gang Ranch was in the late fall of 1977. For Denis and I, this was to be a decision-making journey. I think Rick had pretty much made up his mind to go ahead with the purchase and building up of the famous monster, but Denis and I were holding back a little. This would definitely be an isolated life. Our children were all small: Shan was four, Buffy was three, Dusty was two, and I was pregnant again. What would life be like for them growing up on this ranch out in the middle of nowhere. Would there be enough other children for them to interact with? What would the school be like? Would they miss out on the benefits of organized hockey, dancing, music lessons, etc.? What if they got sick out there? How would I get help for them quickly? We had worked hard to get our egg operation to the point it was now at. The new barn had been built, new equipment had been installed, and the new feed mill was grinding away to make our own feed. Things were up and running. And I didn't know if I could leave the good friends that had become such an integral part of our lives.

We left to tour the Gang Ranch from the prairies, where we set off in Mom and Dad's new vehicle. They had picked Denis and I and our children up on the way, and Rick and Suzanne were traveling along with us in their truck. We drove to Kamloops, B.C., then on to Clinton. Just past Clinton, we turned off at a place called 58 Mile to head in to the Gang Ranch. Somehow I thought we were almost there. A good deal of the property we drove by belonged to the Gang Ranch: 57 Mile, Sullivan Pastures, Meadow Lake properties. We went on and on and on, past trees and lakes, past the Canoe Creek Indian Reserve, across wide expanses of sagebrush and grazing lands. Dust clouds rolled up behind us; there was a compulsion to keep moving faster so none of that nose-clogging powder would catch up to us. I began to wonder if this place even existed, as we had stopped to ask directions from a lady at 58 Mile who had lived there "for years" and claimed she had never heard of the Gang Ranch.

Just when I thought it was never going to happen, Rick stopped his truck ahead of us, waited for the interminable dust cloud to overcome us and settle, then walked back to lean into the driver's window. "Well, there it is," he said, pointing across what we realized then to be the mighty Fraser River down below the snaking switchback road we were on. There was silence as everyone stretched out the windows, squinting to get a better look at the vast expanse beyond us, our dust-filled eyes traveling down to the river then up the other side. Way off in the distance we could barely see a cluster of tiny buildings, nestled like toy Monopoly houses and hotels amidst a panorama of endless hills. But at least we knew now that it existed and we actually had a destination in sight. Eagerly, we headed off. Again, I thought we were almost there when we began to career around sharp switchback corners; Denis was driving and seemed to be having a hard time with every sharp corner he came to.

"I think there's something wrong with your steering," he said, turning to Dad. Dad's car was brand new and apparently did not have the bugs worked out of it yet. After barely making it around the switchback corners a few more times, Denis gave up the steering wheel. "I think you'd better drive, Ted," he said as he climbed out of the driver's seat. "I don't want to be the one to smash up your new car!"

We continued on our haphazard journey around those zigzag turns. Dad seemed to be wrestling to get his car around the corners just as much as Denis had been. The closer we got to the edge each time, the easier it was for us to look down, way, way, down, and take note of the rocks and the old and rusted vehicles draped over the boulders down below, in various stages of decay. I wondered what had happened to the people in those mangled vehicles. I

28

couldn't see any way for them to get back up that steep cliff. Were they decaying down there, too? Mom was thinking along the same lines, I knew, because she was starting to give me long, sidelong looks that said, "What are we doing here?"

"I think it's these new brakes, maybe they haven't been set up properly yet," Dad grunted as he twisted in his seat to get the car around the corner. Mom and I were in the back seat with the kids, Shan, Buffy, and Dusty, but we may as well have been in the front. Our necks were craning around the headrests of the front seat trying to see the next switchback, and by pure motherly instinct, I guess, began to gather the children protectively on to our laps. The renegade car came to the next switchback, Dad began to crank the steering wheel, and we knew we weren't going to make it.

The next thing I was conscious of was standing on the road in the swirling dust with Dusty in my arms, and Shan clinging on to my hand. Through the dust, I saw Mom also standing on the road, clutching Buffy. We looked for the car we had just bailed out of and it was still there, at least the back half of it was. The front half was hanging over the cliff, front wheels spinning freely in space.

Dad was in an agitated state and in a panic to get the car back on to the road. From behind the wheel, he motioned Denis to the front of the car. "Just give me a push backwards," he called out. Denis, in his excitement, headed toward the front of the car, came to the edge of the cliff, then turned to Dad. "What would you like me to stand on? There's only air out there!"

Dad climbed out of the driver's door, and he and Denis stood beside the car taking stock of the situation as men always do when vehicle problems crop up. They walked from one side of the teetering car, around the back, and up the other side, as if doing so would somehow will the thing back on the road. There really was nothing to do but wait until Rick realized we weren't following behind and came back to find us. Sure enough, it wasn't long before the telltale cloud of dust started rolling back up the switchbacks toward us. As Rick came to a stop, accompanied by the faithful powder clouds that covered us up for about the fourth time that day, he exclaimed, "What the..." and fell speechless as he gaped out his window in disbelief at our car teetering on the edge of the cliff. He got out, warily stepped to the edge, and peered down over the sheer drop. The mighty Fraser River was some 1,500 feet below.

After a few "hail Marys" by Dad and a couple of unrequested suggestions by the women, me included, about heading back to the flat land where we might live a bit longer and get out of this everlasting dust, the car was winched back onto the road with Rick's truck. Gingerly, we climbed back in and carried on at a much slower pace, crawling carefully around the hairpin turns. Back and forth we went, looking over the edge at more hapless heaps of wrecked cars that hadn't stopped at the "teetering" stage. At the bottom of the long winding hill, we crept timidly over a narrow rickety wooden bridge that spanned the murky turbulent Fraser River (was this the bridge Rick had told me had been condemned years ago?). Safely on the other side, we now climbed *up* the switchbacks, past more rocky caverns, more sagebrush, more hairpin turns, and more dust, until at long last we came upon signs of habitation: a rail fence, buildings, a trailer-type structure with one whole side of windows that could have been the school, and a cement building beside the teacher's trailer—the bunkhouse, I presumed. On we went to the main yard, a sprinkling of dwellings, corrals, a big red barn, a large old house with a huge veranda that turned out to be the cookhouse, and a rounded steel shop. The first thing I noticed were the hills that encircled the main ranch yard. I still possessed my fascination for hills, but these were all brown.

We climbed out of the car and warily surveyed our new surroundings. It was cold, with a chill wind blowing. Some frozen-looking people walked by, hugging themselves and making some comments about frozen water lines. And that clanging. What was that clanging? Some dilapidated-looking trucks and questionable-looking machinery were heaped here and there.

It was a lot to take in, but I was more concerned about how I was going to get back out of this place without having to go over that road. That annoying clanging was still going on and it was a noise I couldn't quite place. "It's the power plant." Suzanne's voice beside me answered my unspoken question. I remembered now that there was no hydro-electric power here. I had never heard a power plant before, and it violated every sense of decency and privacy I had. "Oh," was all I could say. A few moments of silence passed. I couldn't wrench my mind away from that road. I had visions of my children as teenagers, careening around those hairpin turns for a night in town. No way! I couldn't see any houses that appeared livable. I looked at the eager but dusty faces of my kids, and I thought—they would always be filthy.

Suzanne, I could tell, was thinking along the same lines. "Nobody in their right mind would live here," I said, turning to Suzanne, "leastways, not me."

"Me neither," replied Suzanne quietly. We headed to a small white building with "Gang Ranch Office" inscribed on a sign, where the rest of the family had preceded us. A very pleasant cowboy-type man called Mike Fairless, the son-in-law of one of the present owners, shook our hands warmly and offered us a whiskey; I guess we looked like we needed one. He chatted easily with us for a while, then I watched wonderingly as he reached on top of the desk, picked up a pistol with a well-worn handle, and stuck it into the top of his spurred cowboy boot. Straightening up, he swung the door open ahead of us, "Come on, let's see if the cook's got coffee on at the cookhouse," he offered. Outside, I saw that Dad had already found his way to the shop in search of a mechanic who would hopefully have the

31

answers to the question foremost on all our minds that afternoon: why wouldn't that car go around corners?

We spent a few days on the ranch, trying to take it all in—meeting the people, committing to memory the names of the various fields and different areas we were introduced to. We met Bob Munsey, who was looking after the cattle operation at that time. His wife, Pat, was the teacher at the school, and their daughter was running the Gang Ranch Store. It didn't take us long to discover that the Munseys were well-respected and longtime residents. I am usually not wrong about people, and I liked these people. We learned that the Gang Ranch was virtually an isolated but self-sufficient community. There was a store, school, cookhouse, post office, a "stagecoach" that brought in supplies once a week, and even a traveling preacher who came periodically to conduct services. A traveling health nurse, we were told, visited the school occasionally to check out the children's health needs, along with anyone else who required medical attention. There was no hydro-electric power: the gas-powered power plant provided this necessity. The only telephone line coming into the ranch was an unreliable party line. Every call was long-distance.

The main ranch yard was virtually surrounded by hay fields and, as this was a semi-arid area and only sagebrush and cactus grew naturally, irrigation lines were outfitted on every field to keep a continual supply of water on the growing hay crops from spring until fall. There was approximately 1,500 acres seeded down to alfalfa hay. The main headquarters of the Ranch consisted of these croplands and grazing lands: the wintering area for the cattle and 200-head horse herd—about 17,000 acres in all.

Various crews were needed to operate the massive Gang Ranch operation. An irrigation crew was continually moving the water pipes across the hay fields; a farm crew, working under the "farm boss," operated the farm machinery, worked the fields, looked after the seeding and fertilizing and upkeep of the crops, and did the harvesting (cutting and stacking) of the hay along with some extra help—a haying crew—in haying season. There was a mechanic in the shop whose seemingly hopeless task it was to keep the machinery moving. And when fencing needs arose, a fencing crew took over. A cowboy crew, under the tutelage of a "cowboss," tended to the never-ending requirements of the cattle herd. The success of the Gang Ranch relied on the proceeds from the cattle sales every year. The cowboy crew attended to every aspect of the cattle management: midwifery, treating any sicknesses, branding the calves with the Gang Ranch brand JH, castrating the bull calves, dehorning, and moving the entire herd (at that time numbering 2,500 cows and 2,000 head of yearlings), to wherever they needed to be. A "Cattle Flow Chart" showed the cattle herd starting out from the main ranch and moving around throughout the summer, followed by the cowboy crew, to a total of twelve different "cow camps" situated about fifty kilometers apart in the "backcountry" of the ranch. They would remain at one camp until that grazing area was sufficiently eaten down, then would move on to the next, until they reached in midsummer the high isolated cow camps up in the mountains, the furthest one being Graveyard Valley, 135 kilometers "as the crow flies" from the main ranch yard. They would then continue on the circuit, heading back down toward the ranch in a big circle until they had returned back to the main ranch yard near Christmas Day. This brought them "home" in time for the spring calving, at which time the cycle would begin again.

Mounting excitement as well as a wealth of ideas building in all of our minds about the improvements that could be made on the ranch finally won out. But the decision was to come down to a deadline.

One day I was up to my elbows in bread dough back on our farm in Alberta, shortly after returning home from the Gang Ranch, when the phone rang. I picked up Dusty and balanced him on my hip to keep him out of the dough while I answered it.

"Hi," I heard my brother Dale on the other end. "What are you up to?" "Oh, nothing," I replied, as any mother would when she's surrounded by babies, one of whom is hanging on to her hair with a fistful of dough.

"Listen." I sensed an urgency in Dale's voice. "They've thrown a new deadline at us; they have someone else's offer in the wings, and we have to get our securities in place by this afternoon! I'm not trying to pressure you, but I had to put a deposit of $500,000 down on it to hold it for us, and it's non-refundable if we don't go through with the deal!"

With a glance at the kitchen clock, I drew in my breath. It was 10:30 A.M., Denis was out in the field and, although we had talked about the Gang purchase until we were blue in the face, we were really no further ahead. We had see-sawed back and forth about the pros and cons and had discussions that went long into the night. Sometimes he was for going, and I was for staying; other times I was for going and he was for staying. We didn't want to hold everybody else back from the opportunity either. And I didn't want Dale to lose $500,000!

"I have to get Denis from the field, Dale, and we'll get it figured out." With that, I disengaged myself from the phone, set Dusty and his dough into the high chair, and started scraping the sticky mass from my hands. I heard a machine pull into the yard, and hurried out to call Denis.

After our discussion that day, we both decided to go. I think we had probably both decided already, but neither one of us wanted to feel like we were influencing the other. We were young and energetic, it was an exciting opportunity, and we felt all the disastrous possibilities were taken care of. We knew it was heavy financing—basically 100 percent—but the cattle sales that would immediately follow the purchase would bring in close to a half a million dollars to us. If we didn't put up our security, the deal would fall through for everyone else, not to mention the loss of the $500,000 deposit. The bank was over-secured and there had been discussion that perhaps some of the security could be lifted once we owned the ranch. What could possibly go wrong? If it didn't work, we would sell the Gang Ranch, plain and simple. The $15 million appraisal wiped out any concerns we had about the worth of the Ranch.

The decision was made: We would lease out our farm to a capable person for a five-year period, and give it a whirl.

We phoned our longtime friend and lawyer Dennis Roth in Edmonton. We had discussed this before with him, and he had voiced concern and attempted to caution us, but at that point it was like standing in front of a runaway freight train. He could witness Denis signing the collateral security agreements, but mine would have to be done with a different lawyer, for independent legal purposes.

Two hours later found us bundling all the kids into the car. First we headed to Edmonton, where Denis signed a personal guarantee in the amount of $600,000 using the Laying R as collateral. Legally it was referred to as a Guarantee Bond and Postponement of Claim. Straight from there, we drove to Leduc, Alberta, where I went through the same procedure with another lawyer, pledging $600,000 in a personal guarantee (joint with Denis's). The new lawyer had no idea what we were doing. We had never heard of a personal guarantee before. Everything was in a rush; papers had to be witnessed and documented and sent out by special courier. Little did we know that this was only the first of thousands of fine-printed documents that would pass through our shaky hands over the next ten years.

Rick's papers had all been signed in Maidstone, Saskatchewan; his were virtually the same as ours—putting up everything he owned in the form of a personal guarantee, as security to be an owner of the Gang Ranch. A myriad of papers had to be signed on behalf of IKR, as well, because the Idanell Korner Ranch was also being used as collateral to purchase the Gang Ranch. My father and mother had flown out to Kamloops. There, in the Place Inn Hotel, Kamloops lawyer Derek Donaldson waited. He was the lawyer for the company we had just formed called Alsager Holdings Ltd. This new corporation consisted of all members of the Ted Alsager family. This young lawyer, as well as Bob Erickson, the manager for the Canadian Imperial Bank of Commerce in Williams Lake, B.C., and Dale Alsager, presided over my father signing a "stack of papers a foot high."

Document after document after document was given to him to sign. He gave up trying to read all the fine print; they finally just lifted up the bottoms of the pages where he was to put his signature. He had absolutely no idea what was on all those papers that now had his signature on the bottom. He was flabbergasted at the number of papers involved, but he, like the rest of us, trusted people. That's the way we had grown up—trusting people. Bob Erickson was thrilled beyond his wildest dreams that he could have been influential in assisting to put this giant deal together. He had been flying all over the country and out of the country (to the States) with Dale, wheeling and dealing, and doing whatever he felt had to be done to put the necessary components of this complicated purchase together.

My sister, Donna, and her husband, Ken, had contemplated joining in the foray. As their children were older, it was harder for them to move, and the school at the Gang was only an elementary school. They did take a trip out to the ranch, and Ken expressed an interest in taking over the Perry Ranch operation, a feedlot operation right on the main highway at Cache Creek that we would own as part of the Gang Ranch. Donna and Ken had had more years to become embedded in their community and were going through the same seesawing we had experienced, but I believe they had more cons than pros. The longer you are in a community, surrounded by good neighbors and friends, the harder it is to tear yourself away.

Dale, in his frenzy to have everyone sign up their securities, had made a phone call similar to the one we had received, to Donna. No one had been home. He called the local RCMP detachment in Donna and Ken's town of Wawota and asked them to find her and have her call him for an "urgent family message."

When the police found Donna coming out of their local post office, they relayed to her the chilling message. Certain that someone had died, and frightened half to death, Donna rushed to the nearest phone and frantically called Dale. When she heard that he only wanted her to get papers signed, she was not amused. Donna and Ken made the decision to withdraw their security and continue on with their normal lives.

By the end of that day, all the papers had been signed and all the "what ifs" filed away in the backs of our minds. It was "done." Rick and my father, on behalf of Idanell Korner Ranch, made out the check that would accompany all the paperwork, a nonrefundable cash deposit toward the purchase of the Gang Ranch. The buying price—$4,100,000 plus $200,000 in equipment loans, a $500,000 operating loan, and $500,000 feeder cattle loan.

The famous Gang Ranch, located in the Cariboo region of British Columbia, dust, power plant, cactus and all, now belonged to the Alsager family, headed by Ted and Irene Alsager, who had unselfishly invested more than any of the rest of us—everything that they had accumulated over an entire lifetime.

It was the first time the historic ranch had ever been owned by Canadians. Alsager Holdings Ltd., consisting of all the family members, would own the Gang Ranch. Its major shareholder would be Idanell Korner Ranch, consisting of the original family members. Although it was 100 percent financed, the cattle sales occurring immediately following our purchase would give it a good kick-start. The chain of command had been established. Rick would manage the massive Gang Ranch operation, with assistance

37

from Denis and Oren. Dale would handle the accounting and financial end of it, from off the Ranch. We all owned the Ranch, and we had the bodies, the knowledge, the energy, and certainly the enthusiasm to make it work. We were fired up and ready for anything.

My next trip out to the Gang Ranch was in the spring. The gods who had deserted me on the first visit made up for it this time. The hills were a bright invigorating spring green, the sky cobalt blue. The dust didn't seem so bad, and even the old clanging power plant seemed to have been knocked down a decibel or two. Maybe it was because the pressure of trying to make the decision was over.

Oren was there and, although there were a million things I wanted to see and case out in the main yard, especially living quarters, he kept agitating me about this "special place" he wanted me to see. I finally conceded and climbed into the battered ranch truck parked out front. We left the main yard and rattled over the cattleguard, turned left across the hay field, and headed up through a sentinel of hills to what I learned was Lake Ranch. There were a couple of old leaning grain bins on this large bench, and a small lake on either side of the winding road. Freshwater Lake was on the right, and a gate-type dam control had been installed on the lower end of it to regulate the amount of water being let down to the main ranch yard. The water came down to Freshwater Lake all the way from the mountain glaciers at the back of the Gang Ranch. On the other side of the road was Hog Lake, a smaller water hole that was a favorite for the vast numbers of deer and wild sheep.

Over a series of bumpy little hills, Oren called them the "Rabbit Hills," then up, up we went, to a place called Bear Springs, a huge open hay field. Oren wasn't going to stop here—we jounced around the side of the field and started up a trail through the trees, to an open spot that just kept going up and up. I couldn't see anything specifically different and wondered rather impatiently if we were ever going to get anywhere, my mind falling back to all the things I should be doing down below. But it was a beautiful spring day, one of those remember-for-a-lifetime days when you have to take time out to rejoice.

Oren sensed my impatience and chuckled a little but would not reveal anything about where we were going. Finally, we bounced to a stop on a bunch of rocks. Climbing out, he wordlessly led the way to the edge of some flat-topped boulders and I followed him until there was a straight drop-off and nowhere further to go. I gasped in astonishment.

I know now it had been a trick. Oren knew darn well that once I stood on Table Mountain overlooking the Churn Creek gorge that I would be hopelessly hooked. I caught my breath, speechless. I could see forever up the gorge where Churn Creek disappeared into more cavernous rocky sentinels. And the smell! The sage was just beginning to bloom, and you couldn't help but get half-drunk on its perfume. Straight out from where we stood, a huge, white-headed bald eagle floated in lazy circles. Soft sweet winds tugged at us before carrying on their journey up the endless panorama, taking their secrets with them.

"Just sit quiet for a minute," Oren said in a hushed voice. He leaned over and scanned the sides of the steep cavern directly below us, and finally said, pointing, "There, behind those rocks."

I looked at where he was pointing and could see nothing. Then something moved, and looking more closely I could discern some white-rumped animals moving about, standing straight up on the treacherously vertical slopes, picking contentedly at tufts of dry grass growing from the sides of the canyon.

"California Rocky Mountain Sheep," he informed me before I could ask. "They're always here, but it's really hard to see them unless they move."

I gazed again toward the creek; I couldn't stop looking, drinking it all in. I felt so small and inconsequential.

"That's Cape Horn." I followed the direction of his arm to a point of rocks jutting out over Churn Creek. "And that 1,200 acre flat down there is called Wycott Flats, a good wintering range for wildlife, the bighorns and mule deer; I've already seen a few cougars down there. Old Wycott, they say, was a bit of a loner, lived down there all by himself, and had some longhorn cattle. When he died, they just rounded up what they could, and shot the ones they couldn't catch—I guess they got pretty wild. Joe Haller was here at that time, and he told me what great spreads of horns those cattle had."

I could tell Oren had been around already. He continued, "Sheep Flats is the flat above Wycott, which is a designated bighorn sheep grazing and wintering grounds. We don't graze that anymore, it's been set aside for the sheep. Black Lake is above that flat, and there are a couple of other little lakes, Snake Lake and Brown Lake, up above Wycott."

That trip to Table Mountain did it. I thought God himself must dwell on those perfumed cliffs. Little did I imagine that I would find even more beautiful spots than this. Later, when Table Mountain became my neighbor (Denis and I would build a house just at the bottom of Table Mountain on Bear Springs), it became my haven, my place to escape when the world got too much and I needed to gather myself together again.

Since I have known the Gang Ranch, I have listened to discussions about her vital facts, an endless procession of figures and numbers: how big it is, whether it is the largest ranch in North America or not, and if so, is that acreage or numbers of cattle maintained; the square mileage; how many land titles, government leases, water licences, mineral rights, etc. I have never thought about the Gang Ranch that way. To me, she was an object of beauty and sensitivity, and definitely a survivor against all odds. I saw her stamina, the quiet beautiful strength that upheld her through all the years of uncertainty and human errors, the atrocities that have been committed, government red tape, and the never-ending power struggle between different government departments, bureaucrats, bankers, and crazy people, each trying to tear off a bigger chunk of the ranch for their own use than the others. She has seen the effects of basic human greed, and withstood the staunch refusal of an entire country to appreciate what she is and what she should remain.

I have crossed her clear cold waterways, ridden her lush green valleys, and climbed to the top of her rocky snow-topped crags; her silent forests were full of secrets. I have seen her sagebrush and cactus, her majestic eagles, the stiff-legged cranes that visited Bear Springs every year, the great blue herons that circled the dam eyeing the trout, the baby bears scratching their way up the trees, the multitudes of deer and rocky mountain sheep, the scream of the she-cougar on a star-studded night, the howling of the wolf bitches at Hungry Valley, and I have been filled with respect. My entire family now owned this beautiful ranch, but I instinctively knew that anything this magnificent was not meant to be owned by human beings.

The Move to the Gang

The summer of 1978 saw the Rivard family in Alberta and the Alsagers in Saskatchewan like bees in a full swarm, preparing for the migration west. I was taking flying lessons at Wetaskiwin Air Service, wanting to obtain my license before the big move. Although I didn't have enough time to attend the ground school course, I had sufficient flying hours for a student pilot's license, which enabled me to pilot in the company of a person with a valid pilot's license. Now that the Ranch was ours, everyone was anxious to be on the Ranch physically. It was imperative that the people still on the Ranch, basically a skeleton crew, understand that everything was under control and that the work would carry on without disruption. Dad was semi-retired; he would oversee the IKR operation and also come out to visit at the Gang Ranch, to the little bungalow that was designated as his and Mom's down by Rick's trailer. I knew one of Dad's prime concerns were his meticulously kept ledgers at IKR. He had always kept the big black ledger up-to-date and neat. All the columns and figures were done in pencil, so any mistakes could be rectified without any mess. Rick had taken over, and the ledgers carried on in this dutiful fashion. Dad wasn't going to let them get into disorder now that Rick would be away at the Gang Ranch. People in my Dad's age group did things that way. They knew exactly how much money they had, and tended not to buy something they wanted until they knew they had the cash in their pocket to pay for it. He had always been right on top of his finances, and did not borrow money.

Rick was the first of the Alsager family to move onto the Gang Ranch. He, along with Suzanne and the kids, Lane, Jan, and Heidi, relocated immediately to take control, almost before the ink was dry on the papers. Mike Fairless had been basically running the Ranch for Floyd Skelton but had other commitments that prevented him from being there all the time. The Gang Ranch, from what we could see, had been simply "floating" for years—not growing. Rick's physical presence alone had already made a vast difference to the limping operation, and the working staff there highly respected him. In his efficient and energetic way, he took things firmly in hand. The employees on the Ranch were relieved to see that the slumbering Gang Ranch was awake and moving forward again. And they were overjoyed to have a manager who was up at the crack of dawn each day, working physically alongside them, and at the same time keeping all the problems under control.

We were very much aware of the importance of everyone keeping to their own domain of authority in this complex business. It was set up as Rick being the ranch manager. He would be responsible for overseeing the general management of all ranch operations. He would undertake the supervision of hiring and management of all operation staff. The purchase and acquisition of all equipment required for the Ranch operation would be by his decision. He would undertake the management and husbandry of all livestock and other ranch products. He would co-ordinate the staff and schedule their time off for slacker times, etc.

The responsibility of the day-to-day activities on the Ranch were solely on his shoulders.

As corporate administrator, Dale was responsible for the supervision and management of all corporation administrative affairs. He would handle matters apart from the operational on-farm activities. He would arrange for securing of credit, loans, mortgages, and soliciting of shareholder capital. He would manage the property at locations other than the site of ranch operations. It would be up to him to handle negotiations for the purchase and sales of assets for the corporation all subject to terms of reference to be determined by the corporation. He would co-ordinate activities with bankers, accountants, and others with respect to the overall administration of the company. He was to co-ordinate activities and efforts of shareholders and to provide shareholders with up-dated information periodically on corporation progress and status. As required, he would arrange board of directors and shareholders meetings.

It all sounded very complicated, but was actually quite simple. Rick was in charge of everything happening on the Gang Ranch, and Dale was in charge of things happening OFF the Ranch.

We had purchased two new mobile homes. Rick and Suzanne moved into one about a mile from the main ranch yard beside Gaspard Creek. The cute little bungalow called the "Guest House," just a stone's throw from Rick and Suzanne's place, would be Mom and Dad's living quarters anytime they were on the ranch. These two homes were on the site of the "Big House" that had been the main house on the Gang Ranch before it burned down in 1976. Apparently it had been a beautiful old house, several stories high, with a bunkhouse on the top, and a marble staircase. Sadly, a lot of the ranch records from that bygone era burned along with the building.

Denis and I had expected that the other new trailer would be ours, as there really wasn't much else for accom-

44

modation. We were surprised to learn that Dale had claimed it for himself, and had it installed on top of the hill beside the airstrip. Dale claimed he needed to have accommodation when he flew in periodically. As he spent most of his time in Williams Lake, Kelowna, or Kamloops, he said he would keep his eye open for another mobile for us. It never happened.

Dale and Betty and their family were not going to live on the ranch. For some time they lived outside of Edmonton in a subdivision called Ardrossan, followed by a move to a mansion on Braeloch Road in Kelowna, an exclusive area by the Okanagan Lake. They also bought a house in Williams Lake on Western Avenue and resided there for some time. The office that we maintained at the main Gang Ranch yard held all the records for the immediate concerns of the Gang Ranch operation, but the accounting, banking, and financial affairs were entrusted to Dale. Those of us who lived on the Gang Ranch were isolated, but living in town Dale had access to the banks, lawyers and accountants that were to keep tabs on the finances of the family company. We trusted him totally.

Oren had claimed a little one-roomed shack beside the office in the main yard. Oren had other things on the go— not the least of which was the hunting lodge in Alberta which he ran with his good friend Lloyd McMahon from Edmonton. When Oren was on the Ranch, he was a ball of fire, helping us out with whatever needed doing. When he was gone on one of his guide-outfitting commitments, we were used to going for months sometimes without hearing from him. There usually weren't any phones where he was. We knew when we didn't hear from him that he was on some exciting excursion—perhaps up at the Arctic Circle Lodge, down on the Gulf of Mexico, or on top of some mountain somewhere.

We loved it when he showed up again, because it took at least a few days to hear all the exciting stories about his latest experience. On one such adventure, he had to battle

45

his way upstream on the mighty Mackenzie River. It was a horrendously difficult journey until he finally made it to his destination, Great Slave Lake, the headwaters of the Mackenzie. His small aluminum boat was so battered from the rocks and rapids he had traversed that he feared it wouldn't hold together over the last five miles of the journey to Pine Point. Balancing all his gear in the middle, and gingerly easing his wounded craft straight out into the waves, he slowly putt-putted his way towards Pine Point, his little seven horsepower motor laboring onward. He prayed no squalls would come up, but even the normal swells on this huge lake periodically washed over the side of the boat.

The boat was riding lower and lower in the waves, water slapping around his gear. He cut the motor even more, slowing the boat down so that it would ride on top of the swells. Barely moving now and floating closer to shore, he took time to bail out some of the water, but it was a losing battle. He spotted a dock on the side of the lake, not quite at his destination, but close enough. Slowly, the flagging little boat struggled up to the wooden dock, and Oren leapt off, wet to the waist, hurrying to lift his gear out of the half-submerged boat. He watched the poor little watercraft slowly rocking with the swells, only about six inches now above water. It had brought him on his perilous journey up the Mackenzie, and he felt badly now to hoist his gear onto his shoulders and turn and walk away from it. There was literally nothing left to salvage.

Not planning on being at the Gang Ranch full-time, Oren didn't complain that his living quarters were just a one-room cabin, with a sagging lonely cot huddled in one corner. There was no bathroom, no kitchen, no running water, and definitely no butler.

Nevertheless, someone had to live full-time in the main yard. The mammoth fuel tanks that supplied all the fuel needs for the Ranch operation were located in front of the main shop. They either had an enormous evaporation problem or someone was helping themselves at night. Probably because of the absentee owners, there had been problems with theft in the main yard, and we determined to discourage this from re-occurring. Saturday nights brought off-ranch people drifting in from across the river and beyond, and surveillance was necessary. Most of the Ranch employees lived in the apartments down by the school, or upstairs in the cookhouse. Neither of these had a clear view of what went on in the main yard.

There was also the constant flow of tourists that wound up in the main yard. They usually needed directions about where they were headed to, and many of them had not realized how far it was out there and needed gas to get back. There were always those who didn't know where they were, or how they had got there. People wanted to get into the store, visit the office, look at the maps of the area, sign the guest book; sometimes they just wanted to have coffee and chat for a while. We always took time for them. The trauma of my first trip in to the Ranch was still very vivid in my mind, and I didn't want these people, who had survived the journey in, to be met with indifference once they got there.

It didn't take much figuring to know who was going to live in the main yard in the midst of all the hubbub. By a basic process of elimination, Denis and I were the only possibilities from the family that was left. Oren's shack was in the main yard, but he was not planning on being there full-time. He had a lot of valuable items in his hut, and someone needed to keep an eye on it when he was gone. So Denis and I would be the yard guards, keepers of the fuel, and prime candidates for the loony bin. Denis would throw his energies in with Rick's to whatever was the direst emergency at any given time. Suzanne and I would man the Gang Ranch Store, run the cookhouse, and keep track of what went on in the Gang Ranch office, not to mention the constant demands that came with just being in the eye of the hurricane. Somewhere in there, but not necessarily a priority, were the seven little children, three of hers, and

47

four of mine, that needed some semblance of attention now and then.

The only house left was a small building right beside the main office. I was told it used to be the "pool hall," where the cowboys and other workers used to shoot a few games in their spare hours. This explained the telltale dribbles from chewing tobacco decorating the walls. It was basically one big room, with a small room off each side of it that would become two bedrooms. One "bedroom" had a bathroom, of sorts, attached to it. There was no kitchen (we would make one in the living room), no porch, no closets, no shower, no air conditioning, and definitely no butler.

Rick, thoughtful person that he was, took time from the mind-boggling list of things that had to be done to see that a large picture window got installed in the front wall of our shack, facing the main yard, before we got there. He knew I could not stand to be inside without being able to see out.

One hot summer day, our dusty, Jed Clampett style moving cavalcade pulled into the Gang Ranch yard. Denis drove the green Ford pickup we had previously bought from Oren, pulling the IKR cattle-liner, and I followed with our black Ford Bronco and four kids, Shan, Buffy, Dusty, and baby Lacey. Every nook and cranny was crammed with something. The Alberta farewell parties had all been attended, and we had survived the sad and tearful good-byes to family, friends, and neighbors there. Our poultry operation had been leased out, and our house rented out to what we hoped were suitable people. We pulled heroically out of our yard, Denis driving one rig, me the other, with four children under the age of five, a dog and a cat, and as few belongings as we thought we needed to survive. Behind was left my piano, five-bedroom house, most of the furniture, my best friends, ten thousand chickens, the baby birch trees I had planted along the driveway, good, good people, many fine memories, and, worst of all, my dishwasher. I feigned courage leaving the yard, waving gaily to everyone (I have always tried to avoid those soggy partings), and made it a good half mile down the road before I pulled my rig over to the side of the road to have a good cry. As luck would have it, Denis's brother Omer saw me stop and, thinking I had trouble already, came flying out of the yard toward me. I swiped away my tears and carried on. No time for this.

When we eventually pulled into the Gang Ranch yard the following day, we were met with a beehive of activity. The yard bustled with machinery and crews coming and going; people making plans and changing them; yelling and hollering; horses, dogs, cats, and kids, everybody going somewhere. Rick's organization was in operation—not an idle soul was to be seen. Everybody looked happy, relaxed, yet busy.

It's like a little town, I thought. Here we are in the middle of nowhere, and I'm going to live on Main Street. From the midst of the activity, Rick emerged, then Oren, and I saw Suzanne pull up in their Ford Supercab.

"Welcome to the Funny Farm," said Rick with a grin. I could see he was genuinely happy, and I thought to myself: this challenge suits him.

After we all shared some jokes and joshing about our "new" house, Rick and Denis dashed off to deal with some crisis about the water lines. I heard something about them all having to be dug up. Suzanne whisked away all my kids, calling over her shoulder that "supper's ready whenever you get there." With her truck chockful of little blond heads, she disappeared in a cloud of dust, leaving me in peace to tackle my new surroundings. Suzanne would become much more than my sister-in-law; she was to become my best friend, my strength, the savior of my sanity and, at times, my only reason for staying.

I leaned against the doorway of the "pool hall," wondering where to start and refusing to think about the five-bedroom house sitting empty in Alberta that night.

"You think this is bad. You should come and see my shack." Oren's voice behind me was tinged with laughter.

49

Oren never got excited about mundane things such as living quarters. "Come on," he gestured.

I climbed over a stack of boxes and trailed him past the front of the office, and on to his shack. Oren led the way in through the open door and ceremoniously swept his arm across the single little room. He had gone to work on the place, all right. His guns, reloading equipment, hunting paraphernalia, his trophy deer, and snowshoes hung on the wall, his easel was set up, and his many paint jars lined up beside a host of brushes. Oren was an artist—he already had a partially finished oil painting of a crouching cougar started on a soft piece of deerhide, hanging on a frame. His door was open to everyone on the ranch, and throughout the coming times, evenings would find his little shack filled with people who felt drawn to crowd in and quietly watch him paint. His paintings were good, bold, realistic scenes of nature, animals, and people.

Somehow we made it through that first night, despite the disorganization of moving. All of the kids would be in the same bedroom, which would also be the laundry room, and also the path to the only bathroom. There was no room for a crib—baby Lacey was tucked snugly into a dresser drawer beside my bed, blissfully oblivious to her tumultuous surroundings.

The next day dawned bright and early. Again, miracle woman Suzanne showed up to keep the kids out of my hair. Buffy was still sleeping so stayed with me to "help" with all the sorting out. In the midst of unpacking and rearranging what I had just arranged, I noticed a shadow fall across the doorway and glanced up to see a cute little native girl curiously watching us. She was about Buffy's age, three, I guessed, tiny and fine-boned, with big dark liquid eyes. Someone had taken time to tie her hair in neat little braids on top of her head, a bright yellow ribbon tucked in the midst.

"Buffy, come and see who's here." I called Buffy out from the boxes she was playing in. She slowly straightened up from her "house" and came toward me, looking shyly at the newcomer. I took Buffy's shoulder and nudged her over in front of the visitor.

"Say hi," I coaxed Buffy. "She will be a friend for you." The two little girls stood a safe two feet apart, openly staring at each other eye to eye, as three-year-olds will. They held the stare until I was getting uncomfortable watching.

The little Indian girl broke the duel. She tipped back her head and before I knew what was happening, that sweet little three-year-old girl with the tiny braids and the yellow ribbon had spit forth a stream of some kind of black mass that landed, splat, right on the shoulder of Buffy's white shirt.

Buffy looked down in surprise at her shirt where the "thing" had landed. Horror-struck, she saw what looked to be a black spider with legs going out in all directions. Actually, it was only a wad of splattered chewing tobacco, more commonly known as "snoose," which we would come to be very familiar with.

Screaming in terror, she flew to me and the shirt had to be torn off. "Mom, she can spit spiders," she cried, her eyes like saucers, half in fear, and half in wonder. From that day onward, she developed a healthy respect for "the girl who could spit spiders."

The Gang Ranch was proving to be unbelievably busy. Nothing had prepared me for the constant and never-ending demands. It wasn't what had to be done next, it was whatever had to be done to prevent the next disaster. The yard was like Grand Central Station. Denis and Rick and Oren, when he was around, worked all day and half the night. They did everything—farming, repairing, building, and rebuilding. The underground water lines in the main yard had to be dug up and replaced with new pipe; of course there was no map indicating where the present pipes ran. They put in new dams and rebuilt old ones on the various lakes and creeks above the main yard. These dams

51

would stop the water from flowing down through the main yard and on past, to be lost in the Fraser River. Water was not to be wasted. They constructed a new water diversion to better control the water system coming down from Fosberry, the area where Gaspard Lake was located. The lake housed the main dam that supplied the water coming down from the high country.

They handled the interminable problems that cropped up every day, dealing with employees and sorting out their inevitable squabbles and problems, hashing out solutions for the haying, the machinery, the equipment, the cow camps, the vehicles, and their own homes. They worked from 5:00 A.M. until long into the night. But it was rewarding to see the place changing before our very eyes.

It was a blistering hot summer. We were not used to that dry inescapable heat, and the two babies, Heidi and Lacey, could only get relief sometimes if Suzanne and I took them down to Gaspard Creek and sat with them in the cool water. A sparkling-eyed electrician from Clinton, Walt Adams, who had been in the area for years, felt sorry for me in that hot, closed-in shack and, on his next trip out, brought an air-conditioning fan, one that he said was "just lying around doing nothing." He installed it in my house, wouldn't take any payment, and probably saved my life and definitely made life more pleasant for the people around me.

Our shack did have a few advantages. We had, for instance, some awesome neighbors. Oren was just on the other side of the office. Then directly behind our house, beside the cookhouse, lived a gentleman, native to the ranch, about whom Oren spoke very highly. This immediately made him a worthwhile person for me to get to know. His name was Jimmy Rosette, or Jiggs, or Old Jimmy. He had been born right there in the little tin house he lived in, had worked on the Gang Ranch cowboying, irrigating, and whatever, his entire life. He knew more stories than

52

the library could hold and was an expert in dealing with people and life.

Vanilla extract was a valuable commodity on the Gang Ranch when we arrived there. The black, liquid, *pure* vanilla (not the artificial variety), was a pleasant-smelling, smooth-tasting drink with a high percentage of alcohol. A good dose of vanilla, straight or mixed with coffee, signified a satisfying end to a hard day's work. While Old Jimmy was out working one day, someone went into his hut and stole the bottle of vanilla he had hidden under his cot. This prompted him to make a housekeeping change. Vanilla looked exactly like Coca-Cola. He poured all his vanilla into Coke bottles and kept them right out in the open. He then poured the Coca-Cola into the vanilla bottles, and hid them under his bed. The next day he hooted with laughter when he came back from his long day of hand flood-irrigating, and the Coke-filled vanilla bottles under his bed had disappeared. No one bothered to steal his "Coke" bottles.

Old Jimmy was a professional at flood irrigating. Countless hand-dug ditches carried water down from the higher benches, level by level, to the lower fields. He constantly patrolled these ditches, shovel over his shoulder, accompanied by his faithful horse Marianne and his cowdogs Moose and Bear. He rebuilt areas of the ditches that had caved in and sometimes dug new ones to reroute the stream. The ditches had to be cleaned out constantly to remove branches and other obstacles, and sometimes dams that the beavers had built.

Jimmy had no interest or need for money. He had a whole envelope of paychecks from the former owner that he had never cashed. He said someday he'd cash them. When Oren tried to explain to him that they would be no good, Old Jimmy just laughed. He had no use for money.

That first day on the ranch I had finally got things squared away in the shack to some liveable degree when a knock came at the door. "Yes?" I said. A perspiring man dressed head-to-toe in coveralls, with some hoses and nozzle-type paraphernalia hanging over his arm, was standing there.

"We've been asked to fumigate all the houses out here, and we're giving everyone a half hour or so to get all the things out of your house that you don't want sprayed." He rattled this off quickly since I imagine this was about the fourth or fifth speech he had made so far. "Why?" I asked, incredulously. "I just moved everything in here!"

"I guess the health nurse was out and some kid has bedbugs out here," he answered. "You can leave your furniture where it is, but if I were you, I'd remove any bedding, towels, sheets, blankets, clothing, food, or eating equipment you don't want sprayed with this stuff. It's pretty potent!"

A half hour later found me sitting out in the yard with all my kids, a gigantic pile of clothing, bedding, pillows, towels, and whatever else it had just taken me two days to haul *into* that house. The fumigators, like men at war, with their snorkels and masks and coveralls, clanked through every inhabited building with their stinky, smoky apparatus. Hissing noises and clouds of ill-looking smoke emanated from the doorways as they trooped from house to house. We were not allowed back into our houses for hours and, even when the allotted time was up, I still couldn't go in. A white, putrid, sulphurous-smelling haze hung everywhere—on everything and in everything.

Sitting out in the yard with the other women, who seemed quite unperturbed by the whole affair (this was obviously not a new experience for them), I dejectedly thought about all the scrubbing, washing, and redoing we were in for. This was not my idea of Paradise.

We Get to Know the Place

The initial trauma of moving behind us, we settled in to what we hoped was going to be a normal and routine existence. The first thing we would learn was that there was no such thing on the Gang Ranch as a routine existence. Every day brought new events, new emergencies, new people trying to get on the ranch, and other disenchanted people trying to get off. Usually we'd get right in the middle of something and have to drop everything to cope with some fresh emergency—a forest fire on the hill, or someone that had to be rushed to the hospital in Williams Lake.

The children from our two families—ours and Rick and Suzanne's—became so close it was as if they were from the same family. Although we didn't realize it at the time, the two littlest girls—Heidi and Lacey—were too young to realize they *were* from different families. They were always together and came to think of themselves as permanently that way. We did not foresee the problems that might occur some day if one family moved away and the children would have to be separated.

It seemed I only caught occasional glimpses of the four boys—Lane and Jan, Shan and Dusty. I couldn't catch up to them. They reminded me of a flock of birds. You would see them all in a group with the other ranch kids, one would veer off one way, and the whole group would change direction and follow, the black, well-used rubber of their slingshots flapping out of their back pockets. They practiced spitting, learned to swear, and I'm sure had their pecking-order battles with the other boys on the ranch. If they did, however, we didn't hear about them. All the parents were smart enough to stay out of it, and let them work things out, which they soon did. Their basic boundaries and hierarchy rights established, their skins got browner, their hair got whiter in the sun, and they were, as I had known they would be, totally filthy every time Suzanne or I managed to get our hands on them.

Equipment and livestock were still arriving continually from Maidstone. Vehicles and machinery came out that was needed: farm equipment, the black IKR Ford 4X4 ranch truck, cattle, the buffalo herd that had been purchased by IKR in recent years. My Dad's prized herd of Hereford bulls were trucked out. They looked at first like they didn't really belong there—fat, sleek, monstrous white-faced purebreds that made the rangy mixture of the ranch bull herd seem scrawny in comparison.

The days galloped by in a blur: manning the cookhouse, which was always going full tilt; keeping the store operating and supplied with stock; selling gas; answering the same questions and giving the same directions over and over again; and running back and forth from office to house to store to cookhouse. The office was open and, although we had hired young women off and on to work in there, it still took up a lot of our time. I redid the filing system, making it color-coded so it would be easy to grab a file at a glance. The old party line telephone seemed to ring all day and half the night with people looking for work, people wanting directions how to get there, frantic women looking for lost husbands who had gone hunting or fishing on the Gang, calls from the police. The Gang Ranch, we soon discovered, was a favorite hideout for someone running from the law. It took a pretty serious charge for the police to bother chasing them all the way out there, and there were lots of places to hide if they did come.

They were long busy days; Suzanne, Rick, Denis and I, Mom and Dad and Oren when they were there, starting at 5:00 A.M. every morning, falling into bed exhausted late at night. Our small children got hauled everywhere that Suzanne and I went. They slept in and on and under anything—in vehicles, in boxes, on horses, wagons, and especially in the store, where Suzanne and I would work late at pricing stock and getting it on the shelves. I don't know how many times we jumped into our vehicles to leave, did a head count, and would have to run back up the stairs to the store, unlock the door, and retrieve some little sleeping person curled up in a corner or on a bottom shelf somewhere.

Rosalie Rosette, wife of Raymond Rosette, one of the old-time families born and raised on the Ranch, was always a reliable cookhouse worker and became one of those tried-and-true people that we could always count on.

Between Rosalie and her daughters—Phyllis and Eileen—my Mom, Suzanne, and myself, the 6:00 A.M. breakfast was always on the table. That meant being there at 5:00 A.M. every morning to get the smell of fresh-brewed coffee in the air, and the grills warmed up before the crews showed up. We took turns, repeating the same routine at dinnertime, and then again at supper. Anywhere from approximately ten basic crew members in the slower winter months, to thirty or more in the summertime when all the crews were hard at it, dropped what they were doing to answer the heavy gong of the big "come and get it" cookhouse bell.

The cookhouse was the center hub of all the activity on the Ranch. Everyone had to eat, no matter what they were doing. All the news and jokes and classified gossip got passed around the large rectangular tables along with steaming bowls of wholesome soup, dishes heaped high with fluffy mashed potatoes, home-baked bread and pies, and lots of other good, stick-to-the-ribs food. When they were really lucky, a towering batch of my mother's homemade *lefse*—Swedish flatbread—graced each table. Lunches were packed in the mornings for those employees who would be too far from the main ranch yard for their noon meal. The cookhouse was a happy, happy place. Major problems were solved there, and many a young cocky newcomer learned some basic lessons on table manners and life there. We saw romances begin in the cookhouse, and we saw romances end there. Sometimes we went all out and prepared special suppers, complete with sparkling bottles of wine, for bankers, government officials, special tourists, and European guests.

In the wintertime, the cookhouse was heated by a wood-burning heater in the center of the floor. Rosalie Rosette would run over to the cookhouse in the cold early hours of the morning to start the fire, even if she wasn't cooking that day. The cookhouse would be warm and comfortable with a crackling coziness by the time whoever was showing up at 5:00 A.M. arrived to cook. How we appreciated her thoughtfulness.

In conjunction with the cookhouse, the meathouse at the rear of the cookhouse had to be looked after. This was where the supply of beef for the cookhouse was cured, cut up, and packaged. A well-insulated cool room, it was equipped with special stainless steel meat-cutting equipment, a set of well-sharpened deboning knives, and meat packaging paper. Large strong hooks hung from the ceiling, usually weighed down by a hanging carcass. There was a continual number of "dry" cows (ones without calves) that were kept in a pasture just off the main yard, and fed special grain rations to give us the best meat. When our beef supply was getting low, some of the farm crew, usually Francis Billy, would head for the "meat pasture" with his gun, and soon afterward another carcass would arrive for hanging in the meathouse. The carcass would be left to hang (cure) there for at least ten days, at which time as many of us as were available would converge on the meathouse to help cut, package, deliver to the deep freeze, and clean up afterward. The special stainless steel sawing equipment had to be kept meticulously clean, and the countertops scrubbed with disinfectant after every use. Celina Rosette and her daughters were hardworking veterans at the meathouse, and Suzanne, myself, and whoever else was available would help to put the cumbersome pieces of carcass through the meat saws, producing specified types of roasts, thick red steaks, stew meat, and fresh ground hamburger meat from the big steel meat grinder.

The "stagecoach," an old glorified van driven by Bill Remple from Dog Creek, had everybody waiting for its arrival every Thursday at 1:00 P.M. If you hadn't seen anyone all week, you could be certain they would show up when the stage came. Pillars of dust spiraling up the road would signal the arrival of this happy and good-hearted driver, at a speed only he could handle, and the rest of us could only marvel at. He dropped off the supplies, special orders, and the mail and parcels, hauled passengers into the ranch, and loaded up others to take back out. Celina Rosette was in charge of postmistress duties. She was the wife of Willy Rosette, Raymond's brother, and another longtime Gang Ranch resident. Theirs was a big, happy family and an integral part of the Gang Ranch operation. Willy, like all the Rosettes, had spent a lifetime cowboying and working on the Ranch and was continually sharing with us his endless knowledge of the place.

I used to love to ask Willy how many kids he had. A big grin would spread across his face, he would cross his arms, shuffle his feet around until he was comfortable—we both knew this would take some time—then scratch his head beneath his cowboy hat, lean back on the heels of his well-scuffed cowboy boots, and begin counting. "Well, now, let's see, there's..." and on he'd go, trying to remember all the names and numbers. It usually came out to a different number every time. We would have been lost on the ranch without Willy.

Another "old reliable" was Francis Billy. Of Chilcotin heritage, he and his wife, Adele, and their children had long been part of the operation. Francis's big grin was a vital part of the farm crew, and he took his job very seriously. Seeding, haying, feeding out the huge "bread loaf" stacks of hay to the cattle in the winter feedyards, he was as dependable as the sunshine. The Ranch was not just a job to these people, it was their life.

It didn't take long before we had formed relationships with all these longtime ranch people that would be lifelong, committed friendships. And slowly we were becoming familiar with all the areas and individually named places. Each field, meadow, and valley had been identified over the years and given a suitable name. It was like being in a foreign country and learning all the new provinces and capitals.

Coming up from the Fraser River toward the main ranch yard was Lower Ranch, the hay fields on the lowest level. These fields near the river were heavy producers, with their long growing season and ability to be irrigated. Just above it was Airport Field, where the old airport was. There had been a few calamities on the old airstrip, as it was short, had a few rolling hills and dips in it, as well as a bush at one end and the Fraser River at the other. We heard that Bob Munsey, who looked after the cattle operations on the ranch, had wrecked a plane there, a Cessna 180. Luckily it didn't do a lot of damage, and no one was hurt.

Slim Sherk, a veteran pilot from Springhouse, used to fly in here. He was well-noted for his bush-flying abilities and was the only pilot I knew, besides Oren Alsager, who dared to land his plane on the short Graveyard Valley "airstrip." This was not much more than a bumpy open space surrounded by mountain peaks and glacial lakes and pocked with dangerous marmot holes in the midst of the thick forested Graveyard Valley.

On one particular occasion, Slim took off from the main yard at the Gang Ranch in a Super Cub. One of the propellers was suddenly torn off, and the vibrations caused the motor mounts to break loose from the engine. Shutting the engine off, he descended, gliding down toward the river. The river's banks consisted of three separate flats, like three large steps about 100 yards apart. Slim bounced on each step, and on the last step he bounced so hard the engine came right off and fell down between his wheels. Luckily, the plane came to a halt just before hitting the river.

The following summer, when the spring crews went out to start irrigating, they found the broken propeller blade. It had flown clear across the fields on Nels Point, the field adjacent to Airport Field, and had sliced right through a main line irrigation pipe.

One of the best producing fields, crop-wise, was Churn Creek Field, located down along the rugged breaks of Churn Creek. Just below this field, was a long strip of a bench called Poison Patch.

The Rosette Field was next on the climb up toward the main yard, no doubt named after the many members of the Rosette family, whose history is so embedded in the Gang Ranch area.

The Boneyard, the Ranch dump, was just past the main yard, beside the Gang Ranch airstrip. It used to be called the Starvation Pasture because sometime around the late 1950s either a miscalculation or a mismanagement of feed caused hundreds of cattle to die. Heading past this area from the main yard were the Knoll Yard fields, now under irrigation. Previously a junky old feedlot before we burned it down, it was now irrigated for hay and had a storage area for haystacks. Knoll Yard had a large knoll right in the middle of it. One end of Knoll Yard, where there was shade

61

and lush green grass, became the Buffalo Pen. This was used when buffalo needed to be held in the main yard.

One of the main attractions of the Gang Ranch was that it possessed its very own water supply, from source to finish, entirely self-contained. If you set out from the main yard and traveled eighty-five miles as the crow flies—back to the high mountain country of Graveyard Valley where the headwaters of the numerous creeks sent their bubbling, clear, glacial waters fingering out in all directions, winding and creating paths down through all the valleys and cow camps—you would trace how they eventually became the main water feed in the main yard. If you traveled this route on the ground, you would have to travel about four times the distance, and you would pass through four seasons.

Lake Ranch is the next level above the main ranch area, consisting of a vast grazing area, huge hay fields, and two lakes. Freshwater Lake is the last holding pond for the water coming down out of the mountains, before it is dispersed down to the main yard. Hog Lake is the other lake, so named for the large numbers of hogs they used to run there in the early 1900s. The next flat above Lake Ranch was Bear Springs, but between these two benches was an entire area called Broken Ground. You had to be very careful going across Broken Ground on horseback or on foot. Horses hated going near it. There was some kind of eroding from underneath, shifting ground, and some large cracks that just plain opened up into the earth and went down forever. When you dropped a rock down into these cracks, some of them appeared to be bottomless.

Above Broken Ground was the plateau of Bear Springs, so named as it was a favorite habitat for many of the bears that resided in the area. Bear Springs had beautiful clear spring water that bubbled right up out of the ground. The water on the main ranch was alkaline and barely drinkable. Not so the sweet spring water of Bear Springs. Stump Lake was fed by Bear Springs and was a good swimming hole in the summertime. The Bear Springs area hosted a wealth of wildlife, because of its abundance of water and lush green grazing areas. The buffalo herd was here, as well as hundreds and hundreds of deer and Rocky Mountain sheep, bears, cougars, coyotes, wolves, and fluffy red foxes. Birds of every type congregated at Bear Springs—huge lazy bald-headed eagles, long-legged cranes and the long-beaked snipe, flocks of bluebirds, wild Canada geese, green-headed mallard ducks, and too many grouse to count. Glossy black ravens fought for seniority amongst the tree-tops.

Down below Bear Springs, toward Churn Creek, was Sheep Flats, where the California Rocky Mountain sheep had free roaming range. A gold miner by the name of Sonny Collins had a cabin and quite an establishment built up at the very bottom on the creek. A slight, wiry, practical joker hailing from the nearby town of Clinton, he spent his summers extracting pay dirt from the gold-laden creekbed of Churn Creek. The first time Oren went to Sonny's cabin to get acquainted, no one was home. Cupping his hands around his eyes to peer through the frosted window of the cabin, he was startled to see a body lying on a cot in the unheated confines of the cabin, one frozen-looking hand sticking straight up out of the blanket that covered it.

With a pounding heart, and wondering what he would find under the grey woolen army blanket, Oren pushed the door open and gingerly ventured in nearer to the human outline that was lying so very still on the cot.

Some strands of long blonde hair escaped from under one side of the blanket, and Oren reached down and, holding his breath, drew back a corner of the blanket. A lady was lying there, a frozen smile on her face, and it took a few seconds for Oren to comprehend that the frozen smile was a permanent one—she was a mannequin.

Sonny Collins got many a good laugh out of his lady mannequin—he dressed her up in different clothes for different occasions; once I saw a pretty blonde woman standing in Sonny's yard wearing a red polka-dot dress. I walked

63

over to talk to her and it was my turn to discover the surprisingly lifelike mannequin. Another time, he had her standing at the front door in high heels, her arm bent as though beckoning you in the door.

Sonny Collins had an old crank-type telephone hanging on his wall inside the cabin. If anyone took the time to think, they would realize there certainly weren't any telephone lines around for many a mile. Sonny used to get a big kick out of the people who would come in and ask if they could use the phone.

"Sure," he'd quip, "just leave your quarter on the table."

If, at Knoll Yard, you didn't head up the Bear Springs road but instead went straight, you would carry on past Rick and Suzanne's home as well as my parents' house at Big House near Gaspard Creek. The bridge over Gaspard Creek would bring you to Front Pasture on the other side. At the mouth of Gaspard Creek was the Robinson Lot, named after Wayne Robinson, a one-time manager of the Gang Ranch. Rock Pile, the next field above that, was an expansive rolling grassland surrounded by huge piles of gigantic scattered boulders, evidence of some colossal upheaval in the past.

The flat next to this was Mary's Flat, originally homesteaded by ancestors of a longtime local resident, Harry Marriott. It was actually called Marriott's Flats and over the years became shortened to Mary's Flat. Frog Lake is in this area, named by Jimmy Rosette who was riding by one day and noticed all the frogs who were living in the grass and bulrushes. Carrying on the trail, you can either go down toward the Fraser to River Camp over Ward Creek, or up toward Home Ranch, the site of the original homestead. Taking the Ward Creek way, you will run into High Pasture toward River Camp. The cowboy horse strings run in here when they aren't being used. Below this is Sawmill Camp, where an old sawmill had once been set up. Some of the Haller family worked there over the years, logging the hills between Big Flat and Home Ranch. The Hallers were an old and established family in this Chilcotin area, particularly in the Canoe Creek area. Big, smiling Bill Haller was one of our more dependable people, on the fencing, farming or irrigating crew, wherever he was needed. He was tragically killed in Williams Lake one weekend in a truck accident.

Above this is Big Flat, a huge flat area overlooking the Big Flat River Breaks, a nightmare place for the cowboys because of its steepness and cavernous hidden valleys. The cattle like to go right down to the bottom for water, and it was always a challenge for the cowboys to get them back out.

Below Ward Creek is China Flat—a large flat right along the river. It is very dry, covered in cactus, treeless, and not used very much for cattle because it is so difficult to get in and out of. The high area above, known as Saddlehorse Mountain, shows evidence of irrigation ditches coming from Ward Creek, which were dug by hand by Chinese people. It's claimed that these Chinese grew terrific gardens and orchards down there. Many Chinese spoons, woks, and other utensils have been found, the only remaining evidence of peaceful, resourceful, hardworking people.

The early spring turnout area for the Gang Ranch, called River Camp, was located by McEwan Creek right at the junction where the green Chilcotin River joins the muddy waters of the Fraser River. Cattle could be put in there the first part of April, and it would graze about 500 head for a month or so.

An old mine site, called the Dry Farm, was above River Camp. There was actually no mine there at all. An enterprising fellow managed to put up a bunch of buildings, set up a company, convinced some people there was a mine, and sold shares. He collected money for the shares, and then quite simply disappeared. A local rancher, Bruce Watt, was one of the owners after that, before it was sold to Steve and Vicki Andruss, an American couple who had lived previously in the Anaheim area to the west. The Andrusses were dry farming the land because, true to its name, there wasn't a bit of water for irrigation. Steve and Vicki were very good neighbors and became lifelong friends of the family. Every year, our cattle would go right through their place, grazing and doing considerable damage to their hay crop, a real nuisance for the couple. They were very neighborly about it, and Rick ended up working out a deal with them whereby we would move our cattle through, then replace their hay with stacks from the ranch.

The Andrusses eventually moved out with their two small children Leah and Owen, and sold the Dry Farm to a young Swiss couple, Charles and Astrid Jauch, who also became good neighbors and friends. Astrid and Charlie had two daughters while on the Dry Farm, Amy and then Leah. I marveled at the inner strength and creativity of these young couples, with small children, taking on the challenges of living on the remote but beautiful Dry Farm.

Mercury Flats was on the road leaving the Dry Farm. Poison Lake was on this flat but was fenced off because a type of plant growing on the edge of the lake was poisonous to cattle if they drank water immediately after eating the plant.

Summer Range was our cow camp just past this, before heading down to the beautiful green Chilcotin River. This was where most of the breeding took place, as the cattle drifted here fairly steadily during turnout. The branding would be finished up here, before the cattle headed up to the high country. The Farwell Canyon camp below, right on the banks of the Chilcotin River, nestled on a flat beneath the towering overhead rocks of Farwell Canyon. Here were about forty irrigated acres, a wonderful growing area, with a log barn, shed and a cabin.

Beyond Summer Range, toward the Chilcotin River again, was Jamieson Meadow, where we built, in a joint project with Ducks Unlimited, a holding reservoir for waterfowl refuge and irrigation. Right at the end was Sugar Cane Jack's, the furthest boundary in that direction. Coming back again toward the ranch on the upper road were Six Mile Pasture and Home Ranch.

Home Ranch was the original headquarters of the Gang Ranch. The colony of old, falling-down buildings and an abandoned graveyard, its carved wooden gravemarkers infiltrated by weeds and grass, told us that this particular homestead had many stories to tell. Warren and Pam Farrell stayed at the Home Ranch for the entire time we had the Gang Ranch. Warren had given up a hectic city life in Toronto for a peaceful life in the Chilcotin looking after the bulls we wintered at the Home Ranch. Warren and Pam became good friends to the Gang Ranch people and to Steve and Vicki Andruss at the Dry Farm. There was a lot of musical talent in this group, and we spent a good many entertaining hours listening to the fine guitar playing and singing of Steve and Warren, who also composed a number of the songs they played.

Mud Creek runs toward Home Ranch Valley from Jamieson Meadow. Along this creek you'd find Johnson's Meadow and Burnt Meadow. There had once been an Indian living in an old cabin there who put up hay on the meadow for the ranch. A muskeg fire started there one time and burned right down into the peat moss on Burnt Meadow, leaving great holes and craters in the ground and making it quite unusable. Anyhow Lake was along here, followed by Coyote Meadows. Carrying on you would come to Williams Meadow, a well-used cow camp because it is the first one heading toward the backcountry from Bear Springs. This 800-acre area contains a cabin and barn with corrals, and irrigated hay fields. The Rosettes originated here at Williams Meadow. As far back as the Rosette fellows can remember, they were all raised here. Tommy's Meadow, George's Meadow, and Augustine's Meadow are all named after Rosettes.

Rosalie Rosette once told me how she and Raymond

got married on the ranch so many years ago. When the festivities were over, being young and carefree and without a vehicle, they decided to walk to Williams Meadow for their honeymoon. She described what a hard trip it was. It was a twenty-five-kilometer hike on not much more than a wagon trail through the bush, and she was wearing her wedding dress, lugging one end of a trunk full of supplies while Raymond hefted the other. It wasn't many miles before she dropped her end of the trunk, rummaged around in it until she found more suitable clothing, and stuffed the poor wedding dress into the trunk. They carried on their way happily, lugging the trunk between them.

Raymond was a fun-loving guy who liked nothing better than a good joke. We heard about the time he walked into a restaurant in town and asked a new waitress for "frog's legs, hummingbird eggs, and fried ice cream, please." She dutifully wrote it down and took the order back to the kitchen.

Clair's Cabin, just below Williams Meadow toward Bear Springs, was named for a woman who cowboyed on the Gang for several years. She was apparently a loner, but a good rider, and she used to run the heifers that they were breeding there.

All these places, all these names—and we haven't even got to the backcountry yet!

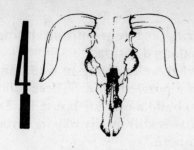

The Eye of the Hurricane

"What's happening?" I asked Rick and Denis as they stood in the midst of a swirling cloud of dusty commotion in the main yard. I suddenly noticed how tired they both looked. It was a good thing calving was nearly over; there had been too many first-year heifers in the herd we had inherited with the ranch, animals that hadn't previously had calves and invariably needed assistance. Rick and Denis were bleary-eyed from taking turns sitting up all night with cowboys, and pulling calves from straining mothers who had given up and needed to be helped along; Rick and Denis would go home toward morning, catch a few hours sleep, then drag themselves out of bed to begin all over again.

It was a beautiful, fresh April in 1979, and spring had arrived in full force, bringing with it all the spring work. On top of the calving problems were the tasks of making sure the farming machinery was ready to go, the fields were prepared for seeding, the range livestock was looked after, the crews were organized, irrigation started, the dams checked and repaired if necessary. The list went on and on. They spent their days running from one problem to the next, organizing and reorganizing, hiring and firing, and constantly making decisions.

"That's what we're trying to find out," Rick answered slowly and in a puzzled tone. "These fellows claim they've been hired to build a new log house for Dale on top of the hill. Their boss is still on his way in. I guess we'll find out when he gets here."

I looked around at the menagerie of people that had just arrived: men, mostly young and well-muscled, long-haired and tanned, dressed in baggy woolen lumberjack pants with suspenders. Some long-haired girls were with them, as well as a cavalcade of trucks, a couple of vans, a jeep, and another high-topped truck with some kind of hoist crane on it.

"Hi. Are you the Alsagers?" A pleasant voice and an extended hand came from a tall, outdoorsy-looking man walking up to us. "My name's Reid Finlayson and I've brought my crew in, as you can see, to build a log house for Dale Alsager."

Rick, Denis, and I exchanged looks as we simultaneously asked each other, "Did you know about this?"

"No, did *you* know about this?" came the chorus of replies.

"I've got the plans right here," said Mr. Finlayson with a smile. "Dale said he liked his house in Alberta so much that he wants this log house built to the same plans."

This time the three of us exchanged glances only, but I could see the same thoughts racing through their heads: Who was paying for this? Why did Dale want a new house built? He was only out here the odd weekend, and he already had a trailer up on the hill. What were we to do with all these people? We didn't have guest accommodation other than the bunkhouse, which was currently filled with staff. If only we had had some warning we could have made some arrangements. As if reading our minds, Reid Finlayson said, "Everyone is more or less prepared to rough it.

70

They have tents and sleeping bags. If they can just hook into some power somewhere...."

"Sure, no problem." I did not want all these people to feel they were not welcome. My mind was frantically making contingencies: the only place where there was any semblance of a flat spot with grass on it in the main yard was the area surrounding our house. They would need water and bathrooms. We did not have any public washhouses or facilities organized.

An hour later, the log builders had moved in. A village, of sorts, sprang up around our house. Trucks, vans, tents, tarps, sleeping bags, lines strung up with blankets hanging on them, laughter, shouts, people playing guitars, and little half-naked kids running around in the sunshine. Our little house had the only bathroom available to these people, and the only electrical outlets. Extension cords snaked out of the house in every direction.

Some of my children were still "afternoon nappers." It seemed I would just get them down for their nap and someone would knock on the door, wanting to use the bathroom. They would then have to sneak through the bedroom where the kids were sleeping to get there. I finally left the front door open; it was easier than answering it all the time.

The only thing worse than having the only bathroom was having the only telephone. Day and night, there was a lineup of people waiting their turn to use the phone. Every call from the Gang Ranch was long-distance so we had to keep track of everyone's calls.

By now, we had got through to Dale by telephone, which was a monumental task in itself. Yes, he was getting the house built, same floor plans as his house in Ardrossan. No, the ranch would not be paying for it. We called a family meeting and everyone voiced concern. He claimed he was paying for it all himself. Later, when it became apparent that ranch money *had* been used, we cornered him and he

71

maintained it would be straightened out later by using his shareholder's loan.

Strange as it may seem, we adapted to a more-or-less communal style of living with all these happy-go-lucky log-building and log-peeling people, who were our "live-in" neighbors all summer. They were good, interesting, hardworking individuals, out in the hot sun peeling logs all day, pulling a curved knife blade with worn wooden handles on either end, back and forth, until no bark remained, just a glistening bare log. Then came what looked like a painstaking job of fitting them together with special notches done over and over again until the logs fit together snugly. Log by log, the monstrous house rose up toward the sky until, by fall, it stood towering above the main yard. Inside, it was like standing inside Dale's house at Ardrossan. It was definitely the same plan, all right, just made out of logs instead of lumber. It was massive—a long many-detailed project for the log building crew—5,000 square feet of hand-hewed notches, special fittings, and sweat, with fireplaces on each of the two levels. The gigantic rock fireplace in the upper living room was hand built by Palle Henriksen Bricklaying from Williams Lake, with help from Bruce Traynor, after the log builders had left.

While the log builders were there, I could have watched them all day, but there was too much to be done; and there were times when I was forced to flee my own home just to be alone.

72

The Big Bet

Later in that same vibrant, bustling spring, Ted and Irene Alsager arrived to stay in their little house down by Rick's. Things had settled down into a sort of routine, and the crews were organized and hard at work in their various capacities. Dad disappeared into the never-ending workforce outside and Mom took right over at the cookhouse. There was something so comforting about having her bustling about behind the counter, turning into a sort of den mother to haying crews, irrigating crews, fencing crews, cowboy crews, farm crews, and anyone else who came along. Mom and Dad would stay for a month or two or until they got the urge to go back home to Maidstone. Dad would get the itch to check on things back there and away they would go.

The business part of the Gang Ranch, from the information provided to us from Dale and the local bank manager Bob Erickson, seemed to be right on track. We had sold $920,236 worth of cattle. It was comforting to know that our livestock inventory at the end of April, 1979, was calculated at $2,692,297, without adding in the value of the newborn calves. The market value of all these animals (appraised at price per pound) was estimated at $4,581,650. Alsager Holdings' livestock now consisted of 194 bulls, 1,150 yearling steers, 1,861 yearling heifers, 2,442 cows,

154 horses, 40 buffalo, and, of course, the new calf crop of 2,385. Over a million dollars had already been paid down on our loan which gave us a good feeling, as Rick and Suzanne, Denis and I, and especially mom and dad, were not accustomed to or comfortable with that big loan hanging over our heads. Although we knew the worth of the Ranch was there, we couldn't wait to get it paid off! At every opportunity, Bob Erickson commended us on the "wonderful job" we were doing out there, and that "everything was going along just great." We were finally starting to relax and enjoy the relentless working routine, knowing that we were headed in a successful direction.

Working on the Gang Ranch was not your normal nine to five job. Breakfast was served at 6:00 A.M. and the crews were working at 7:00 A.M. Some of them trooped into the cookhouse for a midmorning coffee, others didn't even do that. Nobody missed lunch at noon, then out they went again until a mid-afternoon much-needed break, which was their last rest before the gonging cookhouse bell signified supper at 6:00 P.M. In special seasons, such as seeding and haying, when getting the job done meant a race against time and the weather, the crews often went out again after supper, and toiled until dark, or even later. Nobody griped or complained. These were dedicated ranching people who knew what had to be done, and that each job had to be accomplished within its season. They enjoyed their work and they seemed to especially appreciate the fact that Rick and Denis (and Oren, when he was there) didn't just give orders but worked right alongside the crew at whatever was being done.

One night of the week saw a break in the grueling routine. That was Saturday night. The work stopped at 6:00 P.M. and, after the evening meal was cleared away, boots were polished, belt buckles shined up, cowlicks slicked down, and everyone donned their finest Saturday night duds. The evening started out in the Gang Ranch store, where people gathered to pick up supplies, but more so to visit. Shopping was done differently here. People on the Ranch bought their groceries and other needs on their "book," which meant each employee had a special little account book where a record was kept of their purchases. At the end of the month, the amount of their purchases was deducted from their paycheck. This way, no cash actually changed hands. We tried to stock everything needed on the Ranch: groceries, western clothing, cowboy hats, rain slickers, saddles, tack, lariats, kerosene lamps, horseshoes, bubble gum, and, of course, a solid supply of Redman chewing tobacco. It was not unusual for some families to spend their entire paycheck in the store.

When the store closed around 9:00 P.M., everyone would retire to the school or the cookhouse to relax and visit at a bingo, a movie, or, on special occasions such as Halloween or Christmas, music and dancing. Everyone brought baking to be awarded as prizes at the Saturday night bingos, which were one of our favorite entertainments. The bingos were fun because they brought in neighbors from Alkali, Dog Creek, Empire Valley Ranch, and Canoe Creek, sometimes even as far away as Big Creek on the other side of the Chilcotin River. Prospectors that camped at their gold claims along the Fraser River and Churn Creek showed up for the action on Saturday nights. The neighbors might have been far away, but they certainly were enthusiastic.

Movies were shown on the school projector, some of them as mundane as sped-up versions of plants growing. Others were in foreign languages, such as French or Italian, with English subtitles. Nobody cared; they were free, sent out on the "stage" by the Department of Education, and we were there for the laid-back hours of visiting, laughing, and rehashing the week's calamities and accomplishments. This was when the cowboy who got bucked off his horse paid his dues by being the brunt of good-natured ribbing. It was here that the normal and inevitable disputes between any individuals on the ranch were mended and

75

forgotten. Ours was a small intimate community—there was no room for contention.

Entertainment was homemade; it had to be. There were no theaters, clubs, or fancy restaurants. The ranch's people had to rely on each other for their entertainment. We may not have enjoyed all the conveniences, but the Gang Ranch had a very active social scene, and you didn't need any money to attend any of it. The food was provided, the entertainment was live, and the jokes were free. One of the most popular pastimes was betting. As far as entertainment goes, I guess bets were at the top of the list on the Ranch—right up there with story-telling. One of the most memorable contests was between Randy Smulan and Oren. Randy was the eighteen-year-old son of our sister, Donna, and was a happy and welcome visitor at the ranch. On this particular day, his sleeves rolled up over his elbows, Randy was busy cleaning fish with the rest of the group.

"What do you bet I can eat this fish eye?" Oren grinned at Randy.

Delighted chortling passed around the fish-cleaning table, and amused looks were exchanged between the onlookers. "Bet you can't!" Randy had a soft, endearing giggle that accompanied everything he said.

"Bet I can!" Oren egged the situation on, trying to think of something he could force Randy to do if he was successful in getting that slimy fish eye down his throat.

Oren's eyes roved around the now fully attentive group. Gut-stained hands paused in anticipation as Oren's eyes came to a halt at the rolled-up end of a packet of snoose peeking out of someone's pocket. A sly smile slowly unfolded across his face.

"Tell you what," he announced gleefully. "If I eat this fish eye, you have to eat a full pack of Redman tobacco, swallow the whole thing, and keep it down!" Randy raised his eyebrows, contemplating this challenge for a minute. He had never chewed tobacco but he must have been thinking that the bags looked pretty small. Surely it couldn't be

76

that bad if he just swallowed it real quick. Beside, he probably didn't think Oren was going to be able to eat that fish eye.

"Okay, you're on!" he said recklessly.

Without further fanfare and before he lost the momentum of the moment, Oren gripped his narrow, curved, gut-stained filleting knife, popped the slimy fish eye into his mouth and gave a giant swallow. Then, for added effect, without blinking an eye, he dug the other unseeing orbit out of the gruesome-looking fish head, tossed it into his mouth, and gulped it down, too.

"Mmmm, good," he grinned, smacking his lips, ignoring the opposition he felt inside.

"Gross." "Yuck." "Ah-h." These and other responses echoed around the room as the horrified onlookers grimaced at the sight.

"Well, Randy, when's the big tobacco act?" Oren asked jubilantly, wiping the corners of his mouth.

Everyone strained forward to get the goods on the next show. Randy thought quietly for a minute.

"Well, if I eat the tobacco and keep it down, then you have to do something next."

"What's that?" demanded Oren.

Randy sat motionless, trying to think of the most vulgar thing a human being could be made to swallow. The room was silent with the unbroken tension.

Suddenly he burst out, "I've got it!" In his excitement, he began to pace back and forth beside the now forgotten salmon corpse.

"If I get the tobacco down and keep it down," he paused to point a sticky-looking filleting knife at Oren, "you have to eat one of those baby birds that just hatched out in that tree we were looking at!"

Hiding his shock, Oren looked at Randy, trying to appear nonchalant about the repelling horror he must have felt inside, and the recoiling turns his stomach was taking at the mere thought. They had just looked at those newly

77

hatched birds that morning, fat, squat blobs, with a bulging blue-veined sac for a gut, wide beak, and wrinkled featherless skin—truly the ugliest things he had seen for some time. He and Randy had jokingly wondered how the mother bird could stand to look at them long enough to cram food into their gaping mouths.

Groans and moans, and horrified hands-over-mouth whispers resounded throughout the room, as Oren silently weighed his chances. He must have felt pretty sure Randy wouldn't be successful with the tobacco, but what if he was? Still, he couldn't back out now; it was too hard on the pride.

"You're on!" he called out, braver than he probably felt.

Excited people scattered like chaff in the wind. Word spread like prairie wildfire around the ranch circuit. One thing about a place like the Gang Ranch, Ben Johnson himself couldn't outrun a rumor; and any rumors about an ongoing bet, well, they traveled twice as fast. Bets were placed, and replaced, wagers grew by the minute. Everyone was trying to find out when and where all this was going to take place. The whole place was buzzing with anticipation, and the stakes were growing higher with each buzz.

Then came the moment of truth. Randy sat eyeing the open bag of Redman tobacco on the table in front of him, trying to radiate an outward show of confidence. Every eye in the place upon him, he reached for the bag, dipped into it with his fingers, and crammed the entire mass into his mouth, gulping heavily, before he had time to think too much about it.

The package finally sat empty, and Randy sat back, smiling at all the sympathetic, expectant faces.

There, that wasn't so bad, he was probably thinking to himself. All of a sudden, his entire body cramped up in a huge convulsion, violently rejecting the vile substance that had finally worked its way into his system. Eyes bulging, he jumped up in a desperate attempt to get to the door. He staggered outside, clutching onto the door frame, lurched around the corner, and disappeared, the sounds of gagging and retching floating back in through the by-now crowded doorway.

Seconds later, he was found, draped unceremoniously over the pole fence at the back. He hung there like a well-used dishrag and no, the tobacco had not remained where it was supposed to. At no time before, and at no time in the future, would he ever again be this ill.

Oren breathed a sigh of secret relief. He was not at all certain he could have faced the prospect of actually stuffing one of those ugly baby birds into his mouth.

Wagers were steady and ongoing within the cowboy crew: who could stay the longest on any particular cantankerous cayuse, or sometimes a bull; who could rope a certain uncooperative, range-wise cow; who could get from one cow camp to another the fastest; whose gun fired the straightest.

Turkey shoots were also a big hit. Usually held on a Sunday afternoon, everyone showed up with their most reliable guns, a box of shells, and earplugs to deafen the noise. Targets were set up at different intervals, some 25 meters away, some 50 meters away, and so on. Everyone took turns, aiming carefully at the bull's-eye center of each target, the hole left by their bullet marked with their initials afterward. Prizes (usually frozen turkeys or chickens) were given out to the best male long-distance shot, the best female long-distance shot, the best juvenile shot, and so on through all the targets. Poor shots, or shots that missed the target altogether, were always blamed on the gun.

Some Sunday afternoons someone would see a truckload of people heading up to the dam at Fosberry Meadows to fish, and pretty soon a lineup of other trucks, pickup boxes filled with kids, dogs, and fishing gear, would follow. It would inevitably end up with a big campfire and storytelling, the edible goodies anybody brought unquestionably shared amongst everybody. Wintertime saw the same sce-

79

nario, the only difference was that it was usually a woodcutting get-together. Everyone would head out on the backroads with trucks and snowmobiles; the men would chainsaw blocks of wood, others would swing an ax to chop the blocks into firewood size, then everyone would get busy and load all the wood into the trucks. Afterward, people would congregate again around a huge fire, sipping carefully at steaming cups of hot chocolate. The kids would inevitably lose wieners off their sticks, as they always do, but it wouldn't matter in the winter. They fell in the snow and could be picked up and jammed back on the blackened sticks again.

Branding time was an event everyone attended. The new calves had to be branded in the spring before being turned out on the range for the summer months. It usually took a couple of brandings at well-spaced intervals to include the late calves, and later on to catch any "slicks"— older calves that, for one reason or another, had been missed during the first brandings. The calves were weaned from their mothers, separated physically, which forced them to start grazing on grass and finding water on their own. The cowboy crew had a well-organized pattern they followed at branding. Everyone took their place at whatever job they had been assigned to in the assembly line of separating the calves. They would run them methodically through the corrals, one cowboy roping them while another threw the calf to the ground. The calf would then receive the full treatment: a sizzling branding iron would implant the historical Gang Ranch JH brand on its hip, it would be injected with an antibiotic to protect against infection, a plastic ear tag with a number was fastened on its ear as backup identification, it would be treated for any ailments such as pinkeye and, if it was a bull calf, castrated. The testicles that were removed from the bull calves were kept in a container close by, as there were always those people who fried them up for a good feed afterward—a dish commonly referred to as "prairie oysters."

This sounds like a complicated and time-consuming operation, but the cowboys were professionals at this. They had performed these procedures so many times that it was like clockwork to them. Whir-r-r, the rope caught the calf around the neck, and a cloud of dust rose when the calf hit the ground. Before the dust had cleared, the calf would be up and trotting off to join its colleagues, inoculated, ear-tagged, branded, and castrated, and the next calf in line already on the ground. These brandings were usually held at the cow camps outside the main yard—Summer Range or Big Meadow. We women would take all the fixings for a huge meal and prepare it on the wood cookstove in the camp cabin. We made sure it was ready when the crew was nearly finished, because we knew they would be absolutely starving. We would feed all the children, and shoo them away with their plates before the hot, dusty and dog-tired crew clomped hungrily in for theirs. Everyone being fed, and the cleanup accomplished, it was time to relax around the inevitable campfire with strong black coffee.

Roundup was another event performed at the various cow camps when everyone converged to enjoy the activities, volumes of food, and campfire relaxation afterward. The cowboys worked at gathering the cattle herd from the various valleys, ravines, gulches, creeks, and innumerable hiding spots and brought them into one huge herd. Here they would be doctored for any injuries or disease, sorted according to their size and age, and channeled to their next destination. Pregnancy testing was performed on the heifers and cows; the ones that tested "open" (for one reason or another had not conceived) would be shipped out along with cull animals (old, crippled or ill ones). They were trucked to our Perry Ranch feedlot at Cache Creek and taken to market from there.

There were also the marriages and funerals on the Ranch. A cowboy and his girlfriend exchanged wedding vows on Table Mountain; the ashes of Ernest Gibson, a gold miner from down on Churn Creek who was accidentally shot by his twin brother John, were scattered on the scenic climb to Home Ranch. Good-natured, smiling Bill Haller from our farm crew was killed in a tragic truck accident in Williams Lake. Also Jeff, a young worker who had come to the Ranch from New Brunswick, was killed when his truck went over a cliff on the way to Dog Creek. All these events served to bring the Ranch people together, in celebration and in sorrow.

The Cowboy Circuit

The priority of everyone on the Gang Ranch, and the utmost in importance was the cattle herd. That was the reason the Gang Ranch existed. Everyone on the Ranch, from irrigator to fencing crew, to farm hands to cowboys, knew the cattle herd came first, and that the Department of Forestry had to be kept happy.

The forestry department controlled the number of cattle we were allowed to have on the property. It hadn't always been that way. Old Jimmy laughingly recalled the days when the cowboys had the demeaning job of herding and rounding up the thousands of hogs that were raised on Lake Ranch around Hog Lake.

"You hadda run 'em from the front, not from behind," he hooted with laughter at the memory. It seemed that all the cowboys had a long whip-like switch, which they used to direct the hogs' heads in whichever direction they were supposed to go. "It was pretty hard to rope 'em," Jimmy claimed.

There were, of course, other sources of revenue on the Ranch, but they seemed pale in comparison to the cattle shipments every fall that made the Alsager Holdings operation viable. There were 20,000 acres of deeded freehold mineral right lands on the Gang that certainly beckoned with future potential; and there was standing timber, probably around $100,000 worth. We also had advertising companies use the Gang Ranch terrain for their filming—Marlboro Cigarettes came in more than once with their crews and stayed to get that special *take*. We women would groan when we heard they were coming—they needed a 4:00 A.M. breakfast, to enable them to be out and ready with their equipment when the first light of dawn appeared. This meant we had to be at the cookhouse at 3:00 A.M. The first light of day apparently offered the best light for their shots.

The buffalo herd played its part in the operation, too. They were definitely a tourist attraction but, in a financial sense, they offered a diversified form of income. We had a steady stream of buffalo hunts lined up each year, that helped to keep our herd pared to an operable size. They were mostly Germans from overseas, the hunters were flown in, shot their animal, and went away with a head mount. We still had the meat to sell, and the hide. There was a demand for both items. Oren presided over the buffalo hunts. He was the expert at it, and there could never be any mistakes made. A buffalo hunt would net around $2,000 for the Ranch.

Old Jimmy was the keeper of the buffalo. He would finish up his day of irrigating, and then start on his buffalo rounds. He always knew where they were. Dusk would see the huge round-topped cowboy hat come over the hill at Bear Springs, followed by the little straight man sitting so erectly on his buckskin horse. Cowdogs, Moose and Bear, trotted happily and obediently at the rear.

The buffalo were used to Old Jimmy and didn't pay him any mind as he wandered quietly among them. If he wanted to move them somewhere, he simply walked in front of them carrying a pail, and they followed him like lambs. After satisfying himself that all was right with the buffalo herd, Old Jimmy would park the buckskin out front of our house in the grass. She would be left to graze under the watchful eye of Moose and Bear while he came in for a coffee before heading back down to the Ranch.

On one particular evening, all was not well with the buffalo herd. Old Jimmy found a newborn calf that had been abandoned, left behind by the herd. Even the mother had walked away from the quivering red infant, leaving it to fend for itself. Oren was summoned and, between him and Old Jimmy, they managed to lug the not-so-tiny baby over to the Bear Springs house. We mixed up special powdered milk concentrate to substitute for his mother's milk, and he attacked the huge nipple on the jug-type bottle with gusto. When it was all gone, he was not impressed. Less than a day old, he took a run at me and butted me up against the wall of the barn with a force that held me there. I was unable to break away from him. Laughing, we marveled at the inborn neck strength of this supposedly sick newborn.

Although he ate well, and was always anxious for the nourishment, the abandoned calf still seemed to have a problem of some kind. At times he would hang his head down and seemed to have trouble breathing. Antibiotics didn't seem to help. One day his breathing became so labored that I called Oren up from the main Ranch. The kids had become so attached to him that I certainly didn't want something to happen to him now. With great effort, we managed to get him into the blue Bellanca—he was now almost two weeks old and even heavier than he had previously been. If he had not been in a weakened condition, we could never have accomplished it. As he roared off into the morning sky with Oren, I wondered to myself how many baby buffaloes could boast about flying to town.

The veterinarian in Williams Lake met Oren at the airport and whisked the calf off to the clinic. He was not to survive. There was no cure—the diagnosis was that his lungs were not properly formed at birth.

The buffalo herd, starting with the mother, knew that he had a defect. That is why they seemingly so cruelly left him to die. They would not allow a weakness to flourish and be passed on to another generation. It was instinctive for them to allow only the strong and healthy to survive. This was the basis for their historical survival as a species.

The buffalo herd attracted many tourists and curiosity seekers, and promised to grow as a business, but it was the cyclical romance of the cowboys and the cattle operation that made the Ranch flow. It was a well-known fact that the cattle numbers being housed on the Gang Ranch grazing lands now nowhere fulfilled the numbers that it could potentially carry. Presently the leased grazing lands allowed for 27,500 A.U.M.s (animal unit months). The local range coordinator from the Department of Forestry, Ross Fredell, estimated that, with range improvements, reseeding, and proper grazing control, the availability of in excess of 100,000 A.U.M.s could be possible. The method to increase the amount of grazing land available was to expand the land base. We planned to develop new irrigation works at Home Ranch, Lake Ranch, Crows Bar, Perry Ranch, Front Pasture, China Flat, and Big Flat. This, as Rick and Denis and the cowboss had worked out with Forestry, could double our hay production, therefore providing winter feed for twice the number of cattle. The potential for livestock grazing on the Gang Ranch would probably be limitless, if you investigated every possible area that had not yet been developed or utilized.

Rick, in concert with the cowboss and the forestry representative, arranged for over 1,000 acres to be reseeded to crested wheat grass and wild rye. The new pivot irrigation systems installed at Bear Springs greatly increased the hay production for the main Ranch area. Barley was planted at Williams Meadow on the flood-irrigated hayfields there. The 800 acres at Williams Meadow were a perfect location for fattening up the cattle before marketing them in the fall. Williams Meadow was a good central camp for the cattle moving through, to and from various range areas to the west. The trick was to keep the cattle moving in a way that constantly kept good grazing grass in front of them, with the least possible stress on the animals. The Gang Ranch's cattle flow chart pretty well kept the herd moving smoothly. Changes in weather and grass conditions in certain pastures in certain years dictated constant supervision and deviations to the cattle flow sheet.

Visitors to the Gang Ranch invariably had the same desire when they arrived there—they wanted to see a cowboy, a real live cowboy. This was not always easy, as the cowboys spent a good nine months of the year out on the range—it was seldom that they could be found around the main yard. Once the calves were born in the spring and were ready to leave the wintering areas of Bear Springs and the main headquarters, the cattle and the cowboys were on the move. Turnout was around the first week in April. They would head out on their circuitous rotation around the grazing camps and would not return to the main yard until the following winter in time for calving again.

The older and more mature cows were kept at Bear Springs for calving. The younger cows and first-time calvers were kept down at the main yard in close proximity to the "maternity ward" calving barn. This barn was outfitted with special stalls and equipment for pulling calves, and with refrigerated veterinary supplies. The cowboys continually rode through the herds at calving time, looking for the telltale signs of a cow getting ready to calve. If they saw a cow going off by herself, or a tail held in the air or, in the later stages, the front hooves of the calf protruding from the cow, she was watched carefully. If signs of trouble occurred—straining or agitation, or hours going by with nothing happening, the cow or heifer would be herded into the calving barn for assistance. This would sometimes entail pulling the calf—fastening special sterilized stainless steel pullers around the calve's front feet and helping the mother along. Occasionally a cesarean would be required to remove the calf from the mother—if the calf was too large or in a breech position (coming out backwards). The cowbosses were able to perform cesareans if it was not possible to get the local veterinarian in time. An attempt was made not to breed the heifers when they were too small, and not to use too large a bull for breeding. Cesareans were costly, time consuming, and stressful. The best bulls we had were Dad's purebred Hereford stock. It took one bull for every twenty-two cows in the breeding season. Once a year the bulls were performance tested for disease and for semen counts, usually about 10 percent of the bulls would be culled and shipped at that time.

The breeding cow herd was similarly culled and the cull cows trucked out to market to be replaced by the purchase of bred heifers. Depending on the cattle market, these could be purchased at around $600 per head. Sometimes unbred heifers were purchased at a lower price for future production. All our own calves that didn't go to finishing stock as yearlings were kept for replenishing the cow herd. Finished yearlings were sold each year for seventy-five cents to eighty cents per pound.

In 1980 we purchased twenty-three Fraser Red brood cows. This was a new breed that reportedly had been developed specially for British Columbian conditions; their hardiness would cope with the tough terrain, and they were supposedly easy calvers. Our regular cattle herd was comprised of a little bit of everything, crosses of white-faced Herefords, black angus, red angus, a few charolais crossbreds, and the rangy tough Texas longhorns.

The tail end of the calving season gave the cowboss a little breathing space while they waited for the inevitable late-calvers to get their calves on the ground. This gave the cowboss time to assess his crew for the coming year, and hire more cowboys for the coming brandings, turnout, and backcountry circuit. It wasn't that simple to find appropriate people for the back country work. There were the old tried and true reliables who loved that kind of life—the isolation for long periods of time, with no one but their dogs and the black flies to talk to. There were just as many starry-eyed young hopefuls trying to hire on for the romantic life of a cowboy. They didn't realize that romance is hard to find when you're out in the middle of nowhere with no roads, no trucks, and the closest female is about fifty miles away. They might have Oren come roaring down in the little blue Bellanca with a load of salt blocks or other supplies occasionally; other than that, they were on their own. When we installed the solar-powered transmitter on the Marble Mountain site, we did outfit the cowboys in the back country with hand-held portable radios in case of emergency.

One such emergency occurred when a distress call came in from the cowboy camp at Summer Range. Three cowboys were staying at the camp, gathering cattle and getting ready to move them on to the next pasture. A young cowboy named Breezey had apparently disappeared. The call came in from Keith Van Zandt, one of our tried and true cowboys. It was morning now, and they had been looking for Breezey since the previous day. They had all been out riding when Breezey's half-green horse took off with him. Into the bush they headed, and a low-hanging tree limb whacked Breezey off the horse. The other two cowboys, galloping along behind, kept on after the fleeing horse. The last they saw of Breezey, he was lying in a heap on the ground. Breezey had not had a good week. A few days previous to this he was in a wreck with a different horse, who again took off on him. By the time they caught up with that horse, Breezey needed a new saddle and a new gun. He had just returned to the camp with a spanking new saddle and rifle; Keith figured he definitely wouldn't want to lose these now.

Eventually they caught up to the renegade horse, and between the two of them managed to corner him long enough to grab a dangling rein; the other rein was broken off. Breezey would be doing some repair work, but a least the saddle and the rifle were still there. Leading the frothing horse, they headed back to find Breezey and tell him the good news. Returning to the place under the heavy low-hanging limb where they had last seen him, they were surprised to find no one there. They circled around the area a bit, thinking he may have started to follow them. They hollered his name—no answer.

"He must have walked back to the cabin," they reasoned. It was a fair ways, but it seemed to be the only possibility. They headed back to the camp; the cabin was empty.

They were now becoming quite concerned. While they put Breezey's horse away in the corral, and hauled his new saddle and rifle to the cabin, they discussed the possibility of the lost cowboy wandering around in a daze, with a concussion or something. This prompted them to remount their horses and quickly head out for more searching.

They spent the rest of that day, hollering, circling, and trying to follow Breezey's tracks from the scene. They could follow them for a ways, until they became lost in the grass. Finally darkness settled in, and the mosquitos. Breezey the cowboy had quite simply disappeared.

When the call came in the next morning that Breezey could not be found, Oren immediately put the blue Bellanca into action and headed for Summer Range. The cowboys were out on their horses again, searching. The day was spent on a relentless air and ground search. Oren, in the air, followed over every path in every direction that he figured that cowboy could go. They came up with nothing—it was as though he had vanished into thin air. Darkness again stopped the fruitless hunting, and wearily they decided to resume at first light.

The following morning, a call came in to the Gang Ranch office. It was none other than Breezey, calling from Hundred Mile House, the next town one hundred kilometers down the highway from Williams Lake. He had walked to the logging road after he had been skimmed off his horse, and caught a ride with a passing logging truck. Why didn't he stop in Williams Lake? "Cause the driver was going to Hundred Mile House." There never was a clear answer as to why he hitched out in the first place.

Another emergency call came in when a young regular cowboy named Duncan Barnett from Williams Lake became very ill out in cow camp. They had just moved from the previous camp when a violent sickness hit him. Duncan was well-liked and his concerned coworkers were frantic to get him some medical attention. He was flown to Cariboo Memorial Hospital in Williams Lake, where his condition stabilized after a couple of days. Opinions were varied as to what had happened. The other cowboys at the camp claimed he had eaten corn flakes in the morning that had smelled like kerosene. "How on earth could that happen?" everyone wondered. Speculation was that, when they moved from one camp to another, the open box of corn flakes was packed into the same box as the kerosene, and had absorbed a noticeable amount. Duncan recovered to return to his post in the back country.

The first of April signaled the turnout of the cattle herd. They would start moving away from the wintering areas (Bear Springs and the main yard) to Rock Pile, Big Flat, and to the River Camp area, a 2,600-acre area on the warm, early green Chilcotin River slopes.

They would drift around this area and gradually move via Saddlehorse Mountain and River Camp to the 2,200-acre Summer Range area. Sometime between May 15 and June 1, all the cows would be assembled at Summer Range cow camp. This task is not as easy as it sounds. The cows have to be gathered from some tough areas down in the rugged Chilcotin river breaks. This is where the seasoned veteran cowboys proved their value—they could pick out which ones of the myriads of nearly inaccessible pockets were hiding places for lost cows. The cattle tended to gather along the creeks in the back country—the Gang Ranch held water licenses on sixty-one separate creeks.

Here at Summer Range a major branding session would take place, with the whole ranch in attendance. The calves would be branded, castrated, and doctored, ready for the next move. The bulls that had spent the winter down on the beautiful 300-acre Farwell Canyon, or up at Home Ranch, were turned back in with the cows. Another breeding season would now begin.

In the meantime, last year's yearlings have been turned out on their spring range on the 1,200-acre Wycott Flats area along the Churn Creek Valley. The replacement heifers would be kept separate from the main herd here, and would later be moved to adjoining range near Williams Meadow for the summer.

By the first week in July the herd would begin moving into the Fosberry Meadows and Big Meadow areas. Fosberry with its 500 acres and Big Meadow with 300 acres are the main stopover points for the cattle before they move back into the high country. Both camps are equipped with well-constructed corral systems and good cabins.

The first week in July was always a test for the Gang Ranch, and probably every other outfit in the area. It was the Williams Lake Stampede week. It was also right smack in the middle of haying season and cattle moving. One day might not have been so bad, but once the crew got to town and met up in the local taverns with old friends and new ones, it could be a good week before a normal crew would be reassembled on the Ranch. Some of them had to be bailed out of jail, and others met up with new prospects and simply didn't return. The few weeks preceding Stampede Week weren't much better. It was forest fire season, and it seemed that numerous fires would break out just before Stampede week in the Chilcotin forests. Workers would get pulled off their jobs to go and fight fires. They got paid well for this service and everyone needed the extra cash for their Stampede celebrating. It was with uncanny occurrence that the fires would start a week or so before Stampede, giving everyone a chance to get the fires stopped, and collect their cash before the celebrating started.

As soon as all this was over with, the veteran cowboys

would commence the serious task of dispersing the cattle herd into the high back country. Cattle that had been sorted out to be sent to market would be trucked out. These normally went to our Perry Ranch feedlot first, to be readied and sent to buyers and auction markets from there. Here they had a chance to recover any weight lost in the maneuvers. The preparation for the high country took organization and forethought, as they would be leaving behind the half-civilized areas of the lower cow camps, and heading up into the isolated no-turning-back valleys. Equipment had to be gathered together: radios, lanterns, tools for fixing leatherwork, extra horseshoes and boxes of horseshoe nails, bedrolls, axes, food, tack, rifles, bullets, dog food, and a medicine kit for doctoring sick cows. They needed fencing materials to mend any broken fences they came upon. Nothing could be forgotten and left behind— there were no roads past Hungry Valley for supplies to be taken in. Snoose-chewers made certain they had enough chew to see them through, and probably a little extra for good insurance. Oren was invaluable at this time, flying in supplies to various camps, to lighten the load on the packhorses.

The cattle herd would fan out across Hungry Valley or Big Meadow, where they would begin their summer foraging and gradually move higher and higher to the other camps as the grass situation dictated. A lone cowboy at each camp would be responsible for baby-sitting the herd, repairing the fences, doctoring any sick animals, and keeping the wolves, bears, and other predators away. When time came to move the herd to another camp, other cowboys would join him to gather the cattle and move them to the next good grass.

Thus they spent their summer and fall, pushing cattle back to Blue Door, Lost Valley, Beaver Valley, Relay Valley, Little Paradise, Upper Dash Meadows, and Graveyard Valley. The grazing lands in the upper alpine areas such as

Graveyard Valley were very fragile, and the cattle had to be moved quickly from one camp to another.

The cabins at each camp were all outfitted with everything the cowboy would need—wood cookstove, and barrel-type wood heaters, cots, cooking utensils and camp pots, corn broom, etc. The one thing that the camps didn't provide was relief from the loneliness. Some of the cowboys were used to and actually relished the time to themselves. Others found the isolation too much of a challenge.

Women were not supposed to be out at cow camp with the cowboys. We had made this rule after an episode with a girl named Holly. Holly was a nice-looking aggressive young lady who had met one of the cowboys in town on a weekend of reveling and had followed him out to the Gang. She was an artist, of sorts, and we would see her in various places around the yard, sitting in front of her easel with paints and brushes. Although I attempted to catch a glimpse on passing of her work, the paper was usually quite empty. She kept claiming she was starting over. One day I was walking by the corrals when the cowboys were busy branding and castrating some calves and blinked my eyes in disbelief. There was Holly, standing over a calf with a smoking JH branding iron, in her tight blue jeans, tiny tank top, and bright red high-heeled shoes. "Now I've seen everything!" I thought.

The cowboys returned to cow camp, and Holly packed up her easel and moved with them. Rick was a little dubious, but she was already out there before we knew about it, and no one seemed to be having a problem. Someone mentioned it would be kind of nice to "have a cook around the camp."

Once the cowboys were out at camp, we didn't see a lot of them, and they tended to keep the problems they encountered out there to themselves. It was many weeks later before Oren heard a quiet complaint that there were some problems at that cow camp. It seemed that Holly and her cowboy friend were living in the cabin, and the rest of the cowboys had taken up residence outside on the ground. They weren't terribly happy about it, but nobody wanted to radio down with the complaint. Oren flew out to rectify the situation, and Holly had to pack up her easel once more.

Then there was Harold Hawkins, the shadowy cowboss Dale had hired from the office in town. He claimed he didn't need any help from the Gang Ranch cowboys because he had two of his own "crew" with him. They never did come through the main yard, and it was some time before we found out that his "crew" consisted of Rose and Tex—two women he kept out at the camp with him.

After we made the no women in camp rule, I happened to ride out to Hungry Valley with Stephanie. It had been a full day's ride and we were anxious to reach the cabin before dark. As we trotted closer to the cabin, we saw one of the Gang Ranch trucks beside the cabin, and realized we would have company here tonight. While we put our horses away, there was some movement in and out of the cabin as they had no doubt heard us ride up. We noticed one of the older cowboys and his two grown-up sons.

Trooping into the cabin afterward, we exchanged greetings and prepared to make something to eat. Although they made us welcome, I sensed that they would have been happier if we weren't there. "Too bad," I thought, "but we're here now."

One of the sons, in particular, did not look happy, and made numerous trips out into the darkness for reasons we couldn't comprehend. Sometimes he stayed out for quite awhile. When he did come in, he slumped in the corner sitting on his cot, quite openly sulking.

I thought I had better radio down to the Ranch and let everyone know where we were and where we were spending the night. I asked the elder cowboy if I could use the radio that I knew was in the truck.

"Shore, go right ahead!" he answered, but I couldn't help but see the side glances they were exchanging among themselves.

Something strange is going on here, I thought to myself.

Before I could get my coat on and head out the door, the younger son had disappeared outside again. I heard the truck door slam.

Outside, I opened the truck door and climbed in behind the steering wheel, and picked up the mike hanging on the front of the radio. As I started to call down to the Ranch, I reached behind me to remove something I was sitting on. It was a woman's purse, sitting partly open on the seat with a tube of lipstick ready to fall out.

That's strange, I puzzled, a woman's purse way out here? I put my call through, returned to the cabin, and we settled down for the night. The youngest cowboy was still noticeably untalkative, still sulking in the corner, and after a few more trips outside, I was starting to piece together what his problem was. He must have brought a lady out to camp and now, because Steph and I had shown up, he couldn't bring her in the cabin. I wondered what he had done with her; if he didn't have the guts to bring her in, should I say something? There didn't seem to be anything appropriate to say. If he had brought her in, I wouldn't have said anything—nobody is turned away from lodging in that country. The night passed, with the cowboy spending half the time running back and forth outside. Either he had an immense bladder problem, or he was trying to pacify an angry girlfriend, who was no doubt being eaten by black flies and mosquitos in the bush. There was an old fallen down log structure up behind the cabin; I figured she must have spent the night in there, or else in the truck. Neither place was exactly inviting. It must have been a cold miserable night for her—one I'm sure he would hear about for a long time.

The next morning we saddled up and left early, leaving them to whatever devices they were up to. When I returned to the Ranch, Denis told me he had seen the young cowboy in question drive through the main yard in the truck. A girl with long dark hair was in the truck with him.

In the late summer and fall, the cattle began to drift back down toward the Ranch. Grazing season closes on December 30, and the Department of Forestry would have to be satisfied that no animals were on the range past that date. In September the cattle started moving out of the high country to lower grass in Big Meadow, Tony's Meadow, Big Swamp. By October they would be moving into the Augustines Meadow area of the Williams Meadow unit. The cowboys followed this drifting, attempting to make sure none got left behind or lost in the innumerable pockets and endless numbers of tiny meadows that were everywhere. By the time Thanksgiving rolled along in October, the women on the Ranch could be found getting a huge turkey dinner ready for the weaning and late brandings at Big Meadow when the cattle reached that point. This was one of my favorite times—the weather was beautiful, Indian summer, and we could enjoy the Thanksgiving feast without interference from the pesky black flies and mosquitos. Everyone was in good spirits as the cowboy crew could start to see the end of their long isolation. Excitement built up from here on and culminated in the final leg of their journey—the last drive down to the main Ranch wintering grounds on Christmas Day.

All the cowboys were going full-force now, in these days of gathering and searching for strays. The cattle kept moving out of Big Meadow, Little Gaspard, down from Stump Lake toward the main Ranch. Here they knew were stackyards upon stackyards of the farm crew's *bread loaves* of hay that would see them over the remainder of the winter.

The cattle and cowboys had to trail the last few miles down to the main yard around a side hill where it was basically single file. Everyone was out with cameras to catch the first glimpse of the endless numbers of moving cattle that filed steadily down. It seemed the wavering line would go on forever with the bawling and the squeaking of their hooves on the snowy terrain. The cowboy crew drove them on, hunched in their saddles with their backs to the driving wind, faces and cheeks red and weather beaten. They were cold and weary, but happy. They knew a big Christmas celebration of turkey and the works awaited them. And, except for the inevitable strays that would still be gathered, the cattle were back down from the high country, away from the brutal mountain winters. They could now rest up for calving season, which would begin in a couple of month's time. There would be a little space here to relax, clean their rifles, break in a new rope, oil up their saddles and leather chaps, make repairs on their tack and, of course, spend some much-needed time with their ladies.

Ongoing Calamities

"**H**ere we go again," Suzanne exclaimed. "It must be that damned radiator again! How far are we from the Lindes?"

I looked up and saw the stinking brown cloud of steam hissing out from under the hood of the protesting green Ford Supercab.

It was a bright summer's day in 1980, and we were returning from the hot, 100-kilometer drive home from Williams Lake, loaded down to the axles with the store supplies, the shop supplies, and everyone's special orders. The groaning 4X4 truck was always overloaded on these trips with as much as could be piled precariously or stacked on without falling off: everything from cases of Pampers to horseshoe nails, to propane tanks that had to be filled in town and carted back out to the ranch, to people that had been left behind in town from last Saturday night. It was left to Suzanne and I to see to the provisions for the store, the school, the cookhouse, the cow camps, the shop, and the people. Most important of all was the tobacco supply. The cab was also, as usual, full of our children, some of whom were asleep in impossible-looking positions, entwined and overlapping each other like snakes in a pit.

"Can't be that far," I replied. "The cattleguard's coming up." We had done this so many times. The old ranch trucks were not exactly reliable, and the bumpy, dusty trip to town often did them in. The road passed conveniently through the farm of Ken and Kathy Linde. It always seemed to be their yard we went limping into, smoke and steam belching out from under the hood, like today, or else thumping along on a flat tire. Whatever the problem was, Ken and his sons Douglas and Howard took over the vehicle problems while we spilled all our kids into the house and visited happily with Kathy, sampling her latest homemade wine, catching up on all the news from the outside world. It was like an oasis for us.

Ken and the boys would weld up the leaking radiators, patch the tires, whatever it took to get us back home again. They always refused any offers of payment, and lifelong friendships developed with this fine family. Howard Linde later took on the monumental task of building a high-wheeled chuckwagon for us (not unlike the old "prairie schooners"), which served as a movable cookhouse on the Gang Ranch. Kathy Linde spent many hours sewing the chuckwagon's massive white canvas top.

Anyone making the long trip to town was usually delegated to pick up, deliver, shop, mail things, phone people, and a myriad of other favors. You had to leave very quietly if you planned to get away without a handful of "lists." The Gang Ranch telegraph system was usually unavoidable.

One such unlucky individual who didn't get away to town without an errand to run was Susan Prater. She and her husband, Bill, who wound up on the farm crew, had moved on to the ranch and their six children were a welcome addition to our enrollment-poor school. Susan came from a background of "roughing it" and was quite at home with the demanding hardships of the ranch life that met her here. I felt for her at times, crowded into the apartments with all those children, but she was never anything but cheerful, and astonishingly capable—a true community person. What we appreciated most about Susan was that she took over a good deal of the store duties. She lived right next to it, and it was a welcome respite for Suzanne and I.

On this particular day, she offered to pick up the ranch payroll at the office in Williams Lake and bring it out to the ranch, as tomorrow was payday. The payroll was done at the Gang Ranch office in Williams Lake at this time. We previously had a mandatory two-signature check-writing policy, but Dale claimed this was not working because he did not want to have to fly out to the ranch every time he needed Rick's signature on a check. This made sense to us considering the price of aviation fuel and the time it took to fly to the ranch. Everyone trusting everyone, we had it changed to an either/or signature policy for checks.

The end of the day saw Susan and all her kids arrive back from town, dusty and hot, and pull up to the Gang Ranch office. I could see her searching and searching for something, rummaging in the back of the vehicle, moving children, clothing, parcels. The payroll, which she had dutifully picked up in Williams Lake one hour before, was gone. The large manila envelope was still there, but nothing was in it.

"I don't understand this," she cried in desperation. "I know the pay envelopes were all there—" She stopped in mid-sentence and looked, as if for the first time, at her children all suddenly quiet in the back of the vehicle: two little smudge-faced boys, Matt and Jake, and two girls, Pam and Debbie. Her oldest son, Joe, was in the front seat, but Steven, the next oldest, was in the back seat with the four younger ones. He suddenly leaned forward out the window. "The kids were throwing some kind of white paper things out the back window!" he offered.

The mystery was solved. The Prater vehicle turned around and sped back toward town and, sure enough, at various points along the almost 100 kilometers of winding road, came across white envelopes with paychecks tucked inside, some of them caught in sagebrush plants, some of them lying in the dust by the side of the road, some spied

101

over the cliff edges, some possibly carried down to the river by the wind. The ones that weren't recovered were redone, and the next Saturday night's entertainment was the story of how the Prater kids had held everyone's paychecks out the window, then let go of them and watched gleefully as the white airplane-like missiles went flip-flopping in the wind. The entertainment was twofold—they had lots of fun doing it, and we had lots of fun remembering it afterward. Susan Prater took all the ribbing in stride. You had to if you wanted to survive on the Gang Ranch.

Oren occasionally flew supplies out to the ranch, but his cargo space in the Bellanca Scout was limited. Dale's sporadic trips in the Cessna were too few and far between to be of any assistance in delivering supplies. Rick and Denis were busy with the constant demands of working and running the ranch—they simply never left.

Their many improvements were beginning to be very obvious: new fencing, new machinery, new fields, new irrigation systems, a washhouse in the main yard by the cookhouse, the huge barn painted a bright red, the cookhouse also newly painted, and a VHF radio system that now connected us all, whether we were in our homes or in vehicles. It saved many hours of chasing after people with messages.

But in addition to all the cosmetic changes, the Gang Ranch was still a farm and the normal everyday chores had to be done. The "bread loaves" of hay were stacked neatly in newly fenced stack yards, so many that new yards had to be created for storage. The cattle operation was under the capable supervision of one of the rare professionals in that trade—tall, tough New Zealander Paul Jex-Blake. Later, he would be succeeded by colorful American cowboy Lonnie Jones.

These men and their various and ever-changing crews of bandanna-clad, spur-jangling cowboys, top-trained blue heeler and border collie cowdogs at their heels, took pride in keeping constant vigil over the various livestock herds: the 3,800 mother cow herd, the approximately 2,000 head

102

of yearlings at any given time, the bull herd, the 250-head horse herd, and of course, the buffalo. They doctored, calved out, branded, separated, chased, roped, and moved the different animals around to the tune of the "Cattle Flow Chart." They worked in all manner of weather, many times without food and without sleep. It was tough, hard work but enviable to me as they spent a good deal of their time out in the various cow camps and away from the "eye of the hurricane." The pride they held in their individual cowdogs was well-placed; they worked as hard as their masters. The cowboys would travel far and wide and pay extraordinary prices for a special blue heeler, border collie, or sheltie that they heard might have superior breeding or good range experience. These dogs received such special attention from their masters that they became an inseparable team. The dogs were trained to follow at the heels of the rider's horse, and not to go ahead until told. They would wait for their master's signal as to which cows they were supposed to bring in, or which calves had to be kept to the side. They moved the animals by nipping at their heels until the critters moved in the direction they were supposed to go. They were invaluable assets. Some of them, Lonnie Jones's dog in particular, could be sent out to round the cows up in the dark.

The odd hassle confronted us as a family operation, which we felt was only to be expected. Dale would fly in occasionally and interfere with Rick's management of the Ranch. We all knew Dale could be stubborn and difficult, and that his treatment of people was often embarrassing at times, but we couldn't change him and we took his "tough operator" facade good-naturedly. He was a member of our family, he was intelligent, and we loved and trusted him, making allowances for his unpredictable behavior. It was hard on Rick because he was in charge of the basic, routine, and commonsense tasks that needed to be done on any operating farm. Rick would get his crews organized doing something, and Dale might fly in and tell them to do something else, usually something that made no sense whatsoever. It left employees standing scratching their heads, wondering what to do, and made for frustrating times for Rick and Denis. We decided he was just being a typical "big brother" and weathered it out, thinking there would be a lot less friction if he would just stick to his duties as administrator of the financial affairs of the operation. Nobody's duties were supposed to overlap someone else's; that was the first rule we had made.

Dale and I disagreed over the store accounting. Suzanne and I had an ongoing, up-to-date synoptic of the store operation, and it indicated clearly that the store was making a profit. Not a large profit, but more than breaking even most months and in extra busy times such as Christmas and tourist season, doing quite well. Dale claimed it was losing money according to his calculations. I looked over his figures and noticed that he was only calculating in the cash sales as income and not taking into account the largest income the store had—the amounts coming off employees' paychecks to pay for their store purchases. Dale insisted this could not be calculated as income because it was not cash. I insisted it certainly was income for the store—the bulk of the income. Not only that, to close the store down would have employees heading off to town all the time. I eventually tired of arguing about it everytime he flew in (I learned that no one ever won an argument with my brother Dale) and handed the store accounting books over to Susan Prater. She was conscientious at keeping books, and I felt maybe because she wasn't family he would listen to her. I did not want to fight with my brother.

In no time at all, Susan had run up against the same brick wall that Suzanne and I had. We were all beginning to hear the same whining litany from Dale: "You're spending too much money out there; you have to sacrifice, sacrifice, sacrifice!" We were starting to question amongst ourselves just how much HE and Betty were sacrificing. They had bought a mansion of a house on the lakefront in Kelowna, complete with an Olympic-sized swimming pool and a hot tub beside it. We knew he hadn't used his Ardrossan property as collateral to buy the Ranch as we had—it appeared he hadn't put up any property—so we reasoned he must have sold his Ardrossan lot now and bought the Kelowna property. He didn't offer us any answers.

What bothered us most at present was the office situation. Although we had a perfectly good office at the Ranch, where our business operated, we now had an office in Williams Lake with two secretaries, Lisa and Lynn; an office in Kamloops with a secretary named Gus, and an office in Kelowna with a secretary called Debbie. We also saw that Betty, his wife, was on the payroll at $800 per month, and we couldn't for the life of us figure out what for. She didn't even live on the Ranch. Suzanne and I received $400 per month for what we did, and we had to split it. Rick, Denis, and Oren barely got paid anything. Deductions were always taken off their checks for phone calls, gas, store bills, repairs, sometimes things we knew nothing about. Rick and Denis both got check stubs once for negative amounts.

Still, we all were under the impression that we had to sacrifice for the time it would take to get the loan paid off and keep in a healthy position. We thought EVERYONE was sacrificing. Our regular company "meetings" were becoming more sporadic—it was hard to get hold of Dale—and when we did have a meeting, a good deal of the time was starting to be spent in arguments with him. We wanted to get rid of our expensive "secretarial overload." As Rick put it, "This is a farm, not an international cartel!" Dad added, "What we need on the Ranch is cattle, not secretaries!"

Rick and Denis wanted to sell the Perry Ranch at Cache Creek. It was our feedlot operation and consisted of 1,300 deeded acres surrounded by 17,000 lease acres. In bygone days it had certainly made sense, when they drove cattle "on the hoof" to market, and they could use the Perry Ranch to rest them after the long drive, and let them gain weight. Now we could easily truck the cows out straight to

105

market. The Perry Ranch was almost 200 kilometers from the Gang, and expensive to operate and control. Knocking $2 million off our $4 million loan would be very nice. We all agreed the Perry Ranch should go. Dale wouldn't hear of it. Then, he reasoned, the Gang wouldn't be the largest ranch anymore.

In July of 1980, it started to rain, and it rained for a month straight. Rick knew we needed to put the hay up as silage, instead of baling it. Years of experience left him no choice. Not having silage equipment, we asked Dale to approach the bank about obtaining the necessary silage chopper and wagon. Shortly afterward, a call came in from Dale informing Rick that the banker had said "no."

Rick, not being the type of person who would sit help-lessly by as the hay crops rotted in the fields, jumped in his truck and made the hour trip to town in record time to see the banker himself. A surprised Bob Erickson claimed that Dale had never approached him about silage equipment and to, most certainly, go ahead. Bewildered, Rick made the necessary arrangements, headed back out to the ranch, and dived directly into the task of turning the soggy hay fields into potent-smelling green fodder and getting the necessary silage pits dug out to store it in. There was no time to dwell on who had caused the ruckus about the acquisition of the necessary equipment. The disaster that would have occurred without it was too paramount.

Then came the uproar over Bull 107.

"There's only one thing to do," reasoned Rick. He and Denis, Oren, and Lonnie Jones were in the Gang Ranch office contemplating the latest calamity. One of our Hereford bulls was stranded in the snow in remote Relay Valley, which was at the far end of the ranch, high up in the mountains. There was nothing for him to eat or drink, it was impossible for him to walk out, and he was sure to die a slow agonizing death from starvation.

"For him to be there in the first place means that he was culled from the rest of the herd by the younger, stronger bulls," Lonnie said. "His breeding days are probably over in any event."

They all agreed that the most economical and practical route to take would be to get in to him somehow and humanely put him out of his misery.

"For the price of a bullet," they reasoned, "it is definitely not worth the cost of attempting to bring him out."

It was the only sensible ranching decision to make. It would cost a fortune to even think of a "rescue" from snowed-in Relay Valley. And for an animal that would almost certainly not be of any use to us ever again? No rancher in his right mind would balk at this decision. Being way back in the mountains, the Relay Valley would be snowed in until spring. There were no roads, no visible trails, and no habitation for eighty kilometers in any direction.

They began making plans to pursue this route; it was quickly agreed that Oren would be the one to get in there, probably by snowshoe. Then we started to get bits and pieces of information through our Perry Ranch operation at Cache Creek about a "rescue" operation being planned by Dale. We heard rumors about reporters, helicopters, staff, and expensive supplies being flown into the distant Relay Creek area. We shuddered at the expense we could see piling up, but in our isolation we were helpless to stop the big wheels that were obviously already in motion.

Many man-hours and $20,000 later, we heard that Bull 107 was "out," amidst a circus-like flurry of full media attention. Back on home territory, Bull 107 was dazed, weak, and scrawny from near starvation, but definitely out of Relay Valley. Aghast at the mounting bills from this unnecessary media circus, Rick called the local veterinarian in to the Perry Ranch to have Bull 107 semen-tested. As we suspected from the start, Bull 107 was sterile, perhaps due to his age, but more likely due to the fact that his testicles had been partially frozen in the deep snows of Relay Valley. No rational rancher keeps a sterile bull. Bull 107 was destroyed, and we hoped that all the hoopla would quietly die down and we could forget about the $20 per pound carcass.

We weren't to be so lucky. A few weeks later, a truckload of neatly packaged meat arrived at the Gang Ranch, with orders that it be cooked up and served in the cookhouse. This was unusual, as we were in the habit of butchering our own beef for consumption on the ranch. We had a meathouse with all the steel saws and blades needed to process meat from a carcass down into those neat packages ourselves.

I radioed out to our good friends who managed the Perry Ranch, Beth and George Bryant, down-to-earth farming people who kept this busy feedlot operation of ours by Cache Creek under control and opened their doors to any of us who needed a place to stay when we went to Kamloops. Whenever they visited the ranch on the occasional weekend, it was cause for the whole ranch to celebrate.

"Beth, are you by?" I called over the VHF system.

Almost immediately, Beth's cheerful reply crackled over the distance. "Beth here, go ahead."

"Hi, Beth, do you know why this truckload of meat came in here, and where it came from? We're thinking maybe it's a mistake of some kind."

Over the slight static of the radio, I could hear the laughter in her voice.

"That's Bull 107," she said teasingly, and I could picture her barely able to contain her mirth. "Hope you enjoy him, and don't you *dare* send him back out here!"

With that warning, we gingerly opened one of the packages. The meat was dark and rank, smelling exactly like what it was, an old and emaciated bull. "Well, maybe if we cook it slowly for a long time," offered Rosalie hesitantly, never one to waste anything.

The odorous chunk of meat was cooked and simmered, then simmered and cooked some more. Nothing that we could dig out of the well-stocked cookhouse cupboards was spared—onions, garlic, wine, and every spice imaginable were employed in an attempt to make this something that it wasn't. It was no use. It was inedible. The whole ranch rebelled at the sight and smell of it. We tried shifting it over to the store deep freezes to be sold, but word was out on Bull 107. Nobody touched it. We tried to *give* it away, still no takers.

Finally, in desperation, it was doled out free-of-charge to anyone who wanted free dog food, and slowly it began to disappear, along with the sad and expensive memory of Bull 107.

The Move to Bear Springs

"**T**his is the perfect spot for a house," Denis said quietly.

It was late summer now, in 1980, two years since we had moved to the Ranch. Everything was so blissfully peaceful on Bear Springs—the bench 300 meters above the main Gang Ranch yard via a ten-kilometer drive—that you didn't dare speak too loud for fear of disturbing the beautiful Presence you could feel all around you.

"The water comes right up out of the ground over there," he said pointing, "and if we put the house right here facing east, we would catch the early morning sun, and the trees behind would keep it cool in the hot afternoon."

He was right, it was a perfect spot. There was an old homestead down below near a creek—two old log cabins and a barn surrounded by a falling-down rail corral. This had obviously been someone else's dream, too.

We were tired of the lack of privacy in the main yard: the pounding on our door in the middle of the night, the endless procession of phone-users and gas-wanters, the dust rolling in through the doorway. We didn't blame the people; we just weren't used to it. We never had a minute

110

to ourselves. To top it off, the shack we lived in had now developed a major problem with the sewer that required a major excavating and repair job. But as it was haying season, it would have to wait awhile. If you ever want to get rid of a woman, put her in a house with four small children and a sewer that doesn't work.

Here on Bear Springs, there was natural green grass, not to mention the huge hay fields with the two gigantic pivot irrigation systems we had purchased and installed there. They were like walking water sprinklers and traveled around in huge circles, powered by gas engines, and covered the entire area with rainbowed arcs of water. As the numerous sets of wheels had to cross over the irrigation ditch that passed through the entire length of Bear Springs, a sturdy bridge had to be built for each set of wheels to transverse the ditch. Denis was building these now and he wouldn't have far to go to work. There was lots to do on Bear Springs, what with the pivot system and the haying operation. It would save a lot of vehicles driving back and forth for Denis to be right there.

I looked around at the forest, the hay fields, the lush green grass where the springs came out of the ground. A few long-legged cranes were tippy-toeing through the grass, their elongated necks bent to the ground, searching for food. The buffalo herd was heading over the hill to Stump Lake for water, the new red calves bouncing along amongst their tolerant and protective elders. I gazed longingly up the forested hill toward Table Mountain; although I couldn't see it from here, I knew what was there.

"Let's go down and talk to Rick and Suzanne," I said excitedly. I was ready to pack up the kids and move to Bear Springs and live in a tent.

We climbed in the Bronco and headed down to Rick's house, talking all the way about how we could swing it. To Denis, Bear Springs meant being close to work and having a decent house to live in, away from the crowds. To me, Bear Springs signified survival. We had extra income besides our farm lease back in Alberta, in the form of a radio tower lease that paid rental every year. We could use that money. What we were short we could cover with a loan from the bank until our next radio lease came in the following year.

Rick and Suzanne shared our enthusiasm, as I knew they would. A family meeting was called. Dad was cautious. Denis and I were building the house with our own money, and he wanted to be sure we didn't lose it. We thought about buying the Bear Springs house site from the company, but it was situated on an agricultural land reserve and could not be subdivided from the rest. There was also no possibility of building an access road to it. A lease was therefore drawn up between us and Alsager Holdings Ltd., ensuring that should we ever leave the area of Bear Springs, we would be paid for the cost of the Bear Springs house.

Our next stop was the Bank of Commerce, where our friendly banker, Bob Erickson, okayed the lease and voiced his pleasure that there were some new homes going in on that ranch to replace the old ones. He then lent us the amount we would be short until the next radio lease came through. Honest fools that we were, when the lease money came in, we paid off the loan.

Having dealt with the business side of things, we tackled the Bear Springs house with a fervor akin to a thoroughbred at the race track. Every spare minute we had, and Rick and Oren had, was put to the house. They poured cement, hauled supplies, and constructed the foundation; they built a structure into the ground around the natural spring and we had beautiful water, the envy of everyone down below. We purchased a power plant, which I detested, and installed it down the hill from the house, hoping to dissolve some of the noise into the dirt.

The new house was log, from bug-killed pine, and constructed off-site by Dave Webster, a log builder from Williams Lake. I had never seen a pre-fab house go up before.

112

Dave Webster's crew started in the morning when I went down to the main yard. When I went up to Bear Springs later in the day, the house was standing there. I couldn't believe my eyes. I wandered through it, running my hands over the smooth knots of the freshly peeled logs. The best part was the three bedrooms. I could separate the kids into two bedrooms and there was still a loft, which in future times would always be full of company.

We had lots of willing and able hands to help finish it off. Howard Linde went away with blisters on his knees from installing the hardwood floors. Palle Henriksen from Frost Creek, who was a frequent guest at our home, especially during hunting season, grouted and mixed "mud" and polished until all the tile work was finished. Our good friend Ben Wiebe from Alberta went away with a crick in his neck from nailing little boards together on the ceiling, his neck tilted up the whole time. What was worse for him was he fell in love with the Gang Ranch while he stayed with us and began dreaming of valleys and creeks and log cabins in the forest, just as I had done, probably never again to be satisfied with "life on the outside." We loved it when he brought his wife, Helen, out. She was a lot of fun, but it was an ordeal for Ben to get her there. She got as far as the rickety Gang Ranch bridge over the Fraser River and said, "Nuh-uh, no farther, I can't go over that thing." Ben coaxed and cajoled and finally got her to lie down on the floorboards of the car, shut her eyes tight, hold her breath and count to ten, while he raced over the bridge.

It was the fastest move in history. We bade a happy farewell to the little shack in the yard—we had had some good times there—and moved to Bear Springs. As we headed up the hill, I could almost feel the hills closing in protectively behind me. I always felt safe at Bear Springs. I spent hours exploring, and each time found something I hadn't seen before. Sometimes I just wanted to snuggle down against the warm earth, pull a soft quilt of green grass over me, and become a part of this beautiful country called Bear Springs.

It was handy for Oren, too. With lots of room to land, the little blue Bellanca Scout would come nosing down out of the sky, bounce along the side of the field, and roar up almost to the house. Oren's life took a sudden and romantic turn that summer with the arrival of teenaged Jacquie St. Jacques. Jacquie was the daughter of Denis's sister Pearl and her husband, Ralph. We were too busy to pick her up in Williams Lake, so Oren flew off to collect her. From the first day onward, she became an active member of the ranch and our family, and Oren's constant companion. Jacquie was an outdoors girl and shared Oren's enthusiasm for wilderness adventure, hunting, trapping, and fishing. While up until now it had been "Oren and Yukon," his devoted golden Chesapeake dog, it now became "Oren and Jacquie and Yukon."

The creek at Bear Springs became a natural playground for the kids. They didn't have toys—there really wasn't any use for toys out here. The green-headed mallard ducks that spent their days chasing after bugs in the creek seemed to sense that the children were not a threat to them. When the mother mallard hatched out a batch of fluffy little striped ducklings in the late spring, she marched right out to the water, followed by a wavering lineup of the tiny waddlers. She herded them into the creek right amongst the kids and swam proudly around as the ducklings bobbed and paddled behind her. Shan crouched down in the water, and we watched in amazement as one tiny duckling hopped up onto his shoulder and teetered back and forth uncertainly before hopping back into the water again. The kids spent hours and hours in the creek with the ducks and never grew tired of them. Sometimes they chased frogs, or fish, or shiny striped water snakes. The creek was an ever-changing source of entertainment for them.

Now it became an everyday drive for me, back and forth to the main yard, and I didn't mind a bit. That is except for one day, when my trip down to the ranch yard became every mother's nightmare.

There was a cattleguard at the top of the steep hill that came up from Lake Ranch to Bear Springs. Lately, the buffalo had been leaping easily over the cattleguard and heading down on to Lake Ranch, so a rope with a red flag on it had been installed across it.

I had all four kids in the Ford Bronco. Having gone over the cattleguard, I stopped the Bronco, put it in "park," jumped out, and ran back to replace the rope with the red flag across the cattleguard. Turning back toward the Bronco, my whole being froze. It was moving down the steep Bear Springs hill, picking up speed as it went. And, of course, no one was behind the wheel!

I raced after it, knowing it wasn't possible to catch up. Already going at a good clip, it was headed straight for a pile of huge boulders and, if it was lucky enough to miss them, would go directly into Freshwater Lake. I finally stopped, defeated, in the dust, unable to do anything but stand there numbly and watch and pray, certain they were all going to be killed.

Suddenly and unbelievably, the speeding Bronco came to an abrupt stop, enveloped by a cloud of dust.

"Thank you! Thank you! Thank you!" I yelled, as I raced down the hill through the settling dust. I yanked open the driver's door. Buffy and Lacey had fallen against the dash with the sudden stop and were both crying on the floor of the passenger side. Shan was in the back seat, not making a sound, but his white face told me he was scared to death. Where was Dusty? I couldn't see him anywhere. I finally spotted him looking up at me from underneath the steering wheel and understood how the car had stopped its perilous journey. Four-year-old Dusty knew the brake was on the floor. He was too small to reach it with his feet so he had crawled down underneath the dash and had sat on it. He was still crouched there, grinning up at me, but not budging off the brake. It was a face I'll never forget.

This was not the only time that Bronco would jump out of gear when it was in park. Much later, when the receivers came on to the ranch, someone left it sitting in front of the office. It jumped out of gear and rolled down the hill toward the school, smashing through a closed rail gate. Luckily, no one was in the way to be hurt.

Suzanne's sister, Karen Stoughton, had arrived at the ranch to become the teacher at the one-room school. Coming from the same farming background as Suzanne, she was certainly a welcome addition. Growing up in a country school environment myself, complete with good old spelling bees, I was so glad to have my children getting what I knew would be a good, basic education.

Karen fit in on the Gang Ranch like an old cowboy boot and was responsible for organizing many community activities, which are so important in an isolated place where people are rubbing shoulders at all times in every facet of everyday life. A social nightlife is definitely a necessity to put the daily goings-on in perspective. We enjoyed many get-togethers that brought the whole community together, natives and whites, into a very tight-knit situation. No one was any different from anyone else, no one was "boss" or "employee." We were all mothers and fathers with children who went to school together, attended the same birthday parties, rode in the backs of trucks together to brandings, fishing, goldpanning in the creeks. Differences in background, race, personalities, and jobs were overlooked, and everyone got along.

Karen tried valiantly, as I'm sure did every teacher before her, to make the kids go outside to spit their "snoose." She finally gave up the battle and placed empty tobacco tins here and there where necessary on the classroom floor. Suzanne and I watched warily for any suspicious bulges in the lower lips of our children, but if they "chewed" we never found out. They did all start to talk in the singsong Shuswap drawl, and some of them still do to this day. The school's students consisted of Rick and Suzanne's kids, my

116

kids, and the other children from the crew members. They were somewhat of a motley-looking crew, at the most nine or ten students, either very dark, or very blonde. They didn't notice or care.

Actually, we weren't that uncivilized. Mom and I started a Sunday school on the ranch. We got the books from Rev. Paul Davis of the United Church in Williams Lake and every Sunday morning we gathered up all the children on the ranch for stories, cookies, and games at her house. My mother always loved kids; she was in her element, and so were they.

Thanks to the energies of Susan Prater, we also had a 4-H club for the kids, where they learned the basic trials of owning animals, caring for them, and being responsible for their upkeep.

One bright sunny morning, a group of the kids had just come out of the barn from feeding their 4-H calves; laughing and talking, they didn't see a large but gaunt she-cougar crouched on the edge of the barn roof over their heads, her long tail switching back and forth in readiness.

As they started to wander away, the old cougar leapt without a sound and flew through the air, landing in the midst of the kids. Terrified screams and the barking of dogs coupled with the snarling of the cougar filled the air, as people ran from everywhere, not quite knowing what to do. Raymond Rosette fled to his house nearby and emerged again almost instantly with a rifle. Clumsy in his haste, he jammed bullets into the chamber as he ran. There were too many crying children and people moving around to get a safe shot off at the cougar, which by now had Caroline Billy's little dog by the neck and was thrashing around on the ground with it. Raymond moved in closer, took steady aim, and fired.

"Cra-ack." Smoke floated from the barrel of Raymond's rifle, and the writhing she-cougar went still; but it was too late for the poor pup, who lay limp and bloody in the cougar's slack jaws.

Mothers comforted their frightened, whimpering children while the men inspected the old cat. She had been a good size but was gaunt and skinny from starvation. She had no teeth and must have been totally desperate to jump into a group of human beings—one of her worst enemies.

The dead cougar was handed over to Jacquie St. Jacques for a skillful skinning job. The children had by now all recovered, and their immediate fear had turned to excited jabber. The cat was not so formidable in her lifeless state, and the kids would keep this in their memories forever, to be told and retold to future wide-eyed grandchildren.

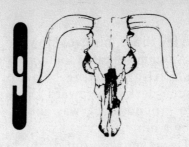

The People

"**S**nuffle, snuffle, snort, crunch."

My eyes shot wide open from a deep sleep. Being a mother with four small children, I was definitely a light sleeper, but this time I was sure I had heard something out of the ordinary. We had been in the Bear Springs house only a few days, and there were lots of creaks and groans from the new log construction, but I knew this was something else.

I turned to Denis, who was sleeping blissfully.

Then I heard it again. It sounded like loud breathing, then some shuffling sounds. They seemed to be coming right out of the wall!

I shook Denis vigorously by the shoulder. "Did you hear that?" I said in a loud whisper. He rolled over sleepily. I knew he hadn't heard it. "Something's in here!" I said. "I can hear it breathing!"

He opened one eye and gave me a quizzical look. I knew what he was thinking: here we are, finally out of the commotion of the main yard, out in the middle of nowhere, not a soul around for miles, and she hears someone breathing?

"Probably just the logs settling," he grunted and rolled over, satisfied that the mystery had been solved. "They'll move for a long time in a new house."

Then as he lay there, his eyes slowly opened wide as he heard it, too. An unmistakable loud breathing sound, a few snorts, and shuffling. Sitting bolt upright, he stared through the semi-darkness toward the wall. A large window, almost to ground level, was about a meter from the bed, covered by a blind.

Gingerly, Denis sneaked out of the bed, tiptoed across to the window, and carefully pulled on the strings that lifted the blind. There, on the other side of the glass from us, not three feet from our bed, was the massive head of a huge buffalo bull, staring curiously through the glass at us with beady black eyes. In the early sunrise, his breath was coming in short puffy clouds, steaming up the window. Looking beyond him, we saw that the whole herd was milling around the house, their feet crunching on the gravel. This particularly curious old bull was obsessed with the early morning sun shining on the glass in the window, sniffing and snorting and licking at it. Then he innocently leaned his massive shaggy forehead against it—and pushed! This buffalo was coming into our bedroom!

I sat stock-still, waiting for the glass to shatter, as I saw the thick windowpane actually bending under the pressure. I had never thought to ask the window people if their product could withstand the force of a 1,400-kilogram buffalo bull.

By now, Denis was out on the step, persuading them to leave. I thought about it for a minute and realized we were actually the intruders. Buffalo are a roaming animal and have a regular circuit they follow everyday: down to the lake to drink early in the morning, up to the flat area to graze during the day, a hike up to the higher bush on the way to Table Mountain in the heat of the afternoon, then back down to drink at the lake about 5:00 P.M. You could set your clock by their movements.

What a shock it must have been for them to go on their daily ritual and suddenly find a house in their path. I didn't blame them at all for being curious.

120

Although the buffalo appeared docile, it became a constant concern to us at calving time when the tourists would arrive, cameras slung around their necks, and head up to Bear Springs to "see the buffalo." I was happy that they had the opportunity to see buffalo in a natural environment, free to roam, but many of the visitors had no idea that a cow buffalo with a calf at her side was a very dangerous situation. I would catch numerous people walking toward these cows with their cameras, trying to get as close as they could to the new baby to get a good shot. I would go tearing out to stop them before they got themselves killed.

The summer always brought many welcome visitors, friends from back home, and of course, lots of our relatives. Our good friends from Alberta, Gerry and Gisele Berube, Bert and Pauline Goudreau, the Handfields, Simone and Emil, and Remi and Audrey, Gisele and Leon Vallee, my Maidstone friends Noreen Donald and the Mitchell girls. I had been so busy on the ranch I had almost forgotten how homesick I was for them all, until they came for a while. Then I cried when they left.

Denis's sister Pearl St. Jacques and her family were always welcome at the ranch. Pearl was a favorite of mine because she was always so cheerful and good-natured. During her visit that summer I was to learn just how good-natured she was.

All the old ranch trucks had names. There was the old red Chevy that was called the "Tomato." There was an old rusted yellow Ford half-ton called the "Lemon." And, of course, when Denis and I showed up with the green Ford F250 truck we bought from Oren, it immediately became the "Cucumber."

On this particular day, I was driving the "Tomato" down the steep Bear Springs hill, with Pearl as passenger. I went to shift gears to slow the beast down, and, lo and behold, the entire gear shift assembly that fitted into the floor of the truck came right off in my hand.

121

When Pearl saw me waving the long gear shift around, trying to fit it back into the floor somehow, she erupted into peals of hysterical laughter.

"Grab the wheel," I cried, realizing my frantic pumping on the brakes was doing no good, and that gearing down was the only way to bring the thing under control.

Pearl leaned over me and steered from the passenger side as I wrestled to attach the gear once more. I could stick it down into the floor but it didn't seem to attach to anything. After a few more attempts, it finally "clicked" into place and we were in control again.

Pearl was hooting with laughter, tears running down her face, and I marveled. She's abnormal enough to live here, I thought. Any normal person would have bailed out.

Rick and Denis were still working nonstop, and I was happy at Bear Springs, driving back and forth down to the ranch. We had various women working in the office. When one would leave, it was not all that easy to find another willing to relocate to the remoteness of the ranch. Lynn Dootoff was one office worker who moved out to the ranch with her two young sons and became a ball of fire within the community.

Jacquie was now a full-fledged irrigator and proved herself worthy of competition with the best of them. Patsy Holst, one of Willy Rosette's daughters, teamed up with Jacquie to keep the irrigation going on some of the fields. She was married to Brian Holst, a longtime reliable member of the farm crew. Maureen Molton was cooking in the cookhouse, a carefree, outdoor girl who relished the ranch life; her good friend Mike Edwards was searching out and verifying all the water-rights licences on the creeks for us.

The cowboy crew was a never-ending stream of separation slips and empty snoose cans. Hordes of young, bright-eyed hopefuls showed up regularly at the ranch office with brand-new saddles, shiny unscuffed boots, and stiff, tight, store-bought ropes that had never been thrown. Once they'd spent a few days out with the real cowboys, they usually had had enough. They had not stopped to realize that they would actually have to walk in those high-heeled boots, throw that rope, get on the back of that frothing wild-eyed cayuse, get knocked down and dragged around in the dirt and the cow dung, go without food and sleep, and freeze to death doctoring some animal because it had picked the best time to get sick or calve—in the middle of the coldest night on record.

The longtime and reliable professional cowboys were few and far between, their well-trained cowdogs their pride and joy, and their trademark. You might insult these cowboys any time, but you better be real careful what you said about their dogs. There was Paul Jex-Blake's crew, Lonnie Jones's crew, and, of course, the longtime Rosettes, Raymond, Willy, Mike, and Leslie. There were guys like John Edwards and Ed Robisson, Pat Johnson, Ross Gruenwald, Frankie Johnson, Bobby Allison, Keith Van Zandt; and Swiss cowboys Phil Gisler and John Schranz, distinctive with their tall, Swiss cowboy hats and a wealth of veterinary knowledge. They were among the few who could harness up the feisty young untrained team of Belgian draft horses and handle them with ease.

The life of a cowboy riding the range, and the dashing figure they cut, certainly seems glamorous, with their jangling spurs, their shiny and all-important belt buckles, their silken kerchiefs, individual cowboy hats, and high slant-heeled leather boots. They packed with them, rolled up and tied snugly behind the seat of their saddle, a long rain slicker, split up the middle in the back so that, when worn, it would hang down on both sides of the horse to protect them from the elements. The dedication of these veteran cowboys was in their love of the life, certainly not their high salaries. Their individuality was assessed by their possessions: the saddle, tack, and cowboy hat they owned, what kind of gun they packed along, whether it was real silver on their gear, whether their lariats were "broke in."

The real honest-to-goodness North American cowboy had to be a tough breed.

Dale sent some fellows out one weekend to conduct a "cowboy school." This went over like a lead balloon. The real cowboys had been born cowboys and had spent their whole life learning and perfecting their trade. They weren't about to stand for the insult of having city slickers with a blackboard show them how to pack a horse, or tie a salt block onto a pack saddle. The veteran cowboys didn't show up for the "cowboy school" and the grumbling and jokes were obvious.

New cowboys did arrive that were serious and stayed: Duncan Barnett from Williams Lake, and Mike Custance from Gibsons. Mike could also drive the huge Ranch Western Star cattle-liner. He later studied to become a lawyer and married Dale's oldest daughter, Kim. We were all thrilled, but especially Mom, as she had introduced them in the cookhouse.

It was equally difficult to get truck drivers brave enough to make the trek over the narrow rickety old Gang Ranch bridge. It wasn't only the narrowness of the bridge, it was the turn they had to negotiate to get onto the bridge, and off again on the other side. There was absolutely no room for error. Some drivers made it in with the rig, then refused to drive it out again. Numerous times Rick and Denis had to go out and help get the cattle-liner, the pup trailer, or both, back on the road after it hadn't made it around a switchback and tipped over. Sometimes they were full of animals; steers going out to market, or cull cows heading to our Perry Ranch feedlot. At times it was easier to trail the cattle over the bridge on foot, and load them on the other side.

New weigh scales and loading chutes were installed out at Home Ranch, near the P&T Road. This eliminated the problem with the Gang Ranch bridge; the trucks didn't have to cross it this way. They loaded cattle at Home Ranch and headed straight to Williams Lake via the back road out of the north end of the Ranch, and took the Farwell Canyon road to town. When cattle were loaded up and shipped out of Home Ranch, we could not see them from the main Gang Ranch yard. It was a good twenty-five kilometers away.

One colorful "cowboss" that passed through the Gang Ranch time sheets was Harold Hawkins. A nondescript drifter with a somewhat murky background, Dale had hired him on from the Williams Lake office. One thing was apparent, and that was that no one ever suffered for lack of entertainment when Hawkins was around. We loved to hear his stories. His imagination was second to none. Around the campfire one night, he balefully told the cowboys how he had lost his best horse. They were riding hard through tough brush, branches and shrubs sticking up everywhere, in hot pursuit of a renegade cow. Suddenly he noticed that his horse was gradually slowing down, losing speed, the cow getting away from him. He couldn't figure out what was happening to his horse, until he finally looked behind and saw a string of steaming guts trailing out behind the horse. His belly had been ripped open by an upstanding stick and gradually, with nothing left inside, he had toppled over and had to be destroyed.

"Hawkins" had an amazing repertoire of eye-widening stories such as this; they were fun to listen to, whether you believed them or not was your affair.

One of the most important people on the ranch was the mechanic. This country was rough on machinery, and parts for repairs were a long way away. We needed someone who could go down to what was called the Boneyard, find a scrap of metal, and somehow transform it into the kind of repair part they needed. Doug Anderson was one such mechanic. He was followed by Bernie Radford, affectionately known as "Big Bird" for his long, storklike legs and beaky nose. Good-natured and easygoing, he and his wife, Bev, and their two boys fit well into ranch life.

Stu Turton, from England, was another such wonder

125

inventor-mechanic, miraculously making a piece of equipment work when there was no part to repair it with. Stu was a crack shot and loved to organize rifle shoots. He also had an almost maniacal love for dynamite. When someone mentioned it was time to get rid of the beaver dams, his eyes lit up and he would immediately head for the black powder in the root cellar.

One of our good neighbors to the south, Frank Meyer, frequently came down from his cabin in the high Blackwater area on the other side of Churn Creek. We would hire him to assist with major mechanic jobs, such as overhauling a motor on the caterpillar. Good natured and of strong German descent, he worked up at the new gold mine on Blackdome Mountain, keeping their equipment in order. On a visit to his property one day, we found a cozy, well-kept cabin tucked away in the wilderness, with a fantastic view overlooking some of the Blackwater valleys. Although it was black fly season and it was difficult to be outside for any length of time, we got a good feel for the beauty of Frank's little homestead. It was surrounded by the immense grazing lands of the Empire Valley ranching outfit. Our closest neighbors to the south, Empire Valley Ranch was owned at that time by Americans Tom and Connie Hook.

Harold Lindberg was another mechanic who sorted nuts and bolts in an effort to keep everything organized in the shop. A single man, he seemed to relish the isolated life on the Gang.

Dan Patten, a clean-cut "go-getter" from the States had arrived. He was a consultant, and we had hired him on to work on the task of getting a recreation program up and running for the ranch company. We already had a fairly good overseas clientele, mostly Germans, for buffalo hunts, which Oren was overseeing very successfully. We wined and dined them in the evenings, usually at Bear Springs, and they spent their days hunting specific buffalo that had been set apart from the main herd. Oren accompanied them and made certain that they got their buffalo head and went away thinking they were the best hunters that ever tracked an animal. We chuckled to hear how one of the hunters had knelt down to feel the buffalo track to see if it was still warm. He must have been watching too many old westerns.

There definitely was a potential for backcountry trips— hunting, fishing, and hiking in the vast outreaches of the ranch. Dan was spending many hours poring over plans and maps and advertising brochures, figuring and re-figuring.

Then there were the people that simply showed up in the yard and stayed, we weren't sure why, and I don't even think *they* knew why. Mike Bailey, an elderly, well-dressed man, obviously from town, showed up and seemed to be housesitting in Dale's new log home. One night he was staying upstairs in the cookhouse, where the cowboy's rooms were. In the middle of the night he heard noises and came to the conclusion that the cookhouse was being robbed. He tried to turn on the lights, but the power plant had been turned off and he was left in the dark. In a panic, and believing someone was sneaking into his room, he climbed up onto the roof in his undershorts and stayed up there for the rest of the night, afraid to come down even long enough to get some clothes on. No one ever really figured out why Mike Bailey was on the ranch, or why he was perched up on the cookhouse roof in the morning, in his undershorts.

George, the maintenance man, was another ranch dweller obviously spooked by the isolation of the place. He was supposed to be in charge of maintenance on the ranch—keeping the plumbing and power plant in working order, and doing any carpentry jobs that needed doing. George had all these skills; his problem was that he was convinced there were devils underneath the trailer he lived in. Brandishing a baseball bat to club any devils he found, he would have half the ranch up looking with him. Rick finally went to George's trailer in the dark and made

127

George look under the trailer while he shone his flashlight around.

"See?" Rick shone the light all around under the trailer. "Nothing there. No devils."

George went back into his trailer. A short while later he would be hammering the trailer with the baseball bat again, chasing devils. This went on every night until he finally had to be let go. He was too exhausted each day after chasing devils all night to do any work, and he was gradually demolishing the trailer with his baseball bat.

A young foreign fellow showed up at the ranch one day. He couldn't speak a word of English. All we could get out of him was that he was from Turkey. Suzanne claimed she couldn't get him to eat anything, and he appeared to be nearly starving. I tried my luck, cooking different things I thought might appeal to him, but he shook his head at everything. We finally figured out that he would eat things like dry cereal if he was right there and saw the box being opened. He was afraid that we might poison him! He had apparently escaped from war-torn Turkey and was afraid of everything. The first night Rick went to drive him down to his house, they went over the cattleguard in the truck—rat-tat-tat. The Turk baled out the passenger side of the truck, absolutely terrified. He thought it was machine-gun fire.

Kees (Casey) Kohke appeared at the ranch one day. Dale thought there were too many machine breakdowns and had hired big Holland-born Kees to be a hard-nosed farm manager, with instructions to "be tough." Kees assembled the farm crew the first morning and explained to them grandly what the new rules were: "The next guy to break down on a piece of machinery is FIRED!"

Everyone shuffled around uncomfortably at this bright greeting, and no one seemed particularly anxious to climb onto a machine. They began to disperse, and Kees Kohke jumped on a tractor with a haying machine on behind and proceeded to head out of the main yard. A short distance from the shop, his outfit suddenly came to a halt. Some-

Judy Alsager with Lady and packhorse Buck.

Ted and Irene Alsager.

Judy Alsager and Richard Keep (1994).

Rick and Suzanne Alsager.

Oren Alsager.

Judy Alsager and Old Jimmy surrounded by Rosette family and Irene Alsager.

Overlooking main yard area of Gang Ranch.

The lower end of Churn Creek.

Judy and Denis Rivard with Buffy and Dusty Rivard in front of the Gang Ranch cookhouse before renovations.

Cowboy John Schranz in front of Gang Ranch horse barn.

Closer version of calving barn.

Closer version of Gang Ranch elementary school with teacher's residence.

Judy Alsager in Gang Ranch cookhouse.

The Gang Ranch school. Back row (left to right): Shan Rivard, Anderson boy, Steven Prater, Caroline Billy, Jimmy Rosette, Karen Stoughton (teacher). Front row (left to right): Corey Dootoff, Buffy Rivard, Dusty Rivard, Pam Prater, Debbie Prater, Junior Rosette, Shane Dootoff. Absent that day: Lane and Jan Alsager, Rick's kids.

Transportation around main Gang Ranch yard in ranch buggy.

Jacquie St. Jacques with she cougar that leaped down from calving barn into midst of children, killing Caroline Billy's dog.

Residence of Old Jimmy (Jiggs) Rosette. He was born in this home and has been there ever since.

Old Jimmy (Jiggs) Rosette.

Buffalo herd after their trek to water, right on schedule.

Buffalo in corral—main yard.

Close-up of buffalo herd.

Buffalo in the Bear Springs corrals. Original old log homestead cabin in background.

One of Oren Alsager's paintings.

Oren Alsager preparing for takeoff in the blue Bellanca.

Gang Ranch airstrip.

The Gang Ranch jeep—suited for rough terrain.

Using the Ranch's track Nodwell machine to pull cattle out of the mud bog.

Perry Ranch operation, Cache Creek, feedlot and shipping area for Gang Ranch cattle.

Cowboss Lonnie Jones.

Dale Alsager's new log house in main yard.

Judy Alsager hobbling horse with Little Jimmy Rosette.

The original old log cabin at Bear Springs.

Relay cow camp.

Trapper Johanson's cabin.

Old Graveyard cabin.

Oren Alsager on Tall Timber - wishing he was someplace else. Photo by Karl Heinz-Raach.

Moving the cattle on foot over the Gang Ranch bridge.

Moving a bunch of cows with calves to new grazing ground. Photo by Karl Heinz-Raach.

Winter scene - winter has its own beauty on the Gang Ranch.

The cowboy "string" of horses - tired but hungry.

Cowboss Harold Hawkins and crew. On far left is Karl Heinz-Raach, photographer from Germany, an occasional and welcome visitor to the Gang Ranch and Idanell Korner Ranch.

"Even cowboys read the news..." Photo by Karl Heinz-Raach.

Hungry Valley cow camp.

Graveyard cow camp.

Farwell Canyon cow camp—the old log barn was carried away by the Chilcotin River one spring.

Farwell Canyon cow camp—the old original cabin.

Cowboss Lonnie Jones (third from left) and crew.

The unpopular "cowboy school."

Home Sweet Home—the Ranch's only "moveable" cow camp.

Cowboy John Schranz heads out for a load of hay.

Cowboy Raymond Rosette.

Cowboy Keith Van Zandt finds a soft seat on the rump of his horse.

Farmhand Bill Haller—tragically killed in a truck accident.

Cowboy Ed Roberson—well known for his cougar hounds.

Cowboy Phil Gisler.

Little Jimmy, Old Jimmy, Judy Alsager and Stephanie Schranz share some campfire stories.

Cattle herd in main ranch yard.

Cowboys sorting cattle.

Glacier-fed Lorna Lake with its milky-green waters was the resting place for a downed plane with its passengers until Old Jimmy and others pulled it out.

The majestic coastal peaks that are the backdrop for the Gang Ranch.

Packed up to go.

Judy Alsager at Indian graves site.

Judy Alsager stands on top of the world.

Graveyard Valley.

The Rivard kids in 1994: Dusty 17, Buffy 18, Shan 19, Lacey 15.

Hesston stacker at work on Big House field.

thing was clunking and grinding in the back, and the outfit would not move. Fuming, he stomped back to the shop where he was met by a group of men silently standing around waiting to see what was going to happen to "the next guy who broke down."

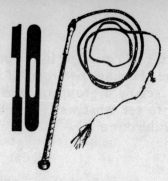

The Christmas Party

Before we knew it, Christmas was upon us, and the ranch party at Bear Springs was in full swing. The kitchen counters groaned under the weight of every kind of food imaginable. Each newcomer had to arrange and re-arrange in order to make room for their contribution. Fancy little girls in starched new dresses chased after shiny-faced boys who, although their shirttails were hanging out, were noticeably scrubbed clean.

The house was full of festive people; I noted with de-light that even our good friends from Empire Valley Ranch, Nancy and Steve Oswald, had made it, a remarkable feat given the shape the winter roads were in. Empire Valley Ranch was even more remote than the Gang Ranch, an-other hour's drive down the Fraser River from the Gang Ranch bridge. Nancy was a substitute teacher at our school when Karen was not able to be there. I could never believe how very lucky we were to be way out here and have the high caliber of teachers that we did. Shan had been fasci-nated with birds since he was very young, and Nancy went out of her way to bring him extra books and tidbits about all kinds of birds. When I wandered around in the bushes with Shan, I was astounded to learn how much he knew about all the different kinds of feathered species, their habits, and where they would hide, and what color their eggs were.

Dancing bodies gyrated to the music blasting in the living room; others were, of course, story-telling, filling every available chair and every bit of standing room around the oversized kitchen table. I heard snatches of animated stories about the "pink grizzly bear" that supposedly roamed Graveyard Valley. More than one excited cowboy claimed to have seen him, and there were written accounts in the logbook at the Graveyard cabin by wanderers passing through claiming similar sightings and "close calls." Oren had, of course, checked this out fairly thoroughly. If there was a pink grizzly bear within a thousand miles, he was going to see it. He had run across a large cinnamon bear back in that area and felt maybe that was what everyone was seeing. But the stories went on.

We had two identical punch bowls from the cookhouse and had wondered just how to go about the beverage situation for the evening's merrymaking. Some people on the ranch liked their liquor, and there were others, the Mormon people, for example, who abstained. We finally decided to spike one of the bowls for the "imbibers" and poured in a bottle of vodka. I wrote "WITH" on a sticky label and stuck it on the side of this bowl. On the other punch bowl went a sticker that said "WITHOUT."

The evening went on, spirits high, laughter reigning, as hardworking, happy people "let go" at the closing of yet another good year. In the midst of the merriment, a group of boys, Lane, Jan, Shan, and Dusty among them, caught my eye. They were huddled together in a corner of the living room, obviously sharing some hilarious secret. I knew immediately, from experience, that they were up to something. It's one of those special powers mothers possess, being able to tell, at a glance, when children are up to no good. I watched them warily out of the corner of my eye. It seemed that every time someone walked over to the

163

punch bowls, they would start giggling and laughing, pointing, and whispering together.

"I wonder what those little buggers have been up to!" Suzanne's voice beside me had a dangerous hint of suspicion in it.

"So you noticed too, eh?" I answered, not taking my eyes off the boys. "I don't know, but I'd sure like to find out!"

We both turned to the boys and, like all good mothers, tried to wither them into submission with the most threatening glares we could muster. With great effort, they straightened their faces and tried to look innocent, failing miserably. Then one of them started, and they all broke into uncontrollable fits of giggling again.

"It's got something to do with the punch bowls," I whispered to Suzanne. "They've probably put a frog in one or something!"

Further scrutiny of the punch bowls proved fruitless. We stirred around in the pink liquid with the ladles, and nothing was in there. With a few more accusing looks in their direction, we carried on.

But as the night wore on, I began to notice a strange situation developing: the people who usually drank were uncommonly subdued tonight, and the ones who abstained were very merry indeed. I watched in interest as one of the Mormon ladies, who never drank, twirled around the living room by herself, skirt swirling out, punch spilling from her glass, singing away happily. The people who should have been laughing loudly and raucously by now were all sitting quietly watching and talking.

Something was very wrong with this picture.

I sniffed at my own cup of punch from the WITH bowl. I took a good sip; it seemed to be only juice.

Maybe I didn't put enough vodka in the WITH bowl, I thought. I couldn't taste anything in it. With that in mind, I opened another bottle of vodka and glug-glugged it into the WITH bowl.

164

Things got even stranger. Mike Rosette was playing the guitar, and people were singing loudly, people who were normally the shy and quiet type.

Curiosity took me over to the punch bowls again. The WITHOUT one was almost empty, but I scraped enough up with the ladle to get a good gulp. This one had the vodka in it! I looked at the label again. Definitely WITHOUT. But I was sure the WITHOUT one had been on the right-hand side before; now it was on the left.

I looked again at the labels. They were crooked, not at all as we had put them on. Someone had switched the labels on the bowls, obviously in haste, and I knew exactly who those "someones" were! At this moment, they were conspicuously absent, no doubt headed for safer territory.

Now both punches were WITH because I had poured the new bottle into the WITH bowl, which actually was the one without any vodka in it. So the Christmas party at Bear Springs became a very jovial one, indeed. No one ever complained, and I never dared ask any of the WITHOUT people if they wondered why they had headaches the next day.

Hungry Valley
Escape

"**H**orsepower?" Rick and Denis said simultaneously. "We hardly have time to get all the work done with modern machinery!" Rick pointed out.

It was now spring of 1981; Dale had flown in for the weekend, and we were all sitting around discussing the recent financial statements he had brought with him, which had us looking in a pretty good position for this year. Alsager Holdings' livestock inventory had increased to 9,032 head of animals. This number came from a physical count of 212 bulls, 1,809 yearling steers, 1,208 yearling heifers, 2,946 cows, 2,600 calves, 207 horses, and 50 head of buffalo. The worth of these animals was valued at $4,638,943. Our livestock sales for the year were listed at $1,369,343. The other income we had seemed pale beside the livestock sales, but was nonetheless important—$65,000 in feed sales, also interest rebates, and the store profits. As everyone was in a good mood, I grabbed this opportunity to find out something that had been on my mind for awhile.

"Dale," I asked him brightly, "someone phoned me about an article that was in the newspaper, quite a long time ago now, that stated the Dale Alsager family from

Ardrossan had bought the Gang Ranch and were the new owners. Wherever did that come from?"

"Oh," he replied with a laugh, "stupid reporters, that's where. I've never met one yet that can get the facts straight."

The moment passed. I didn't really care what was written in the papers, but I did wonder how their information could be so incorrect. I guessed it was possible.

Everyone now proceeded to put in their two bits' worth about how we could operate better and more efficiently. Dale said he'd like to see the operation go back to using draft horses rather than fuel-eating and repair-hungry machinery.

Rick and Denis just laughed. With an operation this size, it was unthinkable.

But Suzanne and I decided to humor Dale. I had always enjoyed my father's team of draft horses at home when I was a kid. When other farmers were out thawing their gas lines and warming up their new tractors on those crackling cold prairie mornings, my Dad would quietly be out hitching up his team to the feed wagon, and away we'd go to feed his purebred Herefords. It wasn't that he didn't have the funds, he just preferred not to put his machinery through the stress of running in that frigid weather. These memories are the best for me, listening to the squeak of the runners on the snow, the jingle of the harness; watching to see if the back feet of the horses would step into the same tracks as the front feet made. My father was a musical man, and his exquisite whistling was a part of the early morning feeding ritual. I used to swear that the horses were stepping completely in time with his lively tunes.

So working with a team now appealed to me, and hardworking Suzanne was always game for anything. She and I decided to take over the task of cleaning out the calving barn every morning—with fuel-saving horsepower. With some difficulty, we managed to harness up the two Percheron workhorses, getting better at it everyday. We

167

pitch-forked the manure from the pen in the calving barn out onto the wagon behind the team, and when the load was full, hauled it out toward the Boneyard and forked it all off onto the field—instant fertilizer. The first time we miscalculated our load and piled so much on that the horses couldn't pull the heavy wagon up the hill.

Our kids would bounce along on the back of the wagon. It was a lot of work and took up most of our mornings. Then, luckily for us, after a couple of weeks of this intense exercise, the traces on one of the harnesses broke. While it was being repaired, Francis Billy, with a smile as wide as his cowboy hat, jumped onto the tractor with the front-end loader, drove into the barn, and we watched thoughtfully as he cleaned out the calving barn pens in about fifteen minutes. He didn't even get dirty.

Suzanne and I looked at each other, threw down our smelly gloves, and never went back to cleaning the barn with horsepower.

Summer set upon us with its multitudes of demands. Suzanne's youngest sister, Sally, showed up for a visit, and we sneaked off for a precious day of freedom to saddle up some horses and take her to visit our good neighbors, Steve and Vicki Andruss. Steve and Vicki owned and lived on the Dry Farm, a good fifty kilometers of riding away. I learned that day the folly of not having a saddle that fit me properly. I think it was Oren's saddle I used, and the seat was too wide for me. We spent some hours being lost on Saddlehorse Mountain, then figured on saving some time by taking a shortcut over the top of the mountain, rather than going around it. That never works, either!

When we finally arrived at the Dry Farm, saddlesore and weary, I climbed off my horse and immediately found myself sliding right down to the ground and squatting there like a mushroom. My legs wouldn't take my weight!

Now that I lived at Bear Springs, I longed more and more to get into the backcountry. Flying back there with Oren countless times had merely whetted my appetite.

168

It was a crisp morning in late fall, and the discussion in the office was over some equipment that had accidentally been left behind at the Hungry Valley cow camp by the cowboy crew. They were making plans for a final branding of the late calves and bigger calves that had been missed at the first branding and they needed the lanterns and the radio that had been left behind.

"I'll go!" I volunteered eagerly. Any excuse would do for me to head out into those glorious, mysterious mountains. Oren had told me: "You haven't lived until you've seen the Mackenzie River at breakup, and you've heard the howling of the wolf bitches in Hungry Valley." I intended to accomplish both those feats in my lifetime, and here was my first chance at the wolves.

A short time later, Jacquie and I were jouncing along in the black Bronco, headed for Hungry Valley. We followed a trail, which had grass growing in the middle of it, through the bush until we hit the P&T logging road. This brought us around by Williams Meadow. A few miles past Williams Meadow, we headed back into the bush, on a more remote trail, until we hit the only real concern we had: the China Freeway. The China Freeway had acquired this label because it ran past China Lake. But the "Freeway" part was a standard joke. It consisted of a mile or so of swampy, boggy, almost impassable territory. Huge ruts crisscrossed it in every direction, as desperate drivers attempted to find a new path across it. Logs stuck up out of cavernous holes, where others had levered themselves out; remains of campfires lined the edges, where people had camped while they attempted to dig their rigs out of the muck.

Putting the Bronco into 4X4 low, we gingerly bumped and clawed our way across the China Freeway. Reaching the other side without incident, we breathed a sigh of relief, slogged our way through Gaspard Creek, and headed toward Fosberry.

Fosberry, where the main dam was located on Gaspard Lake, was a favorite fishing spot. The trout would attempt to jump up against the water spilling out of the dam, and kids could take their hats and catch fish as they fell back down. We passed by the Fosberry cow camp cabins and corrals. The Fosberry corral system was an elaborate one indeed. A division of the Department of Agriculture called ARDA had constructed it under the overseeing scrutiny of Hank Krynen. Hank (Henry) Krynen was the farm manager for the Alkali Lake Ranch for twenty-three years, a veteran and seasoned cowboy who knew every inch of the surrounding countryside by horseback. The Fosberry corral system was constructed with the intention of keeping the flow of the cattle away from the shores of Gaspard Lake.

We continued on past the lake and headed toward Blue Door. Blue Door was exactly that, a patch of blue sky shaped like a door, a pass that led the way between two mountains. Newton's Meadow and Wildhorse Meadows were sheltered grassy areas on Blue Door Mountain, where the wild horses used to graze. The old "wild horse corrals" were still standing in the trees, heavy timber grown up all around them now. The last of the wild horses had been rounded up by Paul Rosette, Old Jimmy's father.

We jounced across the meadow that passed by Chilco Choate's guiding camp. Chilco (Ted) Choate was an eccentric outfitter, and we had been warned long and loudly about his paranoid hatred of the Gang Ranch and everybody on it. Rumor had it that he had been fired from the Gang Ranch years ago and had never forgiven the Gang Ranch people—past, present, or future. I knew how Rick and Denis had to constantly repair the water-retaining gate locks at the dam because of Choate's sabotaging efforts, and I had read the nasty notes he had written and nailed onto trees all over the area. I had seen him in passing, down at the Ranch, up at the dam, and once at a meeting in Williams Lake. At this particular gathering of irate ranchers and concerned citizens, he was advocating the transplanting of elk into the Chilcotin areas, in particular the area around his guiding camp. Not surprisingly, he was met with loud opposition from the ranching community. I was not anxious to meet up with the man, especially today.

We hurried on by, the trail becoming progressively worse. The camp at Fosberry was basically the end of the normal road. From here on it was merely a few tracks through the bush and over the pass. Blue Door behind us, we headed down into Hungry Valley in the late afternoon sun. It was a gorgeous fall day, but we knew it would cool off quickly once the sun slid behind the mountains.

We headed toward the Hungry Valley cow camp cabin. There was still another creek to cross in the middle of the meadow. I had forded this creek before and knew it was fairly deep but had a good solid bottom. Confidently, I nosed the Bronco into the water and proceeded across. Suddenly the Bronco gave a lurch and settled deeply into a hole. Someone had been stuck in here lately and, in their attempts to get out, had dug the creekbed down. Poles and sticks stuck out of the water where they had tried to lever themselves out.

If we opened the doors, the swirling water would come in; it was already seeping in onto the floorboards. Jacquie and I climbed out the windows and jumped to the side of the creek, turning back to see the poor old Bronco, nose down, water nearly up to the side mirrors.

We would have to try to jack it out. Wading through the water to retrieve the cumbersome jack from the back of the vehicle, we found out very quickly just how cold that mountain water was.

Off came our shoes and socks. With pants rolled up as far as possible, we jacked under the water, one side then the other, ramming every stick and pole we could find under the jack, and then under the wheels as the rig got a little higher, swearing our frustrations out as we saw the heavy vehicle settle back down into the creek again. Our feet bright red with the icy cold, we would jump out of the water every once in a while and rub some life back into them. We finally saw the futility of our efforts and flopped down heavily on the side of the creek.

"Well, we're definitely here for the night," I said. "Let's hit for the cabin and try again in the morning. It should be frozen by then, maybe the ground will be harder."

With that bright thought, we sloshed back to the Bronco, crawled back in through the windows and got the few emergency supplies we had brought. I don't know why we worried about keeping the doors closed. The water was already inside the car.

Arriving at the cabin, our first duty was to grab the old corn broom inside the door and run all the packrats out. Packrats are large, smelly rodents that tended to take up residency in any vacant cow camp line cabins. If you planned to leave anything of value there, you were wise to hang it from the ceiling on a string, out of their reach. Before long, we had a roaring fire cozying up the cabin interior, and wet jeans and socks were starting to steam as they hung to dry by the wood-burning barrel stove. The kerosene lamps that had been left there were put to use, and a pot of water was put on to boil. I started going through the supply of canned goods that lined the rough plank shelves on the wall, while Jacquie disappeared outside with her .22 rifle to shoot a grouse for supper.

An hour later, our hunger satisfied, our feet finally thawed out, and the supper mess cleaned up, we contemplated our situation and racked our brains about how to lift the Bronco out of that hole. We had found an old hand winch hanging on the outside of the cabin. A normal winch is an apparatus mounted on the front of a vehicle and has a cable wound around a cylinder. The cable pulls out and attaches to a solid object, usually a tree and, when the winch is activated, the cable winds back around the cylinder, pulling the vehicle toward the tree. This particular winch was a mite archaic. It was operated by hand, in other words we would have to crank the cable by hand to pull the vehicle ahead. Not only that, it had no cable! Not to be defeated, we reasoned we could possibly use instead of cable the snarl of barbed wire we had noticed encasing some fence posts near the creek.

The next morning dawned early and heavy with frost. I thought briefly about whether I'd hear the wolves howling, but wasn't a bit surprised when it didn't happen. Nothing else had gone right on this trek, why should the wolves howl?

We tackled the vehicle problem at first light, hurrying to put our plan into action before the sun thawed out the mud too much. There were no trees close enough to the Bronco to fasten the wire to, but there was a fairly solid-looking fencepost within reach. However, we quickly discovered that the barbs on the wire made it very painful to work with and also that it wouldn't wind or unwind worth a damn. The barbs kept getting caught on each other. We finally threw our contraption to the ground in disgust and fell back to our old "jacking and propping" method. There was a thin layer of ice on the creek this morning, and the frozen mud didn't sink down as much, but the water had definitely not warmed up any. We dug and lifted, pushed and pulled, swore and complained—to no avail. Finally, wet, frozen and muddy, our feet and legs cherry-red, we had to admit defeat. That rig was not going to budge.

Then from the sky we heard an approaching drone, and Oren's little blue Bellanca came dipping down out of no-where. Oren was gaining a pretty good reputation on the ranch for his pilot abilities. His little plane was perfect for ranch work. He could fly almost at stall speed for counting animals; he could drop supplies from low altitude so they didn't smash into pieces—salt blocks, hay, messages, what-ever. After a few instances of dropping notes that couldn't be found by the people on the ground, he started to support the toilet paper industry. He would attach the note to a roll of toilet paper and drop it down. As it floated toward the ground, the toilet paper unrolled, making its descent and point of landing easy to trace. The Scout needed only about forty-five meters for takeoff space, which enabled him to put down into remote areas like Hungry Valley, Graveyard Valley, and the Dry Farm, where the larger planes couldn't. He became somewhat of a legend for his uncanny appearances in that little blue plane when someone was in trouble. It was usually me; he saved my bacon more than once.

Now we could see Oren laughing in the cockpit as he dipped a wing to get a better look. Circling around, he buzzed over us again. This time his arm was out the window and he dropped us a note tied to a rock. Jacquie scrambled to get it. Oren's artistry was at work. On the note was a picture of two muddy girls standing beside a black vehicle in a creek, only the antenna of the car sticking above the water. We wondered how he managed to sketch that picture so quickly and fly his plane at the same time.

The little blue taildragger landed and bounced along the meadow toward us. Oren climbed out and surveyed the situation, removing his cap to scratch his head and periodically breaking into a good hearty laugh. "I think you two had better disappear for a while. They'll have to 'walk' a cat here to get this thing out. It will be a good day's 'walk' each way. I don't think you'll be a popular item!" he said chuckling.

I had already figured this out on my own and didn't really find it that amusing. A bulldozer cat would be needed to get the Bronco out of that creek. There weren't any roads into Hungry Valley for a truck to haul the dozer in—it would have to be "walked" in. This meant someone would have to drive it on its own power into the valley all the way from the main yard, some sixty-five kilometers, at a top speed of five kilometers an hour. The cat had no cab so it would be a cold, twelve-hour trip for someone, not to mention all the way back out again. Disappearing sounded like a good idea. This was definitely not going to fit into Dale's "everybody must sacrifice" plan.

We climbed into the plane and headed off in the direc-

174

tion of Graveyard Valley cow camp, over another set of higher mountains, and down safely into the beautiful higher valley of Graveyard, carpeted now in snow. We started off on the mile-or-so hike through the bush to the cabin, and Oren roared off in the direction of the Ranch. His first stop would be to ask Suzanne to care for the kids for a few days. I imagined him telling her what happened, and could almost hear her laughing from Graveyard.

Four days later, the little blue plane came buzzing back out of the sky and bounced down to retrieve us. We were almost sorry to see him come. Graveyard Valley had engulfed us with its rugged beauty. You could spend a month there and climb a different peak overlooking a different valley or plateau each day. Glacial waters came rushing down from each glacier, filling up the crevices between the upper peaks. The air was cold, invigorating, and totally pure.

We couldn't figure out why the cattle kept running down from the upper alpine pasture beyond the cabin. We kept pushing them back, and they would just run back down again. We found out from Oren that he had spotted a grizzly as he flew over. The huge bear was just on the other side of the cattle, and they were trying to avoid him.

The Bronco was back home when we got there, red carpets still black-wet and stinking like swamp water. But the worst of the heat had died down, and the painful journey with the cat mostly forgotten. All that was left was the inevitable teasing, and luckily for Jacquie and I, the Saturday night ribbing was not totally concentrated on us. While we were away, Paul Jex-Blake's prize cowdog, Mate, had been royally beaten up by Warren Farrell's big white pet rooster at Home Ranch.

Paul had the toughest cowdog on the ranch, and cowboys always have a particular pride about how well their dogs work. Paul and Oren had gone up to Home Ranch one day to see Warren about something. No one seemed to be home at the cabin and when Oren walked up on the front step, this big white leghorn rooster came running around the corner, jumped up on the step, fluffed himself up menacingly, and looked like he wasn't going to let them go any further.

"Just wait," said Paul. "I'll fix that son-of-a-gun." He called to his border collie, "Siccum, Mate. Shake him up, Mate!" The dog and the rooster flew at it. Amid yelps and squawks and flying feathers and dust, it was obvious that the dog had met his match. The rooster held his own, and it almost broke Paul's heart to see his prize dog finally turn tail and run. It was probably the most depressing thing that can happen to a cowboy, and it would be a while before Paul would live that one down.

About a week later, Oren himself was forced to go into hiding. He was pushing some garbage over a cliff in the Boneyard with the skidder when suddenly the skidder stalled. It was not known to be the most reliable machine around, and when it stalled, there were no brakes. He tried desperately to get it started again as it started to go over the cliff. He had a friend, Mervin Hinde, visiting from back home, who watched, horrified, as the skidder, with Oren still pushing and pulling at the levers, disappeared over the cliff. Running to the edge, Mervin leaned over the cliff and watched the skidder hit the side of the ravine, roll once, and crash its way down to the bottom of the sixty-meter ravine. Then it settled in a heap of dust, broken trees, and falling parts. He couldn't see Oren anywhere.

Suddenly, he detected a slight movement and heard a voice underneath his feet.

"Hey, can you give a guy a hand up?" There was Oren, clinging to some tough bunchgrass on the side of the ravine, where he had landed when he jumped off.

Mervin reached out, helped Oren scramble to the top, and they came up to the house. Upon hearing the story, Rick, Suzanne, Denis, and I were just relieved that he had survived; the crumpled-up skidder didn't matter.

"Well, I'm out of here until the heat dies down. I'll

phone you and find out when it's safe to come back."
Dale's recent tirade at the last meeting about too much
being spent on repairs had everybody running for cover.

The Gang Ranch was hard on the people who dared to
live there, but it was even more savage to the machinery,
equipment, and vehicles. Four-wheel-drive vehicles were a
necessity, and expensive to repair. Shocks and springs had
to be replaced time after time because of the continual
jolting. Fuel lines and air lines plugged up with dust, radiators spewed out more water than they withheld. Tires
lasted half as long as they normally would, and brake lin-
ings and brake shoes wore out almost as fast. Tractors,
haying machines, seeding equipment, balers, all paid the
price of continual jarring on uneven, rocky terrain. Me-
chanics and repairs were a routine, normal, and expected
part of every day, every bit as essential as the livestock and
haying operations.

For Oren, escaping Dale's wrath meant climbing into
his Bellanca Scout and flying away. But about a month
later, when the memory of the crumpled skidder had faded
from our brother's mind, he was back.

12

Monsoon Trip

It had rained all spring, constant, never-let-up, downright depressing drizzle. Rick was making preparations for a silage haying season. Denis's parents, Marie and Remi Rivard, as well as his Aunt Rose, were visiting from Alberta. It seemed a perfect time to sneak off again to the backcountry, as they enjoyed the opportunity of having the children to themselves. Denis and I and Howard Linde starting planning for a horseback trip to Graveyard Valley. Although I had been there a number of times by air, I longed to get there the hard way.

We set off in the last week of June. Yes, it was still pouring down rain, but we optimistically thought that, as soon as we put the toes of our cowboy boots into the stirrups, the sun would break through and start shining. Anyway, it had been raining so long now it had to let up soon. No one warned us that it would be a record rainfall year and that it would rain for the next twenty-one days straight.

The first couple of days were uneventful in the continual rain. We splashed our way to Williams Meadow, then on another twenty miles to Fosberry Meadows, spending the first night in the cabins there. The next day we carried on, again in the rain, tucking plastic sheets and raincoats over the packs on the horses in an attempt to keep things dry. We tied our sleeping bags on the backs of our saddles and spread the raincoats we were wearing over them to keep them dry. There is nothing worse than a wet sleeping bag! I didn't even want my saddle to get wet. It was narrow at the top, fit me perfectly, and I felt like I could ride forever in it.

The next day, we saddled up in the rain again and headed on over Blue Door into Hungry Valley. The creek through Hungry Valley, where I had got the Bronco stuck, was now a river. We had to lift our feet up to the top of the saddles to keep them out of the water as the horses slogged their way through.

At Hungry Valley, we lit a roaring fire in the cow camp stove, dried out our belongings again, and made a good meal: ham, french fries, and cream style corn. We didn't have many supplies; Oren had dropped a load of supplies for us from the plane at Graveyard Valley, along with hay for the horses. The next morning I listened intently for the wolf bitches Oren had talked about but still could not hear them. I guess they were too smart to be out in this monsoon weather. Heading out again in the deluge, we were optimistic that it would stop raining today. After all, we had dried out all our gear and clothes.

Oren had given us directions on how to get to Graveyard Valley. We were to turn left when we got to the first major creek. What we realized was that every creek was now a major creek, and that the usually clean-running Big Creek was now a raging brown river. We splashed our way through swamps and water all day, the horses stumbling on stumps and tree branches that were now under the water. We thought if the rain let up, we would build a fire to dry out, but it never did. The normal trail was now under water; we had to travel up above, and we weren't sure if we were going in the right direction. I looked over at the water dripping off the end of Howard's nose and shivered at the dump of cold water that ran down my neck from my cowboy hat. This wasn't fun anymore.

As we climbed into higher country, the going got

179

tougher, and the rain turned to sleet, then to heavy wet snowflakes. The trails were snowed under, and it was becoming dark. We plodded on, making very slow progress, and I began to wonder if we were going to make it at all. We were all soaking wet, and cold, and there was no chance to dry out on the high, snow-covered, treeless slopes.

Not daring to stop, we pushed on in the darkening, snow-filled twilight until we were up past the tree line. I saw in places, where parts of the mountain were sticking out of the snow, that the rocks were reddish and I realized I had seen those red mountains from Oren's plane past Graveyard Valley. Had we missed the place we were to turn off, and gone right past? If we had, I knew the next stop was the town of Goldbridge, on the way to Vancouver.

"I think we better turn back," I yelled. "I think we've gone too far!"

Howard and Denis looked like moving snowdrifts as we rallied our horses around in a football huddle, trying to decide what to do. Everyone was shivering uncontrollably.

"I have to walk for a while anyway," Howard said, "my feet are freezing."

We decided to head back down until we got into some trees, and then try to make some shelter for a camp. We all knew the dangers of hypothermia and we also knew we were all becoming prime candidates. I felt that I was luckier than they were, as I was drier; at least my legs were dry. A few months back, I had wheedled Palle Henriksen, who did fine leatherwork, into making me a pair of chaps. He had fashioned them from soft deerskin, with zippers on the sides, no snaps to bother with. Being a small person, I don't like wearing heavy, stiff chaps. These were perfect, lightweight and soft, yet they were keeping me dry, and the bugs couldn't bite through them.

Back into the trees again, we found a huge old fir whose limbs didn't start until halfway up the tree. It would offer us some protection under its ponderous, snow-laden branches. We knocked the snow off the heavy-needled

180

arms of the tree and started a fire underneath. After unloading the horses we tried to cram as much into that little shelter as we could: saddles, saddle blankets, rifles, saddlebags. We rubbed the horses down, but they quickly got covered with heavy wet snow again.

For supper, we melted snow and drank hot beef bouillon from emergency packets I had in my pockets, and drank licorice tea that Howard carried in his pockets. I could feel cold water squishing inside my soaking-wet cowboy boots but knew if I took them off, I would never get them back on again.

It snowed all night, and we kept the fire going the whole time. The horses stomped around near to the fire, and we felt immensely guilty that we had nothing for them. In the morning light, we had to make a decision: which way to go. The horses were shivering, their wet hair covered in ice. Even their eyelashes were covered with icicles. We walked them around and around, floundering in the deep snow, to warm them up. It was a long way back to Hungry Valley, but we weren't sure anymore just where Graveyard was, with our precious hay and supply drop. We decided to turn back. The unknown snow-covered expanse ahead of us was just too formidable, and at least we knew there would be hay at Hungry Valley for the horses.

We were still wet and loathe to leave our warm fire. We lingered as long as we dared, drinking more beef bouillon and more licorice tea. I wondered if I looked as frozen and bedraggled as Howard and Denis did.

"Howard, whatever possessed you to bring licorice tea? I'm sick to death of it already," I chided him.

"Not as sick as I'm getting of your beef bouillon!" was his quick retort.

Thank heavens for Howard's eternal sense of humor. We really needed it out here.

With fingers that would hardly work, we prepared our horses, rubbing them down as much as we could. The leather straps for tightening the cinches were wet, and our clumsy frozen fingers could barely tighten them. We placed heavy, sodden saddle blankets under the saddles—it really didn't matter anymore—and began a slow, disappointing retreat back to Hungry Valley. Another long day of plowing through the snow, then plodding through the rain, water dripping off our noses and running down the backs of our necks. We didn't even care how wet we got any longer. We had ceased expecting the deluge from the sky to ever stop.

We paused periodically to attempt to warm up, having some difficulty getting a fire going. We would then huddle close to the warmth, and drink more beef bouillon and the everlasting licorice tea. Plodding on again, I heard through the pouring rain a most joyous sound, the distant drone of an airplane. Nearer and nearer it came, and sure enough, Oren's blue Bellanca came zooming down over us, then promptly disappeared into the leaking heavens. We continued slogging along. Not even an hour later, we heard him returning. Swooping down low in front of us, the arm came out of the window, and a large package floated toward the ground and splashed into the water. Not worrying about getting wet, we scrambled right into the water after it. A loaf of bread, a hunk of cheese, and some chocolate bars— an absolute feast.

Three rain-filled days later found us back down at Bear Springs, recuperating from what I'm sure would qualify in *The Guinness Book of Records* as the worst backcountry trip ever, not to mention the overdose of licorice tea.

"What happened to you?" Oren asked as we sat around the table at Bear Springs, me towel-drying my hair after about my tenth hot shower since we returned.

"We couldn't find Graveyard!" I sighed, still feeling defeated.

"Come with me!" he demanded, crooking his finger at me.

Up in the Bellanca we went, rain still pouring down.

In a half hour, we covered the rain-swollen distance that had taken Denis, Howard, and I six days to cover,

182

coming and going. Oren followed our tracks, almost covered up again with new snowfall. Our meandering hoofprints were now mere indentations in the recent deluge, at times floundering back and forth in seemingly aimless directions.

"Here is where you turned back," he yelled over the roar of the engine. Peering down, I could see where our tracks reversed and headed back down toward the tree line.

"Now look where the cabin is," he laughed, pointing ahead.

I gasped in disbelief. There was a bush about one hundred meters ahead of where we had turned back. If we had carried on around the bush, we would have seen the cabin, and the precious food and hay drop! Groaning, I fell back into the seat of the plane.

All was not lost, however. With each trip out, I got smarter. I learned that a very expensive, lightweight sleeping bag is worth its weight in gold. And I learned to cut down on supplies to be carried. I eventually made a list of thirty-five items to take that would sustain me well. This eliminated having to sit and decide each time what to take. I got better at handling the horses, getting more relaxed and letting the pack horses follow, rather than pulling them. I learned to put my confidence in the horses, letting them go their way because, ultimately, they knew where they were going when I didn't. I learned to go in late August and September, when there was no rain, the days were nice, but the nights would freeze, eliminating the black flies, mosquitoes, horseflies, and "no-see-ums."

When we returned, the first news we heard was that Karen Stoughton and Dan Patten had gone into Williams Lake for the July 1st parade and had come home married. That gave us double cause for celebration. We had survived—and normal things like romances and weddings were still happening.

183

13

Back to Graveyard

"Where do we start?" Suzanne groaned in exasperation as she stood in the midst of a whole truckload of huge cardboard cartons, some of them opened and the contents partially out.

The contents were shirts, hundreds and hundreds of them, in every size and color: short-sleeved, long-sleeved, winter sweatshirts, and summer T-shirts. All the shirts had one thing in common and that was the hand-drawn buffalo logo on the front, surrounded by the words "Gang Ranch." This was Oren's artistry at work again, and already the shirts were selling like hotcakes, even though they weren't out of the boxes yet. People were holding them up to their own bodies, and their children's bodies, changing and exchanging for different sizes and colors.

We had our work cut out for us to get them all into the store and sorted by size and price. It was the beginning of the tourist season in 1981, and we needed to get them all out on the shelves before the first tourists arrived.

As we sat categorizing and piling and repiling, we talked about what was foremost in both our minds, the worsening family situation. The ranch was operating at full production, the crews were reasonably stable and happy, and the financial statements showed us in a good position. Our livestock sales for the year were $2,366,443. Our cattle numbers were at 3,300 mother cows, 3,000 calves, 186 bulls, 312 yearling steers, 356 yearling heifers, 204 horses, and 57 buffalo, for a livestock inventory of 7,421. Rick and Denis worked well together, they were both farmers and essentially agreed on all the farming decisions. Running the ranch operation was headache enough without having to worry about what was happening off the ranch. Dale was not a farmer and had an entirely different perspective on the ranch's existence. The result was constant disagreement. People were being hired and sent in that we didn't need and didn't know what to do with. The one-signature check signing wasn't working out either. There were payroll problems and communication problems. Nothing seemed to get resolved at the family meetings anymore. There seemed to be some kind of skirmish with Dale whenever he become involved; literally everything we did was wrong in his eyes.

Rick's health was concerning us most of all. He seemed to have pneumonia but would not stop long enough to make any kind of recovery. Too much work and too little sleep were taking their toll, but I felt it was more than that: he was under too much stress trying to deal with Dale.

Then came the day when he was too sick to get off the couch. Now's our chance! we thought. Suzanne, Oren, and I virtually forced him into the Bellanca Scout and flew him to Williams Lake to the emergency department of Cariboo Memorial Hospital, thinking they would ride herd on him and tie him down for a while. To our frustrated amazement, they sent him home with some pills, saying he was possibly allergic to something out at the ranch, or just needed more rest. The doctors never X-rayed his lungs. Rick would later lose one lung; ongoing bronchial trauma had damaged it beyond repair. Rick had never smoked a cigarette in his life—it wasn't fair.

Our good friends, the Roth family, arrived from Edmonton—Dennis, Veneta, their children Kerry and John. They had also brought with them their niece and nephew

185

Carleen and Colin. This was to be my chance to get out into the backcountry again. Ever since the "monsoon trip" I had thought continually about getting out there again and going that extra hundred meters to the Graveyard cabin and beyond.

Jacquie and I would take the two teenaged girls, Kerry and Carleen Roth, on the grueling backcountry trip to Graveyard Valley, 135 kilometers as the crow flies, and then back again. The backcountry was now like a magnet to me—I could not stay away from it.

For two city girls who hadn't done this sort of thing before, Kerry and Carleen were immensely good-natured and uncomplaining. The first day out, as we trailed our horses past Fosberry Meadows, Kerry became woozy, weaving unsteadily on her horse and finally slumping heavily off the animal and onto the ground.

"A bee bit her!" Carleen yelled, "I saw it hanging around her and I think she's allergic to them!"

Jacquie had a never-ending knowledge of the wilderness and how to survive in it. She quickly dug into her packs until she came up with a raw onion. Using her pocketknife, she sliced the onion in half and placed it, cut-side down, on the swelling red welt at the base of Kerry's throat. The onion drew the poison out of the wound.

Kerry came around in a little while, dizzy and needing some help to sit up and a little time to recuperate. Finally I was able to relax a little and stop trying to figure out how I was going to get help for her from sixty-five horseback kilometers away.

It was a beautiful hot day, although the bugs were bothering us somewhat. We carried on over Blue Door into Hungry Valley, arriving there in the heat of the late afternoon. After caring for the horses, the first thing we decided to do was wash our sweaty clothes in the creek, draping them on the bushes to dry. What a day to be alive, and what a gorgeous place to be alive in, I thought.

Wearing not much more than some footwear and some

186

underwear, we wandered out into the meadow, picking the firm, white, delicious-smelling meadow mushrooms for supper. I could just about taste them simmering in butter and garlic. Picking further and further, we ended up on the other side of the meadow from the cabin. Jacquie was the smart one—she had climbed up on top of the cabin and was lying on the roof getting a tan.

Suddenly, we were caught in a crazy situation. A lone rider on a white horse was loping across the meadow toward the cabin, between us and our clothes. Frantically, we debated what to do. We could run into the bush, but eventually we would have to go back to the cabin. Rules in the backcountry were that no one is ever turned away from lodging. He could stay for days! Quickly, we decided to make a run for our clothes.

Carleen, Kerry, and I ran our fastest on the edge of the meadow, sneaking as much as we could along the trees toward the creek. We knew he could not help but see us. We ripped the still-wet clothes off the bushes and pulled them on. Then, as nonchalantly as we could muster, we sauntered out to greet the visitor.

It was Stiffy, one of the older longtime cowboys, out checking for strays. We waited for him to say something about seeing us, but he didn't. He came in and we made him coffee and watched as he pulled a cold pancake out of his shirt pocket and began happily chomping it with toothless gums. He never mentioned seeing any naked girls, so we thought maybe we were going to get away with it.

After a short visit, he decided to be on his way to Big Meadow, a couple of hours ride away, where our branding corrals were situated. We accompanied him to his horse and soon learned how he had acquired his nickname. He had one stiff leg, and it was an art in itself, the way he got on his horse. Propping the stirrup "just so" toward himself, he backed up about three meters, took a lop-gaited run toward the horse, leapt at the side of the animal, and aimed

187

his toe accurately into the stirrup. Swinging his stiff leg over, he was on.

After he cantered away, we consoled ourselves that he hadn't seen us. "Maybe he's nearsighted and couldn't see that far."

"Maybe his cowboy hat was pulled down too low..."

It wasn't until we arrived back down at the ranch weeks later that we heard about the "nudist colony" Stiffy had run into in the backcountry and, of course, with each telling, the stories had grown more and more interesting.

The higher up we climbed, the worse the black fly and horsefly problem became. Even though we had ample Wipe repellant for the horses, it ran off their bodies continually with their sweat; they danced around looking for relief, becoming more and more agitated, their coarse tails continually switching to keep the bugs away. By the time we reached Graveyard Valley and saw our precious drop of supplies and hay from Oren, the black flies were intolerable. Preoccupied with this problem, we dashed off our horses to check out the cabin for the inevitable packrats and to get a fire going—maybe with some smoke, we would get some relief.

We had left our horses untied; after all, we were one hundred thirty-five kilometers as the crow flies from home. They were tired and I thought ready for a good rubdown of Wipe and some hay. But as we stepped back out of the cabin, the horses had already lit off across the meadow, packs and rifles bouncing, headed for home. Only my trusty old buckskin Buck, which I had bought from Steve and Vicki Andruss at the Dry Farm, remained, and I never did figure out whether he was really that loyal or if he was just too lazy and tired to follow the others.

We chased after the fleeing renegades and managed to catch one horse who kept stepping on his reins, but the others were determinedly disappearing at full speed.

Quickly, we unloaded the packs from the horse we had just caught, and Jacquie leaped on him and took off *to* recover the other horses. We were helpless without them and it was already late afternoon.

Carleen, Kerry, and I set about camp duties, glancing constantly toward where we figured Jacquie would be reappearing. We had supper, cleaned up, it got dark, still no Jacquie. We tried to make light of the situation, but we couldn't hide the fact that we were getting worried about her. I knew Jacquie to be totally self-sufficient, but my imagination started running wild. I knew she had left in a hurry with no coat, and the cold mountain night was beginning to descend. The bugs must be massacring her, I thought. There wasn't even a hint of moonlight tonight, it was pitch black. Still no sign of her.

Finally, I could stand it no longer. Grabbing a flashlight and a few other essentials in my pocket, I hurriedly snapped a hackamore on Buck, led him to the hitching rail, climbed upon the end pole, and slid onto his warm back, bareback. I rode off into the blackness to find her.

If possible, it became even blacker in the bush as I trotted further and further away from the Graveyard Valley and the fading lantern light from the cabin windows. It was a strange sensation, as I could see *nothing*. Normally, I do not feel threatened by anything in the wilderness, but I began to feel disoriented and disadvantaged in the total blackness. This is what being blind must be like, I thought to myself. You can't tell whether your eyes are open or closed!

I figured Buck wasn't able to see anything either since he was stumbling periodically. I fished out the flashlight with the idea of shining the light on the trail in front of him. Big mistake! As soon as he saw the light bouncing in front of him, he went nuts. I ended up on the ground, still hanging onto the reins. Buck was a big horse, fifteen hands tall, and I couldn't get back on him easily without the saddle. I stayed on the ground and tried calling to Jacquie.

"Jacqu-i-e, " I yelled at the top of my lungs.

This started an uproar of another kind. There were

owls in the trees that surrounded me. I couldn't see them, but they hooted in front of me, and they hooted behind me; if I moved, they moved; if I stayed still, they stayed still, continually hooting.

"Jac-qu-ie-e," I yelled again.

"Hoo-hoo-hoo-hoo," was the only reply I got, in front of me, behind me, all around me. If Jacquie was answering me, I'd never hear her. The hooting was getting to me! I headed back in the direction of the cabin.

My flashlight picked out a stump and I climbed back up onto Buck, wondering vaguely if anyone had ever been attacked, carried away, or eaten by a flock of owls. I shut my eyes to the darkness, my ears to the owls, and let the horse go, trusting him to stay on the trail. I figured if he could see to get out here, he could see to get back. And he did.

With sweet relief, I eventually saw the flickering lamp light through the cabin window, and swung down off Buck in front of the hitching rail. As I was looking after Buck, I heard the unmistakable sounds of approaching horses. Who should come trotting nonchalantly out of the blackness of the forest into camp with a string of horses, but Jacquie, a saddle blanket wrapped around her, Indian style, for warmth. She didn't seem to be at all concerned, and I was too sheepish to tell her about being scared back to camp by the darkness and the owls when she had just come through nearly forty kilometers of bush and swamp in the dark with our horses. They had hightailed it almost all the way back to Hungry Valley, she said.

There are no corrals at Graveyard Valley, so we took the precaution of hobbling some of the horses. We fastened their front feet together with special leather hobbles that allowed them to take small steps with their front feet, but not to run. We tethered the others—fastening a long rope onto their halters and attaching the loose end to a stake set into the ground. They could then move around in circles to feed, but would not leave us again. The feeding, watering, and rubdowns accomplished, we all tromped happily into the flickering warmth of the cabin, to tell and retell the day's highlights.

It was all in a day's work for bush-woman Jacquie. I made a mental note never to worry about her again.

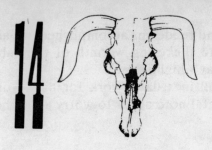

Home Ranch Cattle Drive: Fall 1981

We settled into the rush of fall work: haying, cattle movements, roundups, and last-minute brandings. A couple hundred head of cattle needed to be moved to Williams Meadow from their "dumping out" spot at Home Ranch. The cowboy crew was further out in the backcountry with the main herd so other "movers" were needed. I hastily volunteered my services thinking a day out in the glories of the autumn splendor would do my spirit good.

I never have been one for organized religion; I have never felt, like others obviously have, that God was inside that building called the Church. But put me out in the wilderness where everything you see is a miracle, and I become the most religious person around. I can feel Him everywhere there. I was on a continuous "high" out in the bush.

Dan Patten was presiding over this particular drive. In high spirits, we all headed to the corrals at Home Ranch early in the morning and selected and saddled a ranch horse. Although a late fall chill was in the air, and the morning frost had not yet melted from the slippery rails of the corral and the white crystal-tinged grasses all around, it promised to be a clear, glorious day.

As I sat quietly on the horse waiting for the next step, I looked around at the rest of the "crew" who were in various stages of mounting their horses, adjusting cinches, tying jackets and water canteens behind saddles, applying sunscreen and bug repellant. We were mostly women and children this time, along with Raymond Rosette and Dan Patten. I thought comically to myself that I would sure have a hard time getting hired on as a professional cowboy today. In my mind's eye, I saw the real cowboys with their meticulous white shirts, vests, big belt buckles, distinctive cowboy hats, oilskin slickers, and real silver spurs jangling on the heels of expensive snakeskin, slant-heeled cowboy boots. I glanced down at my corduroy shirt. I had discovered on that bug-infested Graveyard trip that mosquitoes and blackflies did not bite through the ribbing of corduroy. They landed on the raised part of the cloth, and if they did bite, it didn't get down to the skin. Today I wore my comfortable old running shoes—again, not exactly stylish for a cowgirl but my cowboy boots had never been the same since the "monsoon" trip with Howard and Denis. Still, I wasn't as bad as Oren. I remembered, with a smile to myself, the rainy, then snowy cattle drive that Oren had taken part in, and how I had laughed to see him trotting by on his horse Tall Timber with his spurs fastened to the heels of his rubber boots.

Everyone was mounted, and Dan was pointing out directions for different riders to take gathering up the widely spread cattle. We finally got them concentrated into the semblance of a herd, with riders placed strategically on the outer edges. We heard the age-old "Head 'em out" call from somewhere up front and began to move them out, up the side hills surrounding Home Ranch.

I was riding "drag," which meant stuck at the back in the dust, pushing along mothers with small calves and the old tired cows that would soon be wanting to stall at every puddle of water or batch of grass. I didn't mind; it was a beautiful day and I had lots of heavy-duty thinking to do.

For most of the day, we trailed along. True to form, the old cows became tired, and the mothers held back, refusing to move along if their calves hadn't caught up. Gradually, the herd split more-or-less into two herds: the faster group, with Raymond Rosette as "lead man," and the slower ones at the back. Half the riders followed the faster group. We continued to follow happily along the trail, and eventually the faster bunch got so far ahead of us that we lost sight of them. Even their dust settled and disappeared. Soon the faster group came to the cutoff trail in the bush that branched off to our destination, Williams Meadow cow camp. Turning their herd to the right, they quickly got swallowed up on the tree-lined path to Williams Meadow.

When the lead riders at the front of our "slow" bunch came to the cutoff corner, they didn't notice that this was where the first bunch had branched off. They rode right on past the cutoff path, leading our herd with them.

The afternoon went by in a relentless, mindless haze of pushing the slow-moving group. I had cut myself a long, whip switch from a passing willow tree to coax the balky ones along. I kept expecting to break through the bush into the openness of Williams Meadow at any minute. There wasn't a lot of daylight left.

Suddenly, through the dust, I caught sight of Dan's arms waving frantically way up at the front of our strung-out group. He was yelling and gesturing toward us; I couldn't hear a thing over the bawling of the cattle, but it seemed, from the flinging motions of his arms, that he wanted us to turn back. He, himself, was trying to turn the lead cows around!

I left my station at the back and trotted up to where he and the other front riders were pushing the cows back and trying to stop the fleeing animals from going forward around them. The tired cows had obviously smelled the

194

lush meadow grass of the huge clearing I could see up ahead and were bound and determined to get to it.

"What's wrong?" I yelled, over the commotion.

Dan, turning his horse in half-circles, was desperately trying to turn the herd and not winning the battle.

"We're back at Home Ranch! Turn them around," he hollered back at me.

I couldn't believe my ears, but there was no time to ponder on it, or even laugh about it. If we didn't get the lead cows turned around, the whole works would be gone after them. All the riders were now at the front, and finally we managed to get the resisting herd heading back in the direction we had just come from. Some went floundering off into the bush, but a few riders could gather them up once things were under control again.

As we pushed them hard back up the trail, a few kept trying to break away and get back to that open area. I looked behind at the huge clearing through the trees and could hardly stifle a giggle. Sure enough, it was Home Ranch Valley. We had missed the turnoff, gone in a great huge circle, and come back down into Home Ranch again. Following along in my contented, thought-filled daze, I hadn't even noticed when we bypassed the turnoff.

Eventually the front riders came to the cutoff trail and, after some persuasion as it was uphill, the lead cows began the arduous climb up through the trees toward Williams Meadow. We followed, up over the top, through the darkening bush until at long last we started coming down again, straggling into Williams Meadow cow camp just as it was getting dark. The cows were tired and the small calves that followed doggedly behind no longer held their tails up in the air. All of them quickened their pace, though, when they spotted the rest of the herd milling about on the meadow.

A grinning Raymond Rosette and his crew were relaxing at the cabin, well-rested and fed. By now, Raymond had pretty well figured out what took us so long and was chortling away, his well-worn cowboy boots propped up on the windowsill, hands clasped behind his head, ready for a good round of merriment.

After our horses were taken care of, and we had a chance to tromp into the cabin and relax for a while, pull out a few cracked, coffee-ground-riddled cups, and pour ourselves some life-saving and potent "cow camp brew," the humor of it all began to hit us. Many jokes were told and retold about the "great greenhorn cattle drive," when we ended up in the same valley we started in!

The Black Fall of 1981

Back down at the Ranch again, the realities of the problems I had joyously left behind for a few fantastic weeks obstinately hovered over our heads again. I guess I had hoped that they would all have miraculously disappeared while I was gone.

The niggling disagreements with Dale had become major problems. Things seemed to be coming to a head. Unusual matters were coming to light that, in our isolation, we had been unaware of.

The IKR company records had mysteriously disappeared. A property in Alberta, which IKR owned, had been sold and the proceeds of the sale had gone to the Gang Ranch account in Williams Lake, rather than the IKR account in Maidstone. Rick went in and demanded the money back from Bob Erickson and was told it "was not possible." He claimed Dale had used that property as his personal collateral towards the purchase of the Gang Ranch. That did not make sense; Erickson knew that property belonged to the Idanell Korner Ranch company that had purchased it.

Something was wrong with the financing end of things.

We received a letter from the bank that indicated they wanted a meeting. The loan wasn't being paid down the way it had been promised.

We felt employees were getting the "payroll punishment." Unreasonable deductions were coming off their paychecks, for whatever reason. Rick and Denis and Oren vehemently opposed this. They wanted happy employees, and they wanted them treated fairly. Every payday saw a lineup of people at the office door complaining about their checks, and Rick had to somehow deal with it all. It took up precious hours of his valuable time. The paychecks were made up at the office in Williams Lake, and Rick had no control over the deductions. It was a constant source of friction, which did not go unnoticed by the employees.

It was past the "family meeting" stage. There had already been an altercation between Rick and Dale in the front yard, a fistfight between Denis and Dale in the main yard corrals, and a blowup between myself and Dale in the Williams Lake office. I felt Dale avoided coming to the Ranch because he knew we wanted to talk to him about our concerns.

It was time to "end the marriage" and irreconcilable differences were the grounds. Any attempts at reasoning became pointless. We were like a six-horse team, with one of the horses broken out of the traces, trying to pull in a different direction than the others.

Those of us living out at the Gang Ranch wanted to sell the Ranch and its properties, *now!* No piece of property, no matter how beautiful or promising, was worth a breakdown of the family unit.

In the midst of all the commotion, a strange thing happened. A young man by the name of Rick Van Horne had arrived at the Ranch, claiming he had been hired by Dale to "go through the Ranch files and see if they matched up with the Williams Lake office files." Bizarre as this was, it didn't surprise us, and we didn't have the heart to tell him to leave. After a few days, I started to notice that I was

198

bumping into him everywhere I went. If I was in the office, he was in the office; if I went out, he followed. The other people on the Ranch were starting to ridicule him, calling him "Pumpkin" because he hung around the office, seemingly with not much to do. I felt rather sorry for him, as he was always pleasant, and seemed like a nice person. We just couldn't figure out why he was there.

One morning, he was waiting outside the office when I arrived down at the yard.

"Can I see you inside for a minute?" he asked. He seemed anxious and more than a little agitated.

"Certainly," I replied. Once inside the office, he came right to the point. "I'm leaving the Ranch this morning," he said, "but before I go, I want to tell you why I've been here. Your brother Dale hired me to come out here and spy on you, listen in on your phone calls, find out who you talk to, where you go, who you visit. I'm to report back to him on what I find. I don't need to tell you how stupid I feel, and how ridiculous this is. I've been listening in on your phone calls on the extension in the other room. The most interesting thing I've found for him is that you made a call to the health nurse about a rash on Buffy's arm, and you put in an order to Clinton for fuel, also a store order to Kelly Douglas. I'm going in to Williams Lake now to tell him he's nuts!"

I was so shocked that I couldn't even think what to say to him. My first inclination was to laugh. It all seemed so hilarious. What did Dale think I was doing? Entertaining the Mafia out here? I thanked Rick Van Horne for being honest with me and told him I hoped his time at the Ranch hadn't all been unpleasant. Try as I might, I couldn't quit chuckling at the situation, and we finally both ended up having a good laugh over it.

As I watched him leave the office and head out across the yard, I became a little more serious. I really was beginning to wonder about the mental state of my oldest brother.

As far as possible, we had not told Mom and Dad about all the disagreements. We knew how it would hurt them to see any of their children quarreling after all these years of being such a close family. On the other hand, we were determined not to sit by idly while everything they had ever worked for went down the drain; Dad and Rick's IKR had been virtually debt-free, as was Denis's and mine in Alberta. We were not going to "stop asking questions."

We contacted the company accountant, Ben Tokarek, in Williams Lake, who assured us everything was fine. Denis wanted an audit done, but the accountant advised us it was costly and unnecessary. Our financial statements showed we were operating in the black.

I received the following, all within the same week, with strange coincidence: letters from Ben Tokarek, the accountant, the banker Bob Erickson, and the lawyer Derek Donaldson. All the letters claimed they "only wanted to deal with Dale" as they had been dealing with him up to now, and that I should not be "causing trouble" by making all these inquiries. The letter from the lawyer was actually quite threatening, stating I could be sued for "damage to Dale's reputation." Copies had been sent to the rest of the family.

We went to see Bob Erickson, the Williams Lake Bank of Commerce banker. Again, we got the story that "bankers are always nervous—everything's fine. You're doing a great job out there."

My father went to see him and asked him point-blank, "Bob, how much has been paid down on this loan, and how much is still owing?"

Bob Erickson, flustered, hands fluttering with the knot of his necktie, had a very hasty reply: "Ted, that information and those records of payments are all filed away in boxes somewhere. It would take forever to find them today!"

My father now contacted our accountant Ben Tokarek, thinking he would have this information. In October of

200

1982, Ben Tokarek provided by memo to my father the amount that had been paid to the Bank of Commerce since the beginning of the account in 1978. The figure was $3,695,925: $305,346 in 1979, $913,956 in 1980, $1,112,580 in 1981, and $1,364,043 in 1982. We had no reason not to believe him. And we could not understand what all the commotion was about now. Perhaps it was just the way banks operate—trying to frighten you all the time if you have a large loan with them.

Exhausted from trying to deal with a force that would not be dealt with, Rick and Suzanne and the family packed up and moved back to Maidstone. I was beyond being angry at Dale. I was just relieved that Rick would be away from him, as I was convinced this was the source of his ongoing illness.

As we forlornly watched their loaded-down truck disappearing in the dust out of the Ranch yard, the lump in my throat was accompanied by a heavy weight of despair. Along with this was an escalating fear for the Ranch. The employees were totally loyal to Rick, and I felt the operation would not survive without him. They worked fine with Denis, but I knew that when Rick left, Dale would take over management from the Williams Lake office. As it was, when his plane flew over now, employees simply disappeared. No one wanted to be found operating a machine, for fear of having a chunk taken off his paycheck. Throughout all his years of business, it seemed Dale had not learned that you cannot control people out of fear.

Already Brian Holst, one of our best and most reliable farm hands, had come to me.

"I hear Rick's leavin'?" he said, more of an inquiry than a statement. I looked at Brian, his sun-browned face and hardworking calloused farm hands, a wad of snoose bulging comfortably inside his lower lip. He had patiently weathered the seesawing power struggle between Dale and Rick, hoping that the right one would come out on top.

"Well, if Rick's in charge, I'll stay," he had said earnestly, "But if he goes, I guess I'll be movin' on." This last comment was almost a sad apology.

With a sinking heart, I knew he would be going, and others would be too.

In the days that followed, I missed Rick and Suzanne and the kids more than I had ever missed anything. We all missed them. I noticed a direct depressing change in Lacey, and when I talked to Suzanne on the phone, learned that Heidi had reacted the same way, sitting in a corner, not eating, sucking her hand, totally inconsolable. We realized then that these two little girls had been together nearly every single day since they were born, and to them, that was the way life was supposed to be. Separating them had disrupted the security of their worlds.

New people moved into Rick and Suzanne's trailer. We had hired on a Kamloops man by the name of Wayne Jensen, an agrologist with the Canadian Imperial Bank of Commerce there. His wife, Shelley, and three young children uprooted themselves from city life to test their mettle on the isolation of the Gang.

The new family was well-liked, and Wayne took on the manager's tasks in a personable and democratic style. I felt relieved that someone outside the family would be down at the main yard, keeping track of the accounting, and best of all, getting a handle on the livestock numbers. If anything was out of whack, it would surely come to light under Wayne's scrutiny, with his background at the bank. I was also hoping that his presence would end some of the head-butting between Dale and the other family members.

Bob Erickson was acting strangely. He didn't come out to the Ranch anymore. Whenever we saw him in town, he seemed to be terribly nervous, and was invariably in a tremendous hurry, late for some appointment.

"Guess what!" Oren said dejectedly, perched on a stool at the cookhouse kitchen counter, his red-cold hands trying to squeeze some warmth out of a steaming cup of hot chocolate. "Erickson called my airplane loan!"

"Why?" I asked, startled, potato peeler stopping in mid-air. "Haven't you been making your payments?"

"I missed the last two," he admitted, shifting uncomfortably with the memory. "I have to go somewhere and get a job to make some money."

None of us had been receiving paychecks from the company through all the ruckus, so this didn't come as any surprise to me. Oren had been flying and flying, counting cows, and I knew how expensive aviation fuel was. He couldn't afford to carry on like this, with no remuneration. Denis and I had some income from Alberta, so we could at least survive.

"How much does he want?"

"I'm $2,000 behind," Oren answered unhappily. For independent Oren to even hint that he was in trouble was a miracle in itself.

I wrote him out a check for $2,000 from our Laying R account, to take in to the friendly banker. That didn't pacify Erickson. He wanted the entire $9,000 left owing on the loan. This was unusual. It almost seemed like he didn't want Oren to be able to fly. A call was put in to Mom and Dad at Maidstone, and Dad promptly sent out the remaining $7,000 to pay off the debt. Oren could still fly!

Oren left immediately. He hated to be in debt to anyone, and flew off to the States where he had some wealthy friends in Texas that he could always work for. A few months later, as he had promised, we received every cent of the money we had lent him.

As soon as he set foot on the Ranch again, we immediately started spotting for cattle again. He seemed obsessed with verifying the cattle numbers.

"Can you spot for me today?" said Oren, sticking his head in the sliding glass doors of the Bear Springs house.

"What for?" I asked, swishing my rubber-gloved hands around in the dishwater. We had been "spotting"—looking for cattle from the airplane—quite a few times lately.

"There's cows missing," he explained.

"That's nothing new, "I retorted. There were always a few head that seemed to be lost.

"No, this is different," he said, sliding the heavy glass door shut behind him and coming to lean one elbow on the counter. "It's not just a few. I figure we're about a thousand head short!"

I turned to see if he was serious, my eyes riveted to him in shock. I felt he must be mistaken, but I knew he would not be wrong about something like that. I hung my dripping gloves on the edge of the sink, and hurried to get ready.

We flew all that afternoon, and the next day, too, dipping down to the different groups of animals, red Angus, black Angus, Herefords, some Charolais cross, many a mixture of all. I leaned with my forehead pressed against the curved window of the Bellanca, keeping my head steady so that my eyes could move amongst the roving herds without losing my contact spot. On the vibrating notepad I had balanced on my knee, I made a tick for every group of ten I counted. Oren was much better at this than I, and would yell over to me when there was a particularly large group, otherwise we would be almost past them before I could get them all accounted for.

"Seventy-five to the left," he called out, "and forty over there in that draw. Five down there by the water."

We headed back for the Ranch when there were no more places to look. I added up my "ticks" and mentally calculated the number of animals we had seen.

"There are just over two thousand," I told him, as we came swooping down onto the field.

"Hm-m-m," was Oren's depressed-sounding reply, as though he knew the number would be like that, but it wasn't the number he wanted to hear.

There were supposed to be 3,400 mother cows. I added the "ticks" up again. There were no cattle anywhere that could be missed in those significant numbers.

"The only place left is that they must have somehow got

into the Fraser and maybe got swept downriver," Oren said lamely, knowing the remoteness of this possibility.

So the next day we flew the Fraser River, as far down as Big Bar, but found nothing. From there we made one more sweep of the "pockets"—trouble spots such as Big Basin and Little Basin on Churn Creek that he knew of in the high country. But we found nothing more than we had found before.

Oren was baffled, and concerned. Over a million dollars worth of cattle and they didn't seem to be there any more.

"We have to bring the cattle in for an official count," he muttered.

We were not the only ones mysteriously missing large numbers of livestock these days. Our good neighbors from Big Creek, Mary and Ray Thomson from the Sky Ranch and some of their ranching neighbors requested permission to bring some riders over. Thney wanted to go through the animals we had recently rounded up from the grazing range that we shared with them in that area. There were usually some of their cattle that invariably got mixed up with ours. After fall roundup, we would segregate their branded animals, and call them to retrieve them. On one particular occasion when Paul Jex-Blake was our cowboss, one of the animals he was returning to Mary and Ray Thomson was a mother cow with a very tight bag. Obviously she had lost her calf somehow. Paul gave them one of our calves to replace the lost one.

This particular fall the Big Creek people were quite agitated; an appreciable number of their animals were missing. Although they spent a whole day riding among the cattle in the main Gang Ranch yard, searching for brands, the missing animals were not there. This was starting to sound familiar to me. Why were everyone's cattle disappearing? The Thomsons and their neighbors were efficient and honest ranchers—they would not be wrong about their cattle numbers. Their small well-run outfits were such that every animal was significant, and a large loss was very hard

205

to absorb. I thought uneasily to myself that there could be a cattle rustling racket going on in the area. Whoever was doing it would have to be a professional—a real expert.

Through it all, we started getting more and more demanding letters from the bank. They wanted Denis and I to "re-sign" our securities. "Bank policy," they said. No one else had been asked to sign again. We refused on these grounds. They then asked everyone else to sign again, as well. We wondered what the problem was. Why was everyone so nervous when both our accountant and Bob Erickson, who had all the information, told us everything was on track. Had everyone gone nuts?

Denis demanded to see the cancelled checks. They were "not available."

One Friday night Denis came back to Bear Springs very late at night, which was unusual. He had driven to Williams Lake, got into the Gang Ranch office after hours, and brought home a number of bundles of cancelled checks.

What we discovered, as we spent the rest of that night poring through stacks and stacks of Alsager Holdings cancelled checks, led to the ultimate demise of the Alsager family operation of the Gang Ranch.

16

The Holocaust

Our first call was to Bob Erickson, requesting that any sizable checks going through the Alsager Holdings account be held until further notice. We advised him that we needed a two-signature check policy immediately. He claimed he would need a company resolution to accomplish that.

Our next calls were to Rick and Suzanne, Mom and Dad, and Dale and Betty. We wanted an emergency family meeting—immediately. Oren was still away on his fall hunts; we didn't expect to hear from him until they were finished.

At this family meeting, we faced Dale and Betty with the cancelled checks. We had by now categorized them to some extent. Since October 1978, Dale had written some $400,000 worth of checks to himself, Betty, or their personal companies: $69,300 to reimburse himself for expenses; $179,750 to their own companies B & D Aviation Ltd. and Canadian Bio Scientific Ltd.; another $130,000 was just plain paid to them, without explanation. In addition, it appeared every square inch of their uninhabited log mansion overlooking the main yard had been paid for with Alsager Holdings checks. We wanted some answers.

Dale's fury was immediate and expected. He demanded the checks back from us. We refused. We told him we wanted a two-signature check policy immediately. He stood up to leave, a frightened Betty cowering in his wake, and turned to give me a menacing glare. I knew that by exposing them, I now had made a very cruel and dangerous enemy. I didn't care. They had to be stopped.

That difficult year of 1981 turned stormily into 1982, and we hoped all the tension and problems would die with the old year. They didn't; they got worse. Up to now, we thought our only basic problem was that Dale and Betty had gone hog-wild with the bank account. Little did we know that this was merely the tip of the iceberg.

Throughout the winter, we attempted to sort things out within the family company, in addition to carrying on normal operations on the Ranch. Rick was back home operating the Idanell Korner Ranch, and there were many unresolved issues there. Substantial amounts of money were now owed to IKR from the Gang Ranch company for livestock (cattle, bulls, and buffalo) that had been brought out to the ranch. Trucks and equipment had come from IKR. There was still the matter of the property in Alberta that had been sold and the money sent out to B.C., not to mention the original deposit to purchase the Gang Ranch that had been paid by Idanell Korner Ranch. Someone had withdrawn all the funds from the Idanell Korner Ranch bank account at Metropolitan Trust in Edmonton. This was upsetting to Denis and I—we had deposited $30,000 to that account for the shares we had purchased in Idanell Korner Ranch in 1977 and 1978. Idanell Korner Ranch had recently deposited $21,000 there, in addition to what was on deposit there before. Rick was furious. All these things needed to be reckoned with. Rick wanted IKR's ties to the Gang Ranch totally severed. I didn't blame him.

No longer trusting our information sources about our financial situation, Rick and Dad, Denis and I now sat down face-to-face with the head bankers in Vancouver. In January, 1982, after shaking the remarkably soft and well-manicured hands of Stewart Brown and Jack Quinn, we were ushered into their swank, royal, red-carpeted suite. We were offered heavy damask-covered seats at a solid rosewood conference table that was probably four and a half meters long.

"I wonder how many ranches they sold to buy this table!" I whispered to Rick, beginning to feel a touch "under-dressed" in that I hadn't worn a formal gown, and not even one of our men had on a shirt and tie.

The usual amenities about the weather and the state of the roads out of the way, the impeccably groomed, three-piece-suited leader of the tribunal began the proceedings:

"We are experiencing grave concerns over the status of your loan with our bank," he commenced, his papers absolutely straight in front of him, not one out of alignment. His gold-plated and initialled Parker pen was poised importantly. "Now that the amount is close to $7 million—"

"SEVEN MILLION DOLLARS!" we cried out simultaneously.

"There's been some mistake!"

"That's virtually impossible!"

We tumbled over each other's remarks in our eagerness to advise these pin-striped robots that their computer systems had malfunctioned, their secretaries had messed up, they were sorely misinformed, it was not possible for the loan to escalate from $4 million to $7 million when we had been regularly paying it down. Their own manager in Williams Lake, for goodness sake, had advised us everything was right on track—our accountant, our financial statements, our cattle sales...

"Well," he carried on carefully, looking a little worried about the maniacal way these country people had reacted. Perhaps he was thinking about calling security. He continued, "What with that other $2-million loan..."

Again, we broke in, all of us at once. "WHAT $2-million loan?" By now we sounded like a chorus of well-trained frogs, croaking in concert every time the mighty one brought forth a new disclosure.

209

"The $2-million loan that was taken out when your company was cash-poor last year," he calmly replied. "I have the papers right here."

The perfectly lined-up papers were gently shoved toward us.

Four heads craned to scrutinize the fine print and, more important of all, to see whose signature was at the bottom.

They were loan documents, all right, dated June 2, 1980. Two signatures were required on behalf of Idanell Korner Ranch; those two signatures were those of Dale Alsager and Betty Alsager, his wife. Betty Alsager had never, at any time, been a director of Idanell Korner Ranch—I was involved at the IKR incorporation. The signature on the bottom for the Bank of Commerce was Robert Erickson's, manager of the Williams Lake branch.

"He knows who the directors of IKR are!" Rick burst out in disbelief. "What's he doing?"

The remainder of the "meeting" went by in a blur. The big guys upstairs had no information for us. They were there only to collect on the loans, not figure out how they had been carried out, or care, for that matter.

We stumbled out into the drizzly Vancouver streets in a daze and headed for home. The initial shock was wearing off and defence mechanisms started to kick in. Interest rates had soared to an all-time high. They crested at 24.75 percent in 1981, and we learned now that the interest rate on the Gang Ranch loan, for some strange reason, had not been locked in. On top of everything else, on a loan this size, that interest rate quickly spelled disaster.

The first call we made was to the Canadian Imperial Bank of Commerce in Williams Lake. It was late Friday afternoon and while Bob Erickson was there, he was "not available." He would be happy to make an appointment to see my father first thing Monday morning.

On Monday morning, ten minutes before the desig-

210

nated time, Ted Alsager arrived at the Bank of Commerce in Williams Lake for his meeting with Bob Erickson.

"I'm sorry, but Mr. Erickson is not here," a chalk-faced secretary advised my father. "He has been transferred."

"Where to?" was my father's shocked reply.

"We don't know," she said.

We never saw Bob Erickson again. Through ten years of our court cases against the bank, where his name came up more often than "I do not recall," the Bank of Commerce made certain that their man Erickson was tucked safely away, never setting foot in a courtroom to implicate the bank in any wrongdoing. Although Bob Erickson gave evidence at the criminal trial of Dale Alsager, none of the family were allowed to be in the courtroom when he testified. New people were assigned to the ever-thickening "file." Even Stewart Brown, from the head office in Vancouver, was totally removed from the affair. In this way the new "people in charge" could quite honestly say they "knew nothing about it." No banking papers or letters had ever been sent to any directors other than Dale. Nobody knew why.

Our second call that fateful Friday was to longtime ranch realtor Henry Koster. Gravelly voiced, honest, and precise at his job, he had been raised on the neighboring Koster Ranch near Canoe Creek, on the way to Clinton, and became one of our favorite people. Native to the area, and having a lifetime of contacts, he was the logical professional for this job. He already had a buyer in mind.

We officially listed the Gang Ranch, the Perry Ranch, and the assets of Alsager Holdings Ltd. for sale.

The three-ring circus continued on. Dale fought us on every issue: the two-signature check policy, the meeting we wanted to hold for election of new company officers, the sale of the Ranch, anything that meant him losing any authority. Every time we took a step toward removing him, he claimed he didn't have adequate notice, and we would have to start over again. He was throwing everything in our path

211

to prevent us from removing him as president of Alsager Holdings.

Somebody, not us, contacted B.C. Tel and had the telephone on the Ranch cut off. This was our connection to the outside world. I got my hands on an old box-type radio phone. It operated by battery and would only get proper reception from a high place. Calls went through best at night, when the various channels were not so busy. Evenings would find me trudging up the hill beside the Bear Springs house, the cumbersome box telephone under one arm, and a car-size battery under the other. I would perch up on a big rock at the top of the hill, hook my battery up to the telephone, and make my calls. Sometimes I had to wait forever to get a free channel. I would sit there in the dark under a million twinkling stars; the people I talked to could hear the coyotes howling in the background.

When I contacted the telephone company, they claimed the phone had been disconnected at the owner's request. I explained that we were the owners, and we needed it connected. It took a letter from a lawyer to get the telephone reconnected, and all this took over a month.

We made an appointment with our company lawyer, Derek Donaldson of the firm Robinson Morelli Chertkow in Kamloops. Appearing incredibly nervous, he kept jumping up to answer some very persistent phone calls. He listened for a while about our Alsager Holdings concerns, but was constantly interrupted by a harried-looking secretary for more emergency phone calls. Although there was a phone on the table, he went out of the room to answer these calls. After yet another such call, he returned, sweating profusely. He then, rather reluctantly, attempted to serve us with a summons on behalf of Dale Alsager. It sat on the conference table in front of us. Sitting in stunned silence, none of us would touch it. Donaldson explained that Dale was suing the rest of us for two shares, which would give him voting control in Alsager Holdings. Obviously, Mr. Donaldson had attended law school before they

212

taught anything about "conflict of interest." We were his clients, paid his bill, and he had just attempted to serve us with a summons! Rick and I reported him to the Law Society. When we received no response, I later made another complaint, again to the Law Society. Nothing was ever done. We heard later that Derek Donaldson had left the law firm of Robinson Morelli and had become a member of the Bar Association in Kamloops. The complaint we lodged would actually have to go through him. We were starting to learn how the legal system works.

We all stood up and filed out into the Kamloops sunshine. Our company lawyer was not our company lawyer, our company accountant was not our company accountant, and the local bank manager in charge of the company account had disappeared.

A lawyer down the street and $1,800 helped us finally remove Dale Alsager as president of Alsager Holdings Ltd., replaced by Denis Rivard. This same day, although Dale was invited to the special directors meeting, he spent the day loading cattle up at the Perry Ranch and selling them. He kept the proceeds from these sales, indicating to us, the bank, and later the RCMP, that the $66,000 he took that day was for "back wages." Stewart Brown, from the Vancouver office of the Bank of Commerce, telephoned me at the ranch and ordered me to "get that money back from Dale, or else..."

Not particularly wanting to find out what the "or else..." meant, Rick and I went to the RCMP, Livestock Division, in Kamloops and filed a complaint regarding Dale and the missing funds from these cattle sales. This was not easy for us to do. When a week went by and we hadn't heard if they had recovered the money, I telephoned the Kamloops RCMP. They had done nothing, saying they felt it was "a family matter." Later, in court, a judge admonished the rest of the family for "not doing anything" about Dale taking the cattle and the subsequent proceeds that day.

213

We waited anxiously for the ranch properties to sell, but in the meantime, the ranch work had to be carried on in as normal a way as possible. Denis had put Dan Patten in charge down at the main yard—he was energetic and lived in close enough proximity to the main yard to keep an eye on things. The ranch, though rocked by heavy swells these days, was still a marvelous place, and we expected it to sell quickly, thereby solving all the problems. Although our lives were in a total chaos of legal matters, the work on the Ranch went on as normal. The people on the Ranch knew the Gang was for sale, but that's basically all they knew. The same hay fields had to be worked, the livestock had to be cared for.

Henry Koster was in constant, capable contact. He was working terribly hard to get the ranch sold and keep her from going down, basically because he had such a longtime love for the "old girl." We had put a lot of improvements in place: new machinery, new fields, new pivot system, new store, new residences, and a promising recreation program, which was just starting to operate. The Gang Ranch was a full-blown, going concern, and he wanted the right buyer. An appraisal done in May 1981 valued the Gang Ranch at $8.38 million and the Perry Ranch at $2.5 million. What had happened to the $15-million figure we had heard about when we bought the Ranch? Those are just numbers the bank throws around, we were told.

When Henry thought he *had* found the right buyer, he came to us in an agitated and frustrated state.

"Dale is interfering with any offers!" he complained. "He claims the name 'Gang Ranch' and the Gang Ranch JH brand are registered in his name, and he won't give them up. Nobody wants to buy the Gang Ranch without having the name and the brand. Not only that, he claims he won't allow the cows to be counted. No one is going to pay for livestock without counting them first!"

We were beginning to learn that Dale had a particular fondness for putting things in his own name that did not

214

belong to him. By registering the name and the brand in his own name, rather than in the name of the owner, Alsager Holdings Ltd., Dale had now made it pretty clear to us that he had never wanted any of us to be owners. He had only wanted our assets.

Back we went to Vancouver, back to the twenty-fourth floor of the black glass Bank of Commerce mansion, back to the soft-padded damask chairs around the intimidating rosewood table. We shook the soft hands again and prepared to lay out our problems at their black shiny feet. Wayne Borgen was at this meeting, a heavily built member of their banking team who had been to the ranch periodically. Stewart Brown had also visited at the Gang Ranch, ate at our tables, and sung our praises. He sat now, in a presiding manner before us, his fingertips pressed together making a tent with his hands.

I had noticed before that bankers did that a lot—that tent thing with their hands; and when they became thoughtful, they squeezed their fingers together, making the tent go up and down. Maybe it was part of their training, I thought, to keep you from noticing any telltale traces of emotion on their faces.

This time we had brought Henry Koster with us, to confirm that we did indeed have a serious buyer and needed help to get the ranch sold to him. As Dale was creating problems in this area, we wondered if they had the power to take over and sell it around his antics. The offer would easily clear the debt, with a comfortable amount left over.

"We can't sell it ourselves," observed Brown thoughtfully—the "tent" was starting to move up and down—"but we could do it through a receiver. We could put it into receivership, just on paper, and the receivers would have the power to do all things necessary to get it sold. Dale could not stop the sale. It would not be a physical takeover, just a transaction on paper to complete the sale."

We agreed to the "receivership on paper" idea. Nothing

was to change outwardly on any of the properties. All we wanted was to get the ranch sold before the family suffered irreparable damage, financially and otherwise. It was a specific move with a specific motive in mind, to "move" the Gang Ranch, using the legal powers of a receiver, who would deal directly with the purchaser.

By the time we arrived back at the ranch the following morning, receivers had physically arrived at the Idanell Korner Ranch in Maidstone, Saskatchewan, and were running all over the place, placing green tags on all the machinery and equipment to designate their ownership of it. Dad had no warning as to what they were up to or why; it was devastating for him.

They then proceeded to the Perry Ranch and repeated the same procedure there. A surprised Perry Ranch manager George Bryant frantically called the Gang Ranch.

"There are a group of guys here, green-tagging everything. They say the place is in receivership! What shall I do?"

Although I had half a mind to tell him to shoot them all, I thought better of it.

"I don't know, George," I said sadly, "I'll try and find out. It's not your fault, don't worry about it."

Rick was still on the Ranch, having returned to the Gang with us following the Vancouver meeting. He and Denis were over by the shop with the crews. I called them on the radio to come to the office, and then I collapsed heavily into the swivel chair. I felt totally weak and defeated, and so cheated.

When Denis and Rick came to the office, we immediately called the Bank of Commerce in Vancouver. Every name I asked for was "unavailable." It would be days later before I would finally get hold of Stewart Brown. He then claimed that when we had had our meeting that fateful Friday, formal receivership had already commenced, and they could not stop it.

Why hadn't he told us then, that day?

216

It appeared the bank had seen the chance to get their receivership in at Maidstone while Rick was away. It would have been very dangerous to attempt that when he was there! But now I knew that the bank, having publicly put the Alsager Holdings properties into receivership, would invite every "fire sale" offer in the country. Getting a lower price for the Gang Ranch and the Perry Ranch would mean they could also take our other securities—the IKR and the Laying R.

Rick immediately headed for Maidstone, using fury for wings. Throughout the next ten years that the IKR was officially in receivership, no receiver would ever get to set foot on the place again. The one who did dare went away with a few bruises, and one official banker had a heart attack on Rick's front step, even though Rick was nowhere around. Rick's tenacity and determination to save the IKR would carry him through the next ten years of sleepless nights, summonses, threats, court appearances, document services, registered and double-registered mail, and chasing hapless bankers and receivers off the place. They tried everything—and he *never* gave up.

An impressively big, well-muscled Polynesian-looking receiver by the name of Rick Aqui came to the Gang Ranch and planted himself in the office. He stood massively, arms folded in front, trying his best to look stern and uncompromising, as his partners green-tagged the Gang Ranch assets. He remained tight-lipped and silent, but I instinctively knew that the toughness was all on the outside of this guy. I sensed an inner sensitivity that he did not hide for long.

From that day forward, our normal lives were totally changed. We were hurt and angry, and not a day went by that we weren't informed of some new atrocity. We didn't understand what had happened, or why it had happened. Why had Erickson disappeared? Why hadn't the loan been paid down? Why? Why? Why?

George Abakhan, head receiver, and his Vancouverite

crew began to run the Gang Ranch. We watched in amazement as the ranch filled up with their families, girlfriends, aunts, uncles, and friends, driving around in 4 X 4s, looking for deer, sheep, and buffalo, riding horses. No one wanted to miss out on this opportunity to see the great Gang Ranch.

George was a happy-go-lucky and likable guy but very thick-skinned—bent on doing what he was supposed to do. I guess you would have to be to do his job.

A cocky young accountant named Stephen Kaye installed himself in the Gang Ranch office and began to go through the Alsager Holdings accounts; the cattle records were seized from the Gang Ranch, the Perry Ranch, and the office in Williams Lake—that is the ones that were left. Dale had taken most of the records and accounting books. The receivers compiled a two-page list of items that went missing from the Gang Ranch at Williams Lake taken by Dale Alsager. Among the many items on this list were all the share certificates and shareholder information, the minutes of our shareholder's meetings, the IKR files and correspondence, the company seal, all the livestock files and financial records, and the livestock sheets from the synoptic.

I searched all over the main Ranch yard one morning for Stephen Kaye, as I needed a key that he had. No one had seen him yet. I finally drove down to Mom and Dad's little bungalow, that the receivers used for their residence now. I waited some more. Eventually the door opened and there stood an obviously annoyed Stephen, his hair all tousled, wearing nothing but a pair of pants, pulled on in haste. Through the doorway I could see down the short hallway and into the open bedroom door, where a similarly tousled lady occupied a very rumpled bed. I glanced down at my watch—it was 11:30 A.M.

"Yes?" he asked impatiently. My fury was such that I momentarily forgot what I had come there for—these city slicker receivers were on an all-expense-paid joyride—at

OUR expense. I could hardly overcome my desire to drag the both of them out of my Mom and Dad's innocent little bungalow. Since the receivers had come on, they were having a wonderful time. They bought new 4 X 4 trucks to run around in. They had a $6,000 satellite television system installed—something we and the other Ranch people had managed to live without comfortably. They brought out their families and friends, and offered jobs to their city relatives. This was all at our cost, of course. One day I caught a stranger dumping a deer carcass at the dump. When I asked him what he was doing, he claimed he was a friend of one of the receivers and had shot this buck. "I only want the horns," he claimed. "The rest will just go rotten before I get back to the city."

The cattle were ordered to be brought down from the high country for an official count. RCMP cars became a familiar sight, sitting menacingly in front of the office. Strangely enough, the RCMP didn't consider it a "family problem" anymore.

Denis continued to look after the Bear Springs operation, and began the spring work in 1983. Throughout all the hubbub, the hay fields still had to be looked after, and the pivots ready to go.

The investigation went on for months. We were called down to the office in the main yard one beautiful spring day of 1983, to be questioned at length by Corporal Bob Wall of the RCMP.

"Do you know where the missing cattle are?" we were asked.

"No."

"Did you know anything about any cattle loans other than the Alsager Holdings loan, any that aren't listed in your financial statements?"

"No." What on earth was he talking about? The questions went on and on—questions about the canceled checks Denis and I had documented. Did we know that Dale's house and airplane had been paid for by the ranch?

219

Did we know that he had sold his vehicles to the company and then had continued collecting enormous rents for them every month? Did we know that Erickson had paid Dale $200,000.00 back from the original deposit, and then tacked it onto our company loan; in other words, we had paid for Dale's shares in the company? Inquiries were made into our financial affairs and bank accounts from our farm in Alberta. They asked us why we hadn't gone to the police when we knew Dale had taken the proceeds from that last cattle sale. We replied that we had, When they had exhausted their supply of questions, they told us we could go.

About a week later, we were again summoned to the Gang Ranch office. The same Corporal Wall sat waiting, as was George Abakhan, Rick Aqui, and Wayne Jensen, our former manager. Wayne had now moved his family back to Kamloops because his wife, Shelley, did not like the isolation.

The kids had fallen asleep on the way down to the meeting. Denis carried one sleeping child, me another.

Corporal Wall sat on the corner of the Gang Ranch desk, swinging his leg. "I'm happy to say that you have both been cleared," he said smiling at us.

"Of what?" we asked incredulously. We didn't know we had been charged with anything. "I hope you understand," he told us, "but we had to conduct a thorough investigation of all of you. There appears to be a vast amount of company funds, and company cattle, missing."

"It's too bad," added George Abakhan. "If the money was the only thing missing, you'd still be okay, but for the cattle to be gone means death to this operation."

They went on to explain that they had now discovered that other cattle loans had been set up in the Williams Lake Bank of Commerce in the name of Dale Alsager. These did not show anywhere in our financial statements of records and would later be officially called the "phoney loans" throughout all the ensuing court cases. Our cattle sale proceeds, for the most part, had gone into the company bank account so they would show up as a deposit. Then they were removed and applied to the "cattle loans" of Dale Alsager. Eventually "his" cattle loans were all paid down, and the company's were totally in default. Every movement of funds from the company account to Dale's "cattle" loan was initialled "R.E." - Robert Erickson.

By contacting every livestock hauling outfit in the area, they had tracked truckloads and truckloads of cattle that had been loaded up at Home Ranch and hauled out through the Farwell Canyon end of the Ranch, twenty kilometers from the main yard. Sometimes the checks to pay for these cattle were made out to Alsager Holdings Ltd. and/or Dale Alsager. Some of them were simply made out to Dale Alsager. The majority of them were deposited to Dale's personal bank account in Kelowna.

By our understanding there was, of course, only one cattle herd on the Gang Ranch. Every animal on the place had the same brand - JH - Alsager Holdings, and had been paid for with company funds. A good deal of the cattle proceeds had gone directly to Dale, without even hitting the company account. For the most part our company loans had not been paid down, and the interest rates were at an all-time record high of 24.75 percent.

The receivers and the RCMP concluded that as many as 2,200 head of animals had been sold for which Alsager Holdings did not ultimately end up with the proceeds. We heard from them how Betty Alsager had now opened up a meat store called the Rancher's Meat Store in the Aberdeen Mall in Kamloops. She told reporters she owned the store, and that she "had gone through about twenty-five carcasses doing efficiency tests."

There was much discussion in the Gang Ranch office that day about the bank's participation in this setup. It is against the law under Section 88 of the Bank Act to operate two different cattle loans, using the same herd as collateral. Wayne Jensen claimed the bank knew nothing about Dale having any cattle. But Erickson had to have known and covered it up. Erickson was also a rancher—he and members of his family owned the Ochiltree Ranch on Horsefly Road out of Williams Lake. Was all this connected?

A strange ringing was starting in my head. How can this be happening? I thought. First no lawyer, then no accountant, then a disappearing bank manager, and *now* the company had no cattle? What in the hell did all these people think we were doing out here, anyway? How did Erickson and Dale expect the Ranch to make money? Our cattle herd *was* the ranching operation.

A puzzling incident from last fall came drifting back to my mind. One of the cattle buyers had called our cowboss Lonnie Jones and informed him that he was purchasing some cattle-liner loads of cattle from the Gang Ranch. Dale had asked that he make the check out to "Dale Alsager and/or Alsager Holdings Ltd." He felt something was not right and had called Lonnie Jones, who had come up to Bear Springs and given Denis and I this information.

"Go ahead and call Bob Erickson if you don't believe me," he had said emphatically when he saw the disbelief on our faces. "I phoned and told him about this check, and he told me not to worry, he would see it got into the Alsager Holdings account."

The next day I made a special trip to town and sat down across the desk from Bob Erickson.

"Is there any money coming in here for cattle that hasn't gone into the ranch account?" I asked him point-blank. "At any time at all?"

He was totally flustered. I thought at the time that he was angry with me for even thinking such a thing could happen. I began to feel a little foolish.

"Not to my knowledge," he hastily replied, drumming his fingers on the desk. He very quickly changed the subject to inquire about the haying. As I left his office that day, I asked him to let me know if anything like this ever did happen.

I returned to the ranch, thinking Lonnie Jones, who had been butting heads with Dale for a while now, had maybe just had it in for Dale. I never entertained the notion of a bank manager lying to me. When I reached the ranch, Lonnie Jones was gone. Dale had flown out to the ranch and fired him before I got there, which meant that Bob Erickson must have immediately contacted Dale when I left his office. Lonnie had even left behind his saddle and his dog, something a cowboy never does. It must have been quite a "firing."

These thoughts came flooding back to me now, along with the memory of Oren's relentless search for missing cattle, as Corporal Bob Wall continued to totally destroy our basic faith in humanity with the revelations of his ongoing discoveries. Lonnie Jones had been right, and I hadn't believed him at the time. A slow burning anger began to grow in the pit of my stomach. We were a large, legally operating corporation, and Bob Erickson was a professional person that we had trusted. Why had he done it? What was in it for him? Was Dale holding something over his head? If so, why hadn't Erickson gone to the police? A thousand questions crowded my mind.

Denis and I stood, stunned, outside the Gang Ranch office in the bright sunshine, the sleeping kids now hoisted onto our shoulders. The Gang Ranch office door banged shut behind us, and Wayne Jensen joined us. I looked at him blankly.

"Hey, don't feel bad," he said, leaning up against the log fence and crossing his arms. "I worked here for over a year, and I never heard of Dale owning any cattle. There's nothing in the books about it. Every cow on this ranch has a JH brand and, as far as I'm concerned, belongs to the company!"

In the myriad of court times to come, Wayne Jensen would be the only banker who honestly and stubbornly stuck to his story that all the cattle on the ranch belonged to the company of Alsager Holdings. The rest of them had

223

to acknowledge what I fondly refer to as the "phoney loans" to keep their bank out of trouble. We kept thinking that Wayne Jensen would at some point buckle under to his superiors, but he relentlessly and tirelessly defended the company of Alsager Holdings.

A short time later, Dale Alsager was officially charged with seventy-two counts of fraud, embezzlement, and cattle theft.

Reporters hit us full-force. The Gang Ranch going into receivership, with criminal charges involved, was big news. I quickly learned that if you refused to talk to the media, they wrote lies about you. If you talked to them and told them the truth, they *still* wrote lies about you. The headlines emblazoned across the front page of the local *Williams Lake Tribune* read: "Father Against Son, Brother Against Brother." Every paper and magazine we picked up had some unbelievably inaccurate story about us and the entire family. The reporters usually contacted Dale for information, and the stories we read were, to say the least, incredible. We read that Dale Alsager became the first Canadian owner in the 127-year history of the Gang Ranch—west of Williams Lake—when he paid $4 million for it in 1978. "Dale Alsager, Gang Ranch owner"—it was as though the rest of us didn't exist. We had bought the Ranch with our assets. Dale had put up nothing. We now knew that the $500,000 deposit he claimed he had put up simply had not happened. Bob Erickson was aware of that. We weren't.

At about the same time as criminal charges were laid against Dale, we were served with notice that the Canadian Imperial Bank of Commerce was putting the Laying R in Alberta into foreclosure. Why not receivership? They felt it would sell quickly and, as it was already being leased out, they would not have to put a receiver on the place.

Oren phoned innocently from the States one day. He had just come up from Mexico, and had lots to say. He finally asked what was new on the Ranch.

"You don't want to know," I replied. "And if you want to stay sane, stay away! The Ranch is in receivership, so is IKR, and the Laying R is in foreclosure. Oh, and Dale has been arrested for cattle theft."

There was absolute silence on the other end of the phone. Finally, he asked, "How many cattle are missing?"

"About two thousand," I answered. It was something I think he already knew, he just wasn't sure of the number.

I thought it would kill Oren to see the Ranch like this. There was nothing he could do anyway. We spoke very briefly—this was a party line and neighbors could hear the conversation.

"We've got to find a good buyer for the Ranch," he said. "I've got some leads down here, and I've got some work to do for George Vogt, then I'll be back," he said. "See you then."

The bank threw the Gang Ranch company of Alsager Holdings Ltd. into bankruptcy, claiming it would stop the debt from climbing higher. Still, inexplicably, the "debt" went from $7.2 million in 1982, to $11.7 million in 1986, when the bank finally got a judgment. Denis continued working at Bear Springs. We could not go home to Alberta because the people there still had an active lease. Besides, Denis did not want to leave the Bear Springs house; we had paid for it ourselves, and doggone it, they weren't going to get it! We hired a lawyer in Williams Lake to file a *Lis Pendens* to protect our interest in the Bear Springs house, in the event of the sale of the Gang Ranch property.

That left me running full-time now, hauling my kids with me, making long, hot, dusty trips to Bankruptcy Trustee meetings, court appearances, meetings with accountants, meetings with lawyers for the purposes of hiring them, firing them, and hiring new ones, meetings with MLAs. I even made an appearance at a Farmers' Survival Group meeting, where I found Dale and Betty Alsager busy soliciting support from the sympathetic group gathered

225

there. The people at this meeting were all trusting honest farmers.

Denis and I were the only ones left in B.C. now. It was too expensive for Rick and Dad to keep coming out every time an appearance was required. Process servers came all the way to Bear Springs to serve us with summons after summons. They would get stuck on the muddy Bear Springs hill, we would pull them out, and they would rather sheepishly hand us a summons afterward. I'm sure we singlehandedly supported Canada Post with the number of registered and double-registered letters we received. Tempers flared from impossible situations, and marriages were strained to the limit. Mine was not to survive. I no longer had the energy to fight for it.

There was nothing that could be done here. At that time we were still naive enough to believe that the wheels of justice would eventually turn, but I knew it would take a long time.

Even though the midsummer sun was shining down in an abundance of glory on the Gang Ranch, this was definitely the winter of my life. I knew that my time on the ranch was limited and I still hadn't heard the wolves howling at Fish Lake in Hungry Valley. I knew exactly what I needed, the only thing that could straighten out the confusion reigning supreme in my head—a generous and therapeutic dose of the backcountry. I went to see Jiggs: "Old Jimmy" Rosette.

To the Backcountry with Old Jimmy

"I'm gonna rope 'im by the tail," chuckled Old Jimmy. "I don't think grizzlies have tails," I answered back.

We were discussing the famous pink grizzly of Graveyard Valley and wondering if we would be lucky enough to find him. When I went to Old Jimmy and suggested we "hit the backcountry," his immediate response was "okay." Life was that simple and uncomplicated for Jiggs.

Old Jimmy was born in the little shack in the main yard where we now sat, planning our "tomorrow" getaway in the semi-twilight of the late afternoon. His father had been Paul Rosette, the longest-standing cowboss on the Gang. Jimmy's mother died when he was young; he didn't know what her name was—no one ever told him. He was the youngest of four children, two older brothers, and an older sister, all of them dead now. At that moment, in August of 1983, Old Jimmy was sixty-nine-years old, but he seemed to be more like forty or fifty. I hoped I'd be able to keep up with him in the backcountry and wouldn't make a complete fool of myself.

Small, wiry, and tough, but always happy, I envied him his life of simplicity and his not-to-be-equaled knowledge of the country all the way from here to the west coast. I also envied him for another reason: through sixty-nine years of living, Old Jimmy had never even seen a lawyer—much less talked to one—not even once! Or a banker!

Also heading out on the trail of the pink grizzly with us would be my good friend Stephanie Schranz, wife of cowboy John Schranz. Quiet and trustworthy, and ten years younger than I, Stephanie became my anchor in many a storm. Her brother was Phil Gisler, known to me as the "Whistling Cowboy." I had been riding in the bush one day when I'd heard this exquisite whistling. Briefly I had wondered if maybe my father had somehow come out to the ranch and was wandering around in the hills, whistling his praises to the heavens. The sweet notes echoed down the valley, resounding clearly off the surrounding trees and hills, trilling and shrilling in the crisp morning air. Closer and closer it came until the telltale Swiss cowboy hat came into view, and there was Phil searching for strays. I thought to myself that if all those cows heard that melodious whistling, he wouldn't have to go search for them.

Also coming with us was Raymond and Rosalie's son "Little Jimmy" Rosette. As we felt we had too many "Jimmys" along and it would get confusing, we quickly renamed him "Charley" just for the trip.

Having made all the arrangements for my kids, I was now raring to go. I was terrified something would happen, some subpoena or court appearance notice, a call from a banker, or a lawyer. The horses Jimmy had assembled were in the corral in the main yard, well-fed, well-rested, feet freshly shod, and ready to go.

My two horses were ready at Bear Springs, and the others would ride up there first thing in the morning so we could get an early start.

The next morning dawned bright and sunny, a gorgeous day to be off, and I was ready and waiting. I hadn't been able to find Oren's pack boxes where he usually kept them in his shack, and this was worrying me; these receivers had a bad habit of saying everything was theirs, grabbing it, and forcing you to fight about it "after the fact." Thankfully, I had Oren's pack saddle up at Bear Springs, out of their clutches. I reasoned that it would be easy to identify those missing pack boxes, as they had the initials "O.A." burned right into the wood.

In place of the rigid-type wooden pack boxes, I was now using two large packbags, heavy canvas bags that fit over the pack saddle, hooking over the supports on the opposite prongs of the saddle with long, strong, leather straps.

I was ready to go, and had been for some time, but still no one showed up. In my impatience, I finally drove down to the ranch to see what had happened. Overnight, someone had let all our horses out of the corral, and Old Jimmy was out rounding them all up again. Someone obviously did not want us to go on this trip!

It was late afternoon by the time they all arrived at Bear Springs: Old Jimmy on Penny, Stephanie on Roanie Jo, Charley on Marianne, and two packhorses Judge and Summer Range. Old Jimmy's two dogs, Moose and Bear, trotted at the heels of his horse. They immediately flew into a frenzied, snarling battle with Stephanie's border collie Jesse, I guess to determine amongst themselves just who was going to be "boss dog" on this trip.

Stephanie, Charley, and I already knew who our "boss" was, and I fell into line riding Lady and trailing my big buckskin Buck as a packhorse. I didn't fail to note with a certain amount of envy how neatly Old Jimmy's pack boxes were secured—ropes crisscrossing in neat X's with diamond hitches tying everything solidly together.

It was to be a rocky start. It was nearly dark and in our haste to get away, we had forgotten to tighten the cinch on Summer Range's pack saddle and lost the whole pack before we had got a hundred yards from the house. My packs came loose on Buck after some trotting, as the soft-sided packbags re-adjusted themselves with the movement, making the rope longer. Then Stephanie lost her packs. After some "adjustment" time, we finally got everything under control and headed out on the trail to Williams Meadow, under a brilliant full moon, the Ranch and its problems falling further and further behind with every hoofbeat. I felt the familiar old feeling of security as the forest and hills closed in around me. Three hours later, we trotted into Williams Meadow, heading straight for the corrals, which were easy to find in the bright moonlight.

The next morning I awoke early to the gurgling of the creek right outside the cabin and knew I was in the right place. Thus began the highlight of my years on the Gang Ranch, and probably of my whole life. I never dreamed I could have such a relaxing time. On my other trips out it had always been quite a bit of work just caring for the horses: checking their feet for stones caught up inside the inner tender soles of their hooves, replacing horseshoes that got knocked off on the rocky trails, checking their bodies for sores from saddles rubbing, tightening and retightening ever-loosening packs, rubbing them down with insect repellant, on and on. We had always spent a certain amount of time being lost, wasting precious hours pondering which creek to follow, or which trail to take, sometimes backtracking many miles.

This time Charley became our "happy horse wrangler" and our official grouse-plucker. Stephanie and I didn't have to worry about shoeing horses or chasing them, and we didn't even think about getting lost. We were with the most expert trailblazer in the province of British Columbia, and maybe beyond.

Old Jimmy had blazed all these trails in his younger days, and had left his initials carved in trees to mark the trails. Sometimes, as Oren had laughingly warned me, he intentionally led people astray with his blazings. You would follow the trail for miles and miles, and then it would abruptly end. Old Jimmy hooted with glee recalling the number of cowboys who had been ready to "shoot him dead" for this.

The days flew by in sunny oblivion. Old Jimmy, with the patience of Job, made us tie the "diamond hitches" over and over again until we got it down pat, chuckling and giggling whenever our clumsy fingers messed it all up. We had lost a couple of pairs of hobbles from our packs that first night on the way to Williams Meadow, so Old Jimmy now taught us how to make *proper* rope hobbles for the horses, so they would not take off when grazing.

We headed out toward Fosberry the next morning, Old Jimmy animatedly telling us all the way of all the things he was going to do to Chilco Choate when he got there.

Stephanie and I exchanged some is-he-really-serious looks as Old Jimmy went on about all the horrendous things Choate had done in the past, not the least of which was shooting Old Jimmy's dog. A feud had raged furiously ever since.

I learned so many things I never knew before: that the mountain where the Devil's Rock is located beside Williams Meadow is called Echo Mountain; and that the mountain I had passed through so many times, beside Blue Door, actually had a name—Will's Mountain.

As we approached the dam at Fosberry, we watched with interest as a great blue heron circled slowly above the outpouring torrent. Suddenly, using his long knobby legs as rudders, he swooped down into the spray. Then he rose, propelling himself up and away with wings that probably spanned one and a half meters, and gripping securely in his long beak a struggling, arching rainbow trout that glistened in the sun. With long, ponderous, flapping motions, the heron headed for the solitude of the nearby forest to savor his prize.

As we passed by the Gang Ranch's log corral system, past the Fosberry cow camp cabins, Old Jimmy pulled Penny up short beside the new log-pole gate that had just recently been installed. It leaned curiously and, as we followed Old Jimmy's gaze and heard him start muttering something about "that goddamn Choate," we saw that every support post of the gate had been neatly sawed almost all the way through with a chain saw.

Stephanie and I exchanged somewhat nervous glances and proceeded to head our horses to the far side of the meadow to skirt Chilco Choate's camp.

"Come on," Old Jimmy waved us back with his arm, "we'll take a shortcut," and he headed straight for the outfitter's camp. We followed uneasily, brazenly crossing the meadow right behind the cabin. We saw no sign of life.

A short way further, we stopped off the trail for a feast of wild raspberries and gooseberries. Old Jimmy would do that every once in a while, suddenly veer off the trail into the bush and, lo and behold, there would be a totally hidden delicacy in a forested pantry: raspberries, blueberries, hooshums, or gooseberries. We stopped by a small lake and picked wild bay tea to save for later on.

As we sat happily in the berry patch, stuffing our berry-stained mouths with handful after handful, picking out and discarding the odd twig or bug, Old Jimmy told us about a horse he once had called Propane Tank.

"Why did you call him Propane Tank?" I asked.

"'Cause he was always explodin'!" Old Jimmy laughed with glee at the memory.

John Dodds and his son Mike were at the Hungry Valley cabin when we arrived and, after the evening meal, we settled back with our nightly snort of Yukon Jack. This definitely livened up the molasses-like campfire coffee, and the story-telling.

John Dodds was another seasoned old-timer who had cowboyed and wrangled his way around this area for years. In earlier times, he had taken quite a few jobs delivering supplies by packhorse over the formidable mountain pass ahead of us to the Goldbridge area on the other side. One specific lady he talked about lived on the other side of the pass and couldn't exist without her newly acquired brass bed and her purebred pet cat. John took on the job of delivering these items to her.

232

The shiny brass bed was wide and bulky, too cumbersome to tie on the horse's back. When he did get it balanced precariously up on top, it kept getting hung up on the overhanging branches in the bush. Finally he lifted it off the horse's back and tied it behind the horse, dragging it along the ground like a travois.

The cat, in the meantime, was rigged up in a cage on top of the horse, but that wasn't working out either. Whenever the cage tipped or swayed with the movement of the horse, the cat would reach its paw out of the cage and claw the sides of the horse's back. As one might imagine, this caused all kinds of pandemonium.

The only thing left to do was to tie the cat's cage onto the brass bed "travois" that bumped along the swampy and rock-strewn trail behind the horse.

By the time he got his cargo over the mountain pass and into the settlement of Goldbridge on the other side, the shiny brass bed was no longer shiny and you couldn't tell it had been brass. It was bent and mangled, and the cat wasn't in much better shape. But the delivery had been made.

Old Jimmy led us on a time-saving shortcut to Graveyard Valley that eliminated the need to ride to Big Creek and follow it up, bringing us into Graveyard camp in record time. It was an exquisite day, not only observed by us, but by the countless varieties of wildlife who paused but briefly to wonder why we ambled through their territory. Countless head of peacefully grazing deer momentarily ceased their sideways chewing motions to stare at our passing. A beady-eyed, fluffy-tailed marten watched us warily from his perch overhead in a towering, silver-barked balsam tree. There were wolverine tracks, bear tracks, wolf tracks, coyotes, and foxes, lazy circling eagles, and, as we climbed out of the swampy area closer to Graveyard, hordes of mountain marmots.

Another group was already at the Graveyard camp. A very friendly Swiss couple from Langley, Lara and Marten Gabriel and their daughter Judy, were on a pack trip with a lady rancher from Lillooet and her helper. With them was a beekeeper from Lillooet who wore a crown of thorns on his head. They called him "Jesus."

Old Jimmy took his trusty Winchester, and he and Charley disappeared into the bush, emerging shortly with some dangling grouse for supper. I loved mealtime in the backcountry. We always ate like kings: white ptarmigan breasts or larger grouse breasts sautéed along with fresh meadow mushrooms in garlic butter. These traveling people even had refrigerated pack boxes and treated us to a feed of fresh lettuce salad with firm, red tomatoes.

After supper, everyone relaxed with coffee, spiced up with a nip of Yukon Jack, and some hot cornbread biscuits, and stared into the crackling campfire as Old Jimmy entertained us with stories of Graveyard Valley and how it was named.

An Indian hunting party, a band of twenty, had been traveling across the wilderness here years ago. This not being their normal territory, they became disoriented in the first valley, and it was named Lost Valley. Instead of heading out the easier route to Relay and Big Bar, they mistakenly headed in the other direction, which eventually led them to remoter areas higher up. In the next valley, they could find no food, as the icy winter was upon them. This valley became Hungry Valley. Starving, they headed on over into the next valley where, willing to eat almost anything now, they managed to shoot, with their bows, some of the mountain marmots. Old Jimmy claims that the oily, stinky meat of the marmots was poison to their systems, and they were all found dead around their campfire, pieces of unfinished marmot meat alongside their frozen bodies. No one was left alive to tell what really happened. This, of course, became Graveyard Valley; the actual graves are still there in a tiny valley to one side of Graveyard Valley called Little Graveyard. Each grave was covered by now-rotting logs. The next valley beyond, high up on the top, was now, of course, Paradise.

Old Jimmy had been a visitor to Graveyard throughout his whole life. He had come in the middle of winter, hauling hay in with a dogsled pulled by a team of twelve dogs; he had battled his way in through the swamps with a horse and wagon; he had come through on horseback when the snow was so deep he had to walk ahead and shovel a path for the horse to be able to get through. I could relate to this story. I think Denis, Howard, and I were nearly at that point on our "monsoon" trip.

The gods were smiling on us now weather-wise—crisp bright mornings followed by the beautiful blue skies of Indian summer days, and nights so cold the bugs were frozen.

The following morning, we exchanged gifts with the Graveyard Valley visitors—some of their honey for some of our smoked salmon—and bid them a fond farewell. We were heading up one of the glacial valleys that fed down into Graveyard Valley, Tosh Creek. At one point, Old Jimmy veered off on one of his "detours" into the trailless bush. Beating our way through the underbrush, we soon came upon an old and abandoned log cabin hidden away in the forest midst, long grasses growing now from its sod roof, a sagging testimonial to a bygone era in Old Jimmy's memories. Retracing our path through the bush, we continued our precipitous climb right to the top of the narrow Tosh Creek Valley, past the timberline and into the snow. The horses labored up the steepness beside beautiful crystal-clear waterfalls, blanketed on either side with mossy carpets, tiny fragile alpine flowers growing out of the soft greenness.

Old Jimmy stopped and dismounted to examine a large grizzly track. We let the horses rest, their sides heaving, their breath coming in cloudy short spurts.

Finally the horses would climb no further, and we climbed down into the snow, gazing down on the panorama laid out below. Tosh Creek snaking out from the glacier on which we stood and trickled down its mossy bed on its

235

never-ending journey into the valleys below. I closed my eyes and breathed it all in, not letting it go.

"Whee-ee-ee-ee" I heard from behind me. Turning, I saw Old Jimmy and Charley sliding down the glacier. They had taken off their leather chaps and were sitting on them, leaning back and pulling the chaps up between their legs to use as toboggans. Down they flew over the bulging ice, legs tucked up in the air, yelling and hollering and skittering off-course.

Later we headed back toward Graveyard, the horses jerking down in short steps to counter the steepness. The elevation here was 2,400 meters, and I felt a sweet relaxing tiredness. I was starting to "unwind," and the acuteness of missing the kids was wearing off a little. I had even thought of taking them along, but they were just too young. I thought about Old Jimmy, and the deepening respect I was feeling for him at every turn. He's so comfortable out here, I thought to myself, and he loves every inch of this place.

On the way down, Old Jimmy got enough grouse to last us for a couple of days. He had only one eye, but you would swear he had three. The old Winchester never missed.

Lady, and all the horses, had lost weight with the exertion of the last week. The cinch had to be continually tightened, and I could feel it wasn't tight enough now. The antics she had gone through getting down the steep Tosh Creek Valley had worked it even looser. I figured if I sat very still I could last until we got around the bush to the cabin.

Old Jimmy had been quietly watching my saddle, too. When he knew I wasn't going to make it as far as the cabin, he said quietly, "Your saddle's fallin' off."

I half-turned toward him.

"It's okay," I said, "I think I can make it to the ca-a-a-b-in..." As I was talking, the saddle went over sideways, and I went unceremoniously with it. I spent the next while trying to organize myself and the horse again to the accompaniment of everyone's laughter.

236

I listened very carefully to whatever he said after that.

Beautiful days drifted by in a beautiful blur. Old Jimmy wasn't satisfied until we climbed right to the top of every mountain. We struggled up rocky, velvety moss inclines to the glaciers of Sluice Creek and Grant Creek. We sat mesmerized by the milky glacial waters of Lorna Lake, as Charley plucked an unlucky grouse, and Old Jimmy told us how he helped to pull from the lake the remains of an airplane that had crashed, the dead passengers still seat-belted inside.

Old Jimmy veered off the trail once more on one of his jaunts into the unknown bush and brought us suddenly upon a tiny one-man cabin tucked away in the trees. If you didn't know it was there, you would never find it. It was apparently built by a trapper named Johansen, and the rough-hewn wooden front door was only a little over a meter high. Inside, covering almost the entire expanse of one wall, was a stone cooking fireplace.

We stood one day in the mountaintop wind on the very top of Graveyard Mountain, where you could see forever in every direction. We looked down on the Cluckata Range, Powell Pass, Lorna Lake, and Tyaughton, and toward Paradise and Relay. I was on a continual natural "high." As I stood at the peak of Graveyard Mountain, looking down into Grizzly Valley on the ranch side, I had passing thoughts of the receivership, the family problems, the bankers and lawyers, and realized none of it really mattered in the whole scheme of things. We are just specks of fleeting existence in this vast universe. This realization is what I had come out here for. And the quiet peaceful people I had come out here with were what my soul had needed.

One of Old Jimmy's favorite pastimes was climbing right to the top of a mountain, as far as we could humanly make it. Then, finding something to pry with, he would work away at the base of the biggest rock he could find, until it broke loose. Sometimes this would take hours. His

237

hearty laugh would then echo out over the vastness as the boulder went bouncing down until it crashed explosively into the trees below.

"Let's go to the Dill Dill Plateau," said a grinning Old Jimmy, his skin still bright-red from his early morning ritual of "washing-up" in the icy creek waters.

I knew the corner-post of the Gang Ranch was on this plateau so was anxious to go.

We rode back toward Big Creek and crossed it, the mountain water so cold that Jesse, Stephanie's border collie, did not want to put his feet in to follow us across. Whining and agitated, he paced back and forth until, realizing we were carrying on without him, took the icy, shivering plunge.

We clambered up, up again until we reached the Dill Dill Plateau, an eerie place that the snorting horses didn't want to walk in. It was a huge flat high-altitude plateau, full of dangerous potholes and "niggerheads" sticking out of the ground, spooky walking for the horses, and they knew it. Hunters rarely went there, so wandering moose were abundant, standing black and stark under their massive racks. Fat, white, feather-footed ptarmigans enjoyed the holes that made good hiding places, and made us a welcome change from grouse for supper.

We moved over into Little Graveyard Valley and set up a camp in the trees. Old Jimmy preferred to sleep outside rather than in a cabin, and I came to see why. Waking up and opening your eyes to the sun rising over Paradise Valley is probably the kind of experience that happens to you only once in a lifetime. As far as comfort was concerned, Old Jimmy showed us how to make beds out of pine boughs that put the hard wooden cots in the cabins to shame. At least the pine boughs had some "spring" to them.

We ambled contentedly across Little Graveyard one morning, listening to the warning "whistles" of probably ten thousand fat-bellied grey-brown mountain marmots. They differed from the marmots down near the main yard

238

of the Gang, who were smaller and yellowish brown. Little Graveyard was pockmarked with the pushed-up dirt of their dwelling entrances, and the soft earth held the tell-tale claw marks of grizzlies, where they dug everywhere, attempting to unearth the marmots.

Two mounted riders waited for us in the middle of the meadow. We took note of the baseball caps tilted on their heads and, when I saw that they were wearing running shoes and riding on their pack horses, I thought, oh, oh, Old Jimmy's not going to like these guys. To make matters worse, they had their worn-out-looking horses parked right smack on top of the logs that covered the twenty sacred Indian graves.

We drew closer and reined our horses up to face them. They were definitely city-slickers, their tired horses weighed down to the maximum, no horseshoes on them for this rocky terrain, their hooves jagged and split. One man was fairly young, sandy-haired, with wire-rimmed glasses, the other one older, dark, and heavyset.

"Hi," the bespectacled one greeted us. "We've been looking all over this valley for the old graves everyone's talking about. Do you know where we can find 'em?"

None of us spoke. They were *standing* on them.

Old Jimmy finally bent toward them, leaning his elbow on his saddlehorn.

"Yeah, sure," he drawled, without cracking a smile. "You head out the trail that way,..." He pointed off toward the distant side of the valley.

I had to lower my head to keep them from seeing my smile and saw Stephanie out of the corner of my eye doing the same. They were right on top of the graves, and Old Jimmy was going to send them on the wild goose chase of their lives. I guess they had expected to find polished marble headstones, not the log graves under their feet.

"Over toward that mountain ridge there, 'bout three miles up. When you hit the creek, follow it up 'bout two hours until you come to a meadow, and there they are...kind of hard to see in the grass..."

"Gee, thanks." They both smiled excitedly, kicking their reluctant horses into action and moving off the graves, anxious to be off before they forgot all the directions. "Thanks a lot!"

As they bounced off across the meadow to their new "destination," we couldn't contain our laughter any longer, and Old Jimmy gave a low laugh. "That should take care of those guys for a while!"

That night, as I relaxed pensively by Old Jimmy's usual huge campfire (forestry officials had, in the past, dropped down with their helicopters numerous times to warn Old Jimmy about his grandiose campfires), I noticed that the soles of yet another pair of cowboy boots were worn right through, no doubt from all the rock-climbing. I was averaging a pair a trip!

The next morning was grey and overcast, and it started to rain lightly on us towards noon. This camp in Little Graveyard Valley was in a low spot, and the ground soon became pretty soggy. We moved as much of our supplies and tack under the trees as we could, then spent the remainder of the day in a steady drizzle. Luckily, it let up before dark, or it no doubt would have turned to snow. The next morning we were glad to see the sun, as the night had been one of the coldest we had so far. It soon clouded over and, fearing more moisture, we decided to move to higher ground.

We made the move over into Paradise Valley, a beautiful alpine valley just over the pass from Little Graveyard Valley. We made camp just about at the tree line.

We were starting to have to make repairs on some of our equipment. On the way over the top of the treeless pass between the two valleys, Lady's leather martingale had broken. This is the piece of leather that encircles her neck and includes a strap that fits between her front legs and fastens to the saddle, keeping it in place. Then the tie-rings on the back of my saddle fell off. Fussing with all these minor irritations, I didn't notice until we got to Paradise Valley that my 35 mm camera, which Oren had brought me from the States, was no longer in my shirt pocket. It was a valuable item, not available in Canada at that time, a 35 mm camera with a retractable zoom lens that fit into your shirt pocket. As we had been traveling through shrubby territory all day, and I didn't think I would see it in the dark anyway, I decided to wait until morning light to go and look for it.

Stephanie quietly turned an unwilling Roanie Jo around and trotted back down the trail we had come in on. Much later, she came riding back into camp. I couldn't believe my eyes when she wordlessly pulled my camera out of her coat pocket and handed it to me. It was such a small camera, and thinking of the shrubs it could have fallen underneath, I really didn't expect to see it again. She got an extra ration of Yukon Jack that night.

It was a dark night, no moon, the only light our crackling campfire. Old Jimmy was oiling up his cowhide chaps with the grease from a marmot we shot, rubbing the inside of the skin back and forth, back and forth on the well-worn leather. As he worked away, he told stories and laughed, and laughed and told stories. I was deliciously tired—a beautiful fresh-air tired, not like the draining mental fatigue I had known lately down at the Ranch. It wasn't long before we arranged our sleeping bags in respective spots around the glowing embers of the fire, and promptly went to sleep.

I awoke to the low throaty growls of the dogs. Twisting myself awake in the restraining sleeping bag, I saw their crouching forms in the dim light of the dying fire. All three were making menacing movements toward the same part of the bush, the hackles on their back bristling straight up in the air. They retreated backwards toward the fire, still growling, not wanting to venture any further.

"Ho-o Moose, whatsa matter, boy? Come 'ere, Bear," I

241

heard Old Jimmy speaking quietly to the dogs. Jesse was sticking right by Stephanie's bedroll—I could see her arm around his neck. "What is it, Jesse, what's there?" I heard her whisper.

We were all wide awake. We could hear the horses stomping around in a frightened state, and suddenly a loud crashing and breaking of branches in the bush. I slid out of my sleeping bag, pulling clothes on as I grabbed for my boots at the foot of the bedroll. "What's that smell?" I whispered loudly. I could detect a strange, unpleasant, rotten smell. There was more snapping of limbs and thrashing around in the trees.

"The horses!" somebody cried. "Something's after the horses!"

I headed around the side of the bush to where we had tied the horses the previous evening. Stephanie and Charlie were in the meadow, too, looking for their horses. I could only see fleeting shapes of them in the darkness. Old Jimmy had sneaked off toward the bush with his gun to try and see just what was out there.

I found the low shrubs where I had tied Lady with a halter on a long lead rope. She was gone. Her halter hung emptily from the end of the rope, one strap broken. I had hobbled Buck, and now I headed across the meadow toward a moving shape that I hoped was him. By the time I got to where the shape had been, it wasn't there anymore. I headed back toward our fire, and the commotion that was still going on in the bush. I could hear Old Jimmy's voice, but I couldn't see him.

"Who-a-a girl, thatta girl, who-a-a now," he was saying.

"Jimmy, what's happening? " I called, as softly as I could.

"This crazy horse, Summer Range, has got herself all tangled up in her rope in the bush. I'm tryin' to git her unsnarled. Think I'm gonna have ta cut her rope," he answered. "I don't know what spooked 'em—I think maybe

242

that grizzly. Sure smells like grizzly, anyways, prob'ly after that marmot carcass."

I left him thrashing around in the bush with Summer Range and continued my search for Buck and Lady. All kinds of things were running through my mind. Grizzlies can see in the dark. I can't. Grizzlies have an extremely good sense of smell. I wanted to be as far away from the skinned marmot as I could get, yet I didn't want to be out on the meadow where he could see me. I crouched in the darkness of the trees, not moving a muscle. It seemed like I crouched there forever.

Things became eerily silent. Old Jimmy must have got Summer Range out. Stephanie and Charley were probably doing the same thing I was—hiding and quaking in their boots. I didn't know where anyone was. Even the dogs seemed to have disappeared. The fire had pretty well died away. Gradually the pounding of my heart settled back to normal, and I got brave enough to stand up.

"Steph," I whispered as loud as I could, straining my eyes in the darkness. Then a little louder. "Steph!"

There was a rustling of shrubbery and Stephanie answered from somewhere to my right. "I'm over here!" Then Charley's dark form appeared in our camp clearing. Stephanie and I left our hiding spots and moved stealthily toward him. Old Jimmy was nowhere to be seen.

"I'll get a flashlight," I volunteered, having located my sleeping bag. I rummaged for my pack that had been at the foot of my bed, but it was gone. Stephanie and Charley were doing the same—finding their bedrolls and feeling around for other belongings. We scrounged around then for kindling and dry branches to get the fire up and roaring again. I wanted the biggest fire we could make.

Suddenly, as silently as he had left, Old Jimmy appeared in the clearing, rifle in hand, Moose and Bear close at his heels.

"She's gone," he said, half-laughing, "took off with the marmot up thatta way." He pointed up toward a nearby

243

forested hill. "She won't be back tonight. She got what she wanted." He laughed again as he set his gun up against a tree trunk and came to warm his hands by the fire. It was a frosty night, but I didn't think it was the cold I was shaking from.

We climbed back into our bedrolls, deciding to find the horses and missing gear when we had some daylight. It was a sleepless night, I heard every sound in the bush from then on. Every time one of the dogs perked up its ears, I was sure the grizzly was back. Dawn soon started to lighten up the eastern sky, and we were able to take stock of our camp situation.

I couldn't believe my eyes. It was as though a hurricane had gone through our previously organized camp. While we had been preoccupied with the horses, that bear must have investigated every scrap of supplies and gear we had. Packs were dragged everywhere, contents strewn about. It looked like a war zone. Old Jimmy had hung his freshly oiled chaps on the high limb of a tree. Unbelievably she hadn't got them. She must have been satisfied to find the marmot carcass and move on.

Now Old Jimmy spread out his hand, fingers extended, and placed them into one of the pawprints she had left. I think that's when it hit me just how close this encounter had been. The hair rose up on the back of my neck as I wondered aloud. "How could something that big make so little noise??"

Old Jimmy laughed quietly. "That ol' bear could come and chew on yore ass, an' you wouldn't hear her comin'!"

I could tell he had a pretty healthy respect for that "ol' bear." As soon as it was light enough, we went looking for the horses. They hadn't gone far, except for Roanie Jo and Penny, who were nowhere to be seen. Old Jimmy saddled up Marianne and trotted out to round up the horses and look for the missing ones. We knew he wouldn't be back until he found out where the grizzly had got to.

Slowly we got breakfast going, nothing was where we

had left it. After a good stout cup of coffee and hot chocolate to warm up, we set about the task of re-organizing and repacking. When Old Jimmy returned, hours later, the camp was back to being respectable again, except now we had a pile of broken halters and lead ropes to repair.

"She's holed up on that hill, alright," he told us, "a big ol' female grizzly. I think she's gonna stay up there." He added with a chuckle, "She ain't pink either."

Old Jimmy decided, much to my delight, that we should move camp. I had already thought about that old she-bear coming back snooping for more marmot grease. We very graciously conceded that the grizzly could have that camping spot if she so desired. We always prided ourselves that, when we left a camping spot, not a trace of us was left behind. But I'm sure the marmot scent was still in the air.

As we headed out, the horses trotted eagerly. Even the packhorses were trying to get ahead of the others. They did not like the smell of grizzly and were happy to leave. I kept glancing up toward the hillside where the old bear was probably monitoring our every move. I wasn't afraid of her anymore. She could have done a lot more damage than she did, and not only to our packs and supplies. We were the intruders; she had every right to investigate us. We were trespassers in her territory.

So we moved camp again, over the next ridge into Little Paradise Valley, higher up yet, and no bush. Now we didn't feel so vulnerable. If something came, we would see it. Old Jimmy had brought along some marmot fat in a tobacco tin, and spent the evening greasing up everyone's cowboy boots. I watched him, wondering vaguely to myself how fast I could get those boots off if a grizzly came again. I would just give him my marmot-smelling boots and maybe he would be satisfied. As Old Jimmy rubbed the boots and polished them, then rubbed and polished again, he related to us how he and two other cowboys had once caught seven guys butchering a rustled beef in Relay Valley. The seven guys had guns and threatened to kill them if they were going to "squeal." Old Jimmy and his friends quickly insisted they "were rustlers themselves, and would never tell!"

Later, they managed to sneak back to the ranch and call the police, who eventually arrested the seven guys. They each got a $3,000 fine and a jail sentence.

The nights were decidedly cold way up here. Even with Jimmy's gigantic blazing fire going all night, we kept moving closer and closer to the fire. We all laughed at the holes burned in the bottoms of Stephanie's socks; the bottoms of my boots weren't much better.

We eventually and begrudgingly tore ourselves away from Little Paradise Valley and headed toward the next camp, Relay Valley. One of the Gang Ranch riders, Bernard, was there at the cabin when we arrived. He told us it was September 5, and I couldn't believe my ears. I had thought it was still August!

We slept in the cabin that night, the first time in a while, and the next day headed out past some high, craggy, reddish rock sentinels that typified Relay Valley. Old Jimmy informed us that there was a gold mine around Relay somewhere called Lost Mine, owned by an Englishman by the name of Haunted Jack. He had died, and his body had been found in the main Gang Ranch yard in an old bin where he had apparently crawled in for a sleep. No one was ever able to find the mine.

We trailed on out of Relay Valley toward Beaver Valley. Charley was now leading my packhorse Buck. Lady had developed a small sore on the upper side of her tail where the rope from me to Buck had lain, and she didn't want anything that even hinted of a rope near her rear end. We had continued to pack up our own packhorses every morning so that we would not forget how to perform the now-familiar knots. As we passed by Prentiss Lake, supposedly a good fishing hole, Old Jimmy and Stephanie headed for a blueberry patch on the hillside, and Charley and I threw our hooks into the placid water. I crouched by the shore, my elbows propped on my knees, occasionally giving a jerk to the line dangling from the end of a long sapling we had cut. I gazed pensively up at the strikingly blue sky, half expecting Oren's little Bellanca Scout to come roaring out of its blueness. I remembered then that Oren was still down in the States with his good friend George Vogt, trying desperately to sell the Ranch to interested people there. I felt relief that he wasn't down at the Gang trying to fix all the impossible dilemmas there. I thought about Rick and felt a sharp pang of guilt. Poor Rick had worked so hard that he never had much chance to get out into this beautiful backcountry.

Much later, we carried on, eventually coming into Lost Valley. Here was a fork in the trail and we had to make a choice: head to Big Meadow or Hungry Valley. As Big Meadow was a longer ride by two-and-a-half hours, which would put us there in the dark, we chose Hungry Valley. It was a decision that fate no doubt had designed for me.

The next morning, in the darkness of the Hungry Valley cabin, my eyes opened wide from a deep sleep. I listened to the soft night sounds around me, the snorts and grunts of the others, the rustlings of their sleeping bags as they moved, and I wondered what had disturbed my semi-consciousness.

Then I heard it. First, a short yipping cry, then another, this time longer, mournful and haunting. Other cries joined in, some died out and then started again.

The wolves! Sliding hastily from the coziness of my smoke-imbued sleeping bag, I fumbled for clothing, then strained to pull my stiff leather boots over my bare feet. I jabbed my arms into my heavy woolen shirt, grabbed my now tattered down-filled vest, and quietly lifted the heavy wooden latch of the cabin door and stepped out into the frozen morning.

The log sides of the cabin were covered with frost and I leaned on them, feeling the chill seep into my body. Then, closing my eyes in the pre-dawn darkness I opened my ears and my soul to the she-wolves.

The wilderness otherwise was deadly silent. It was their turn, and *only* their turn to speak: one by one, sometimes all together. Periodically one would take over as the cries of another seemed to be dying out. Long, lonely, sorrowful howls, echoing and resounding across the valley and up into the darkened pines of the mountainside, building strongly to a high-pitched crescendo, then gradually fading away almost to a whimper, like the thin weeping of a lost child.

Motionless, cold forgotten, I absorbed every ghostly wail as prickles crept along the back of my neck, teaming my own griefs with theirs and allowing my sorrows to flee, out into the very bowels of the forest, fading along with their dying wails. I felt the light on my frozen, tear-streaked face and opened my eyes to the wonders of the sunrise, no doubt summoned by the she-wolves. Slowly and haltingly, the lonely cries subsided, and finally stopped.

Now I had only the breakup of the Mackenzie River to see. Now I could go home.

18

The End

The situation on the ranch had gone from bad to worse. I had expected that, and was prepared for it now. Nobody was going to hurt me anymore. I was brown from the sun, re-fortified now, and strong, inside and out. My slow-burning anger had turned into a determined resolve to find some justice. I had heard the she-wolves.

The receivers were supposed to be looking after the ranch, but they hadn't followed through with a sale yet; they seemed to be having too much fun on the place. They claimed they couldn't get the name Gang Ranch or the brand back from Dale and that, as a result, the buyer had withdrawn his offer. We got the distinct impression that they did not want the ranch to sell until they had at least got one hunting season under their belts.

I didn't really blame the specific receivers; this was a job to them and they all had families to support. What I didn't understand, and I still don't to this day, is why our society has tolerated the concept of receivership. It's a no-win solution for *all sides*. It's like two dogs fighting over a bone, and a third dog is called in to eat the bone. It doesn't make a lot of sense!

Assets were disappearing: the buckboards, buggies, wagons, tack, six sets of draft-horse harness probably worth around $12,000, the Belgian draft team harness, Oren's pack boxes, and, worst of all, the original, 1870 antique saddle that had belonged to Jerome Harper and was kept locked up in the tack room.

The receivers claimed someone had broken the lock on the tack room door and stolen the saddle, but they never called the police to report the theft. Why not? "It was just an old saddle," they claimed. This saddle was easily distinguishable by the name "Harper" carved right into the typically high back seat of that era, and to me, the "theft" was akin to someone robbing a grave. I ordered them to find it. As long as our money was still running this place, I was going to be stuck like a cactus to them.

Rick and Suzanne were just as busy in Maidstone, trying to fight them off the IKR and keep the business going. The receivers emptied the company bank account, bounced checks Rick had written, threatened him, and sent nasty letters. Eventually, Rick and Suzanne stopped reading their mail.

Suit actions were popping up like the marmots in Little Graveyard Valley. Dale was suing the rest of the family for two shares. The Crown was prosecuting Dale for embezzlement and cattle theft. The bank was suing all of us for nonpayment of the loan. Dale was suing the bank for $20 million and suing the bank's lawyers as well with a "nuisance suit." This meant that because the lawyers were now defendants, they could not represent the bank. In desperation, they settled out-of-court with Dale and *presumably paid* him money to drop the suit. In later years when I learned of this cash settlement with Dale Alsager, I wrote to Vincent Morgan, lawyer for the Bank of Commerce. I requested that he provide me with details of this "settlement" and advise us of the amount. No doubt it was our money that had been paid to him. The written reply I received from Vincent Morgan stated that, yes, there had been a settlement of cash. As for the amount they had paid to Dale, Mr. Morgan wrote that he "was not at liberty to disclose that information."

Dale also commenced a similar suit action against the receivers, as this had worked so well for him. The receivers, as the bank had done, made an out-of-court settlement with him. Dale and Betty had also taken one of the expensive ranch horses (Dale valued it at $7,000). The receivers made a feeble attempt at getting it back. Dale claimed that Alsager Holdings had "gifted" the horse to Betty "for services rendered." The receivers let them keep the horse, buggies, and countless other items they had removed from the ranch operation. The irreplaceable Harper saddle was among those items. Years later, Suzanne saw an ad in a western magazine where the Harper saddle and other antique Gang Ranch artifacts were advertized for sale. The phone number to contact was that of Dale's son in Kelowna. It seems they allowed him to keep the Alsager Holdings assets he had taken from the Ranch in return for dropping the suit action against them. It appears Dale was making money at this! So much for the receivers protecting the assets of the company of Alsager Holdings.

We, the rest of the family, were suing the receivers, challenging the passing of their accounts. In other words, we were trying to stop the theft. We also counter-sued the Canadian Imperial Bank of Commerce (via Robert Erickson) for unspecified damages.

Those who weren't suing us were writing about us. I stopped buying magazines or newspapers. I had not yet read a true account of what had actually happened.

The receivers did not appreciate my newfound aggressiveness. When we received an eviction notice to vacate our house at Bear Springs—the house that we, personally, had paid for—we refused to leave. Someone shot Lady's two-year-old sorrel foal the kids had named Copper. Whoever did it left him lying by the side of the road where the kids couldn't help but see him on the way home from school.

The expensive and horrendous "mistakes" were unfathomable. The calving barn mysteriously burned down, and the receivers did not have insurance on it. The pup trailer on the big white cattle-liner tipped over on the icy roads, fully loaded with cattle. They didn't have insurance for this either. More than 200 head of heifers did not get bred and were accidentally sold along with the cull cows. They spent $15,000 on an irrigation ditch that was built on the wrong angle and water couldn't flow into it. It appears the receivers did not know that water would not flow up-hill.

A horse hung himself in the barn trying to get at hay in another stall. Someone had gone to town for the weekend and forgot to tell anyone he had left a horse tied in the barn. They applied the wrong kind of fertilizer ($30,000 worth) to one of the fields, resulting in a total crop loss. All of the longtime and conscientious staff on the ranch left. Anyone who cared about the ranch couldn't stand to watch what was happening. I couldn't bear the thought that Denis kept working for them at Bear Springs.

Oren came flying in one day. He had returned from the States and had traded his little blue taildragger Bellanca Scout for a newer, bigger one of the same type that had belonged to Darcy Christianson out west of Williams Lake. We had always bugged him to get a bigger, more stable plane, worrying about the fierce downdrafts in the mountains where he always flew. I recalled vividly the jarring downdrafts we had hit in the back country on a couple of occasions. These happened frequently when we flew just over or around the top of a mountain. When the plane hit a downward movement of air, it would basically stop flying and fall straight down until it hit more stable air again. When it hit bottom it was like hitting solid ground. Everything on the floor of the aircraft lifted to the ceiling as the plane fell, and then came tumbling down on top of you when the plane stopped its descent. I found that out the hard way when one of the heavy portable radios went into flight on one vicious downdraft. Now that the Bluebird was gone, and I sat in the quiet, purring cabin of this newer model, I almost longed for the shuddering, vibrating cabin of the little blue Bellanca, where you had to use two hands on the top side of the door to hold it or it wouldn't shut properly. The little bluebird had saved my butt so many times and I missed it already.

As we piled the kids in the new plane (there was even room for them in here!) and roared off to try it out in the backcountry, I poured out to him, over the headset earphones, all the things that had happened in his absence. His face got grimmer and grimmer and, by the time we taxied back down onto the Gang Ranch runway, he had decided to immediately go and follow up his efforts at selling the ranch. It was the only solution.

"There's a guy by the name of Garry Bradley who is interested in buying the ranch," he said, "and maybe even George himself. I'm going to see if I can't hurry them up."

With that, Oren roared off into the dusk. It was the last time I would see him. On a clear but frigidly cold December 9, 1983, his new "safer" plane crashed on its way to Maidstone as Oren went to see Mom and Dad. The lengthy investigation concluded that a bolt was stripped. Although the plane had passed a forty-hour check, the stripped portion of the bolt was on the inside of the plane's wing fabric, where it had escaped detection. One wing subsequently broke loose from the bottom strut and folded up over the plane. Oren never had a chance.

There was now an empty, icy pit inside me where my feelings used to be. Nothing could help, not even Table Mountain. In that terrible black period before Christmas 1983, I left the Gang Ranch with my four children and never went back.

That is except for one time, years later, when I would trudge up the hill once more to Table Mountain. On a huge gnarled tree that leaned into the sagebrush wind blowing up from the Churn Creek gorge—a tree that looked as if it would lean there forever—I picked up the hammer I had

253

brought and pounded a gold-plated plaque onto the tree
with a big spike:
IN LOVING MEMORY OF
Oren Louis Alsager Jan. 24/57 - Dec. 9/83
FLY WITH THE EAGLES, OREN

19

The Aftermath

The Gang Ranch went into receivership on November 24, 1982. A lengthy investigation followed, culminating in Dale being charged in the early summer months of 1984 with criminal breach of trust, fraud, and cattle theft. Adjournments followed adjournments, and the trial did not proceed until the first months of 1986. The trial was set to be held in Prince George. We testified at a preliminary hearing at Prince George in December of 1984 to determine if the charges warranted that a trial should proceed. The judge ruled that they did. During this preliminary hearing, Dale convinced the judge into having the proceedings held in Williams Lake. As the rest of the family had been subpoenaed to testify, none of us were allowed to hear any of the evidence. We could be in there only after our own testimony was given, and we were among the last witnesses called. Bob Erickson did give evidence at this trial, but we were not allowed to hear it.

Bob Erickson was asked by Crown Counsel Rowan at this trial about his early discussions with Dale regarding the purchase of the Gang Ranch. "What was he (Dale) going to put into the deal?" queried Rowan. The answer Bob Erickson gave was, "I don't believe there was—very little. I don't believe there was anything."

When asked if he was not concerned about various cat-

255

tle that were purchased and then sold to the company, the exceedingly large checks being made out directly to Dale Alsager, Erickson replied, "In this particular case, we were very, very concerned to follow this closely because, no, Mr. Alsager did not have any particular cash of his own into these purchases."

We learned through reading Erickson's testimony later that in March of 1980, he asked Dale Alsager to reduce his personal cattle "loan" by $85,000 as he had promised to do previously. When it became apparent that Dale Alsager could not or would not make this payment, Bob Erickson lent him the $85,000 and, of course, made the company of Alsager Holdings responsible for it. Unbelievably, he did not advise the guarantors (us) of this and countless other questionable and curious transactions. Even more unbelievable was the fact that the $85,000 didn't go to reduce the "loan" in Williams Lake; it was used toward the purchase of Dale's house in Kelowna. We wondered amongst ourselves what had been in it for Erickson. Was he just operating out of fear, or did he benefit in some way? We would find out, years later, that JH-branded cattle had passed through the corrals of the Ochiltree Ranch, partly owned by Bob Erickson. We had no record of any cattle sales to this ranch.

Erickson had supposedly lent Dale money to buy cattle. Yet his testimony in court when asked if there were any animals, that is cattle, identified as being personal animals, he replied, "No, there was not. There were no cattle, cows, yearlings or otherwise identified to me as being the property of anybody other than the company. At either location." When we read this afterward, we wondered about a jury that listened to this testimony and then thought it was all right for Dale to pocket the proceeds for over a thousand head of cattle. There came to be a familiar pattern: cattle were being bought, paid for with a company check, then sold again to the company by Dale Alsager, with Dale somehow still retaining ownership. In addition to all the

256

cattle he had "sold," Dale Alsager still claimed that 1,135 head were "his" after the receivers came on the Ranch. That was basically most of the herd that was left on the Ranch.

We testified, time and time again. Dale's lawyer, Joe Gordon from Kelowna, kept telling us we knew about Dale's cattle and other transactions. We kept saying we didn't. He shoved paper after unfamiliar paper in front of us, insisting we had seen them before. We answered, no, we hadn't. When Denis was in the witness box, Joe Gordon asked him if he owned a high-powered rifle, and if he had used it to shoot at Dale's plane as it flew overhead. I didn't know someone had shot at Dale's plane. Apparently there was an indentation on the bottom of Dale's plane that they claimed had been made by a bullet. Joe Gordon gave the impression that Denis was the only one on the Ranch who had a 30-06 rifle with enough power to shoot that distance. I thought back to our "turkey shoots" on the Gang. Nearly everyone on the Ranch owned a high-powered rifle.

Joe Gordon claimed his client had retained the proceeds from the cattle sales and other funds because he believed he was "operating in the best interests of the company." How it was going to benefit the company to have no cattle herd, and be forced into receivership because its loan wasn't paid down was something he wisely didn't go into. Crown Counsel Rowan was confident with the case he had against Dale Alsager. All the evidence was there—written and spoken. In his final instructions to the jury, Judge H. J. Hamilton explained to them the matter of "color of right" that Joe Gordon was trying to use as a defence. Color of right in legal terms means an honest belief in a state of fact, which, if it existed, would be a legal justification or excuse to perform an act that would be, otherwise, unlawful.

The jury sat for two and a half days and came back with a surprising decision: Dale's acquittal on all seventy-two charges. Williams Lake is a small town. Early on in the

257

trial, one jury member had been kicked out of the trial as he was seen talking to Bob Erickson in the parking lot of the courthouse. Another jury member I learned afterward had felt the bank was equally at fault. "What in the hell was that bank doing?" he asked. The jury had sat for eighty-one days, on a trial that had been slated for a duration of three weeks. They were business people, and some of them were losing their businesses. One member of the jury was a member of the Farmer's Survival Group and stubbornly refused to be swayed by the others' "guilty" votes. Finally, they didn't care about the decision. They just wanted to get out of there. They all swung over to his side. Such is our justice system.

I now lived at Chimney Valley, a small subdivision between the Gang Ranch and Williams Lake. I rented a trailer there. All the kids except for Shan, the oldest, were back in the same bedroom again. Chimney Valley had a small, country-type elementary school, and I had thought this would not be such a shock for my kids, who had never known anything else but the one-room, semi-formal Gang Ranch school. But they would have to be in different classrooms, something they had never experienced before. On a snowy winter day before Christmas, I drove the four of them down to the Chimney Creek School for their first day. They were terrified. They had never seen so many kids. They stuck together, totally silent, like one person with eight legs. Shan was the oldest, ten years old, and the others hid behind, beside, and underneath him when they could. They would not be separated to go to any classrooms.

The principal, good-natured and relaxed Byron Kemp, told me to "Go home, they'll be fine." With leaden feet, I turned my back on them and walked away.

Byron Kemp and his staff finally won the kids' confidence. They allowed them to stay together for a few days, then gradually funneled them off into different areas. In no time at all, they blended into normal school life. The only noticeable difference between them and the other students was their singsongy Shuswap way of talking. The little Gang Ranch school, with the Shuswap and Chilcotin words written on wall posters, and the snoose pails on the floor, was now just a wonderful part of their past.

Denis had remained at Bear Springs. He was determined not to let them have our new house, and he still worked on the hay fields there. I thought that, by being apart for a while, our marriage might have a chance to repair itself. It was not to be. Both of us had changed too much. Our peaceful farming lives were gone. We had been cast overboard, and we were both floundering in the wake, swimming toward different shores. We were both filled with anger about what had happened: I got tired of dealing with my own anger, and having to deal with his, too. Denis returned to the Laying R in Alberta, and in 1986 our divorce became final. The house at Bear Springs stood empty. Our family pictures still hung on the wall.

The court actions did not stop for all this personal trauma. Whether we were in the middle of a divorce, or burying one of our family members, the subpoenas and registered letters continued to be placed in our hands.

We went after the bank. When they sued us, we filed a defence and counter-sued. It was May 1986 before we could get the whole convoluted mess before the Supreme Court system in Vancouver. The lengthy and high-priced trial would last fifty-one paper-filled days.

At last we filed into Courtroom 52; our long painful wait was over, and now justice was going to happen. We would lay out all the clear-cut evidence that we had painstakingly brought together in one lengthy package. We had pared it down as simply and concisely as possible, sworn out our truth in thoughtfully prepared affidavits. The learned judge would read our submissions and listen carefully to our sad story; he would listen just as carefully to the bank's excuses. Then he would smile kindly down upon us from his elevated wooden bench, bang his heavy gavel in finality, and rule fairly and squarely, making everything right again. At least that's what we, in our naivety, *thought* was going to happen.

Soon the starting-to-bustle courtroom filled up with boxes and boxes of papers. Delivery boys labored up the aisles, pushing squeaky two-wheeled carts piled with stiff cardboard cartons bulging with files and records and documents. They were followed protectively by lawyers in elegant, billowing black cloaks and stiffly starched white collars, and more lawyers, and more lawyers. The lawyers outnumbered the other observers and reporters. The bankruptcy trustees were there with their lawyers. The receivers were there with their lawyers. The bankers arrived with a battery of lawyers. I think even some of their *lawyers* had lawyers. Dale Alsager was there with his lawyer and, last but not least, the lawyer for the defence of the rest of the Alsager family, prestigious George Davis, and his assistant lawyer, Dr. Marion Price.

Most of the lawyers had wide-eyed, notepad-clutching articling students in tow, and at least one assistant. There weren't enough counsel tables at the front of the courtroom for them. Vying for positions, they piled up like the conventions of bickering blackbirds that flock onto the overhead wires in the fall, the odd one getting squeezed out and scrambling for another toehold down the line.

Another flowing black cloak entered from the front of the courtroom behind the oppressive and gigantic bench. This was Justice Josiah Wood, who strode briskly to the heavy oak chair in the middle to preside over the proceedings.

My mother leaned over, her ongoing sense of humor still very much evident throughout all the months and now years of coping with the agony of what had happened to the family.

"We're dressed all wrong!" she quipped in a whisper. "We should have worn our black dressing gowns!" I looked over with acknowledgment at her and at my father, who sat expectantly beside her. Their peaceful and honest lives had been so rudely disrupted, thrown into this totally alien world of lawyers, courts, documents, sworn affidavits, and nosey reporters. They were in their seventies; they didn't need this. Yet through it all, they had steadfastly and quietly maintained their integrity and their faith. The bank might take all monetary assets away from these people, but there were some things they couldn't take.

We knew that the bank would be a formidable adversary, one that would "fight dirty." These were not people we were up against. It was more like a giant steamroller machine that simply ran over you and crushed you if you got in its path. They had done this many times before. We were just another pesky debit weed to be eliminated from the garden of irreceivables. We had no experience in dealing with professionals like this. We had already been warned that the success rate for fighting a bank was 25 percent. But we were still optimistic. After all, this was Canada, and things like this didn't happen in Canada.

Rick, Suzanne, and Denis were lined up on the other side of me, waiting impatiently, as we all were, for our chance to swear on the good black book, get everything out in the open, get back home to our children and our lives, and put this all behind us. For Rick there was seeding and all the other work at IKR to worry about. It was a major undertaking for him to fly back and forth to B.C. for court case after fruitless court case. It never seemed to fail that the receivers would pull some kind of dirty trick down at Maidstone while they knew he was away at court.

Dale Alsager sat apart from us, on the opposite side of the courtroom, a strange situation that was now becoming familiar to us. Oddly enough, I felt no animosity toward him. I wondered what strange forces had entered into his life to compel him to stoop to such depths in a desperate attempt to dig himself out. I wondered more surprisingly about Betty. What kind of wife would support her husband through such outrageousness? Was it fear? If there was a psychiatric problem, as I was beginning to suspect, why hadn't she got help for him? Didn't she care? How could any one person live a lie for so long, let alone two people?

I gazed thoughtfully then at the reassuring back of George Davis, ex-guide and outfitter-turned-lawyer, and remembered fleetingly the six other law firms we had gone through before finding him. It had been nearly impossible to find a lawyer who would go up against one of the big banks—the success rate says it all. We went through countless lawyers who appeared to be willing to take it on. But we noticed that, after extracting as much money from us as possible without putting themselves out, they were basically just cushioning us for defeat. When we sensed this happening, we would fire them. We had one lawyer in Vancouver who charged us $20,000 and then forgot to file our defence.

When our company lawyer, Derek Donaldson, had deserted us, we had hired a lawyer by the name of Andrew Berna, of Berna Horne Marr & Coates in Kamloops. We realized this avenue was getting us nowhere, and that nothing was being accomplished. We paid him what we owed him, but he wanted more. We refused. He sued me personally for the company legal bill, as I was the only one left in B.C. I knew he couldn't do this, it was not a personal file. We went to court, and I defended myself as there was no way I was going to hire another lawyer. Rick flew out to testify that all dealings with this lawyer were company concerns, and the bill was exorbitant. Mr. Berna didn't even bother to show up; he sent his secretary. Unbelievably, I lost.

When I returned home, I got a call from a man in Kamloops who said he had heard that day about me losing the case against Berna. He had lost a similar case involving the same lawyer and judge and, in doing some digging, discovered that the particular judge I had been in front of was a golfing partner of Berna's. "Appeal it," he said. "Get a different judge and you'll win."

I appealed. This man, whom I had never even met, took the particulars of my case over the phone, prepared a properly written defense, and sent it to me by Loomis. I returned to court—and won. Again, Mr. Berna sent his secretary to court. This time, the judge expressed some dismay and surprise at the previous decision that had been handed down. The lawyer who had helped me was Jack Cram. He was one lawyer who had an absolute intolerance for corruption. I was learning very quickly about "the system." I began to think it must be very hard to be an honest lawyer. People tend to mark all lawyers with the same black label. I have met a few honest and conscientious ones—embarrassingly few.

In April of 1994, we read in the papers how this same lawyer, Jack Cram, was physically ejected from a Vancouver courtroom for "going berserk." He apparently berated the judge and everyone present about how rampant corruption was in the particular case he was involved in, and in the legal system in general. It turned into a brawling fiasco, as he had a vast number of supporters in the courtroom who came to his assistance when the court deputies tried to haul him away. The last item I read told of how he had to be physically brought back into the courtroom for some kind of sentencing and was subsequently sent for psychiatric assessment.

I can certainly relate to Jack Cram's frustration, after being a close observer and participant of our legal system over the past fourteen years. I think I, and Rick, and my whole family, came close to being carried out of a few courtrooms. It really hurt to find out how agonizingly inadequate the system is. It especially affected my father. He was such a believer in his country, justice, and the political system. It was hard for him to lose this lifelong respect. Judges can walk away from a case, reserving judgment. By the time they submit their decision, months and months later, they are far removed from the situation and do not even have to face the people involved. Lawyers accept the situations with a "win some, lose some" attitude. I guess they have to, to survive.

I quit looking for corporate lawyers and started looking for lawyers who had "beaten the bank." There were two lawyers in all of Vancouver who had such a reputation, and one was George Davis. When I first sat patiently in his outer office, a typed-up, condensed version of our woes in my hand, I marveled at the number of other desperate-looking people coming in and going out, laden down with bulging briefcases ready to burst, their faces worried and frowning. I knew what they were going through.

At long last a slight but well-built man with glasses, greying and fatherly, came hurrying out to say a few words. I knew instantly that this man was to be the "captain of our lifeboat." I was surprised, though. I had heard how tough George Davis was, and this man didn't look tough. I sensed an inner sensitivity, which was later confirmed. Here was a man who would "take on the big guys" and never give up, but was unable to sit through the movie *Fatal Attraction* because the pet rabbit got thrown into the stew pot.

"I'm sorry," he explained, as gently as he could muster, his hands held wide open in helpless gesture, "I am snowed under with cases, and it is not possible for me to take on anything new right now. I'm sorry..." He was already walking away.

"Please..." I begged, holding forth the prepared story. "Just take five minutes to read this...please."

Reluctantly, he turned around, took the outstretched papers and, after a slight hesitation, said, "Okay, I'll read it, if it's short, but I'm telling you, I am stretched too thin now; I can't take another case on."

He sat down quickly behind his paper-laden desk, adjusted his glasses, and rapidly scanned over the papers.

Ten minutes later, he took the case on. He would not take payment until he won; we would pay disbursements and court costs.

Thus began a long association between the Alsager

family and the man who took our problems on as his own, entering into the fray as one of us. Like us, he became outraged at what had happened to the company of Alsager Holdings Ltd. and couldn't believe the extent of the Bank of Commerce's involvement. He scribbled notes, tagged pages, examined and cross-examined, extracting truth and untruths from the various hapless players squirming uncomfortably in the witness box, gestured respectfully to the bench, and annoyed the judge at times by correcting his mistaken facts on corporate law. George knew his corporate law inside out; some of the honorable judges didn't. George was an honest man. He didn't fabricate documents, forge signatures, or try to distract the judge and courtroom from the main issues. He didn't have to.

This was an alien world to us. It seemed as if the basic facts just couldn't come out. Hours and hours were spent dissecting silly points of law. We spent one whole morning watching in stupefaction as they argued back and forth about whether an argument was an argument or not.

The trial dragged on, frustrating in its tedious progress.

My father was fit to be tied. He was used to getting up early in the morning and working until his day was done. The courtroom was a new area for him—listening to all this fussing around about legal details, then, just when we thought the testimony was going to get somewhere, a recess would be called, or an objection would be made that would take half a day to deal with. We wasted a good part of one day watching a slide show that Dale had brought! It turned out that Dale was an absolute expert at leading the entire courtroom off on some frivolous issue that meant nothing, but wasted hours upon hours of valuable court time. Sometimes the judge stopped him, but not often enough to suit us.

We could see this was not going to be quick. We rented an apartment on Robson Street, within walking distance of the courthouse, just a few blocks from downtown Vancouver. It was to be our home for the next five months.

Day after lingering day we attempted to absorb all the testimony, theirs and ours, listening in amazement as the top bankers with whom we had dealt personally "did not recall" anything. We had to practically hold my father down as Stewart Brown testified under oath that he did not recall being at a meeting with Ted Alsager or talking to him at any time, or even having met him. Even the judge remarked on the banker's "total absence of memory."

The courtroom was warm and quiet; sometime during the morning of one brisk cool day, an unsteady, unshaven, bleary-eyed derelict wobbled unnoticed into the warmth of the courtroom and slumped down into the seat directly behind my mother. A distinct, musty, alcoholic odor wafted up to us from the depths of the soft seat into which he had sunk.

The courtroom was silent. The judge was writing, deep in thought, and no one was to disturb him. Shortly, from the area directly behind my mother, came distinct and heavy snoring noises. Our friendly drunk had fallen immediately into a sleepy, noisy stupor.

People were starting to turn around, attempting to find out who had lost control of their wakefulness and was making this racket. There would be silence for a few seconds, then the noises would start again. My mother squirmed uneasily in her seat. The drunk was not visible behind her, and people were beginning to stare at her, thinking she was the culprit.

Another loud snore, and a snort. Justice Wood looked up from his papers and, peering over the glasses that were pulled down on his nose, fixed a stern glare on my mother.

Poor Mom wiggled uncomfortably in her seat and finally, when every eye in the courtroom was fixed on her, she turned and pointed to the seat behind her. George Davis stood up and moved around the seats to find the slumbering invader, practically down on the floor now in his relaxation.

The bailiff was summoned, and the poor man was removed.

As we sat through hour after hour of testimony and sworn statements, and literally thousands of pieces of paper being put "on the record," it became very obvious to us that Dale had wanted everything to be "his." The rest of us didn't figure into the picture *at all.* We saw evidence such as the letter he sent to Peter and Kathleen Kiss from Buck Lake, Alberta, where we had purchased the buffalo herd. We (Alsager Holdings) had paid for the forty-five-head herd with company checks: $5,000 on March 2, 1979, as a deposit, and $41,000 on March 13, 1979, to complete the purchase price of $46,000. On April 20, 1979, Dale wrote a letter to the Kisses, stating, "For tax purposes, I would very much appreciate if you could re-issue the receipt for $41,000, also the Bill of Sale, and put both of those items in my personal name (Dale E. Alsager) rather than Alsager Holdings or Gang Ranch."

This pattern unfolded again and again. We watched as the damning evidence was presented. Dale would buy cattle with a company check, then *sell* them to the company, issuing a check to himself, and then still claim the cattle as his. We got to the point where nothing surprised us anymore. Head Vancouver banker Don Ellwood swore that changes to the original loan, evidence of further borrowings, and evidence of Dale's "phoney" cattle loans financed by the company, were not communicated to the other guarantors (us). When asked who would be responsible for passing this information on to the directors of Alsager Holdings Ltd., he replied, "probably between inception (of the loan) in 1978 and late 1981, it would be Mr. Erickson. Between late 1981 and the end of 1982 I would imagine Mr. Stewart Brown would be the most knowledgeable." But Erickson had now disappeared, and Stewart Brown could barely remember his own name, much less who the Alsagers were. We sat and listened angrily as he murmured,

267

"I don't recall" or "I have no knowledge of that" to basically every question that was put to him.

The supplemental $2-million loan we knew nothing about was a major issue. Now, fearing that Betty Alsager's signature might not suffice, the bank pulled from their magic mountain of documents, a resolution backing this loan, apparently signed by Rick Alsager. Rick denied ever seeing the document before. "For me to sign a resolution to that, it would have had to have been brought up at a meeting or discussed with any of the other family members, and it never was. It was never ever mentioned—anything about borrowing $2-million more and especially having Idanell Korner Ranch backing it."

Someone showed us afterward how easy it is for documents to be forged. Putting a blank piece of paper over a paper with an authentic signature on it, and then holding it up to the light of a window, a new signature was easy to trace, with a little practice. "They do it all the time," we were told. This one was done a little sloppily, though. The document with Rick's signature was dated March 26, 1980, and the loan debenture was dated June 2, 1980. The loan hadn't even been thought of in March.

Although we had heard it before, we now learned, formally, that Dale had not put up the $500,000 he had told us he had. The bank (through Bob Erickson) had advanced him $200,000 of this, and it had been repaid by the company. The $300,000 he did put up was set up as a shareholder's loan, not to purchase shares. Dale Alsager had not purchased any shares in Alsager Holdings, and had ended up owning 49 percent of it. The shareholder's loan was a never-ending source of revenue for him to draw on.

To our consternation, weeks and weeks of court time was now spent haggling over Dale's phoney "cattle loans." We found it totally frustrating. Dale had owned no cattle on the Ranch. If he had, there would have had to have been some written agreements between himself and the company with regard to grazing fees, etc. There were none, and none of us had any knowledge of this setup. The big bankers now had to say Dale did own some of the cattle. They (through Bob Erickson) had lent him personally $615,000 for the purchase of feeder cattle. This was in direct conflict with the cattle loan carried by the company, and a brazen violation of the fundamentals of banking. It was against the law. The personal loan to Dale was guaranteed by Alsager Holdings, and the interest from the loan charged to the Alsager Holdings account.

When asked if there was any information about Dale's personal loan given to any of the guarantors (us), Mr. Ellwood replied, "No, I cannot recall any such evidence." It was also established through testimony from all the bankers and receivers present that at no time were the cattle "purchased" by Dale through the phoney feeder cattle loan, distinguishable from those cattle owned or bought by Alsager Holdings. We now heard Dale testify how he could distinguish "his" cattle from the Ranch cattle at a glance. He could tell just by looking at them, in a herd of over three thousand cows, just which ones were "his." What was also amazing was how "his" cattle herd multiplied. It appeared that even "his" steers and yearlings had calves.

Papers kept popping up with Dad's signature on them. We recalled now how Dad had been horrified at the stack of papers he had had to sign in front of Derek Donaldson, Bob Erickson, and Dale Alsager, that fateful day in Kamloops before we purchased the Ranch. He had not read them. If he had, he would probably still be signing his name today. There was a paper with his signature on it stating that Betty Alsager was suddenly a director of IKR, whose directors were only original family members. When asked if he had signed this, Dad replied, "Why would I sign this?" Some of the missing Idanell Korner Ranch papers were mysteriously reappearing. Dale shoved one particular paper in front of Dad. It was a list of directors for IKR and Betty Alsager's name had been added in pen. This of course would clear her of any wrongdoing when she signed

269

on behalf of IKR for the disputed $2-million loan. Dad's reply was that Betty had never been a director of IKR. There was even a document with Dad's signature on it guaranteeing the past, present, and future debts of Dale Alsager. To all of these queries about his signature being on these strange papers, he quietly replied that he did not recall signing them.

Dale Alsager called his wife, Betty, to the witness stand to testify. She dutifully responded as though well-rehearsed to the questions he asked her, until one particular question seemed to stump her. "Yes," she replied. "No—I mean yes—" She stammered and looked confused, then in front of the judge and a whole courtroom of people, she leaned toward Dale from her perch in the witness box and whispered loudly, "Is that what I was supposed to say?"

Tittering and shocked murmurs resounded throughout the audience, and a surprised Justice Woods looked over toward the witness box in disbelief. He then very carefully laid his pen down and leaned back in his magistrate's chair. Although he allowed the questioning to continue, he made no movement toward picking up his pen to record any of the testimony. None of the lawyers wished to cross-examine the witness.

Of all the inexplicable transactions that had secretly gone on, one of the strangest was a loan in the amount of $85,000 on May 7, 1980, to Dale Alsager. It wasn't for cattle, and no one seemed to know why it was given out, other than that he wanted the money. The loan was paid out on April 27, 1981, by, who else, the company of Alsager Holdings. This loan transaction came up numerous times in court; every banker who was asked about it was "stumped" as to the reason for this loan. Even the judge, in his comments, admitted "total confusion" as to the nature of this loan. Because it was so "confusing," nothing was ever ruled about it. It became very apparent in the proceedings that whenever Dale Alsager wanted funds, Bob Erickson simply handed them over to him and made the company responsible for the payback. As one lawyer in the courtroom so aptly put it, Bob Erickson was "in love" with Dale Alsager. Thomas McNabb, a private investigator we later hired to assess the bank's involvement, stated "at some point Dale Alsager began to manager the bank manager."

Throughout the proceedings, the bank's lawyers were trying their best to make the bank look like the poor guys who got caught in the middle of a family feud. We totally disagreed. The family feud was the result of the actions of the Bank of Commerce. There would not have been a "family feud" had the bank not been totally negligent. These were professional people, and we had trusted them to be honest. Alsager Holdings was a legal, highly financed corporation. This was not a little family farm but a multi-million-dollar ranching business. What kind of bank makes out a loan for $2 million and doesn't let the people responsible for repayment know about it? What kind of bank sets up a system of personal "phoney" loans and uses company money to pay them down, again without telling the guarantors? They had to know the company was going down. How could it possibly survive? All it would have taken was for the bank manager to say, "I'm sorry, Dale, we can't do this without advising the guarantors." Or for him to advise any of us at the Ranch about what was going on. This was his duty, and his job. Even when we had asked him, he had lied.

We now saw a document from the bank that infuriated us. On an interoffice memo with letterhead that read Wayne H. Borgen, and dated December 11, 1981, was the following hand-written communication:

Al Cranswick, Office Manager, B.C. Livestock Co-op (salesyard) reported to Wayne Jensen that Dale Alsager has requested Mr. Cranswick, to whenever cattle were sold through B.C. Livestock Co-op, to make check out in name of Dale Alsager, instead of to "Gang Ranch."

Mr. Cranswick is "aware" of the situation—but request we send him letter stating—All checks to be made

271

out to Gang Ranch and directed to C.I.B.C. Williams Lake B.C. Livestock Producers Association.

Not only had Bob Erickson been in on the diversion of funds since the beginning, but now we knew that the head bankers in Vancouver had know since December of 1981. They had not made us aware of the situation, or basically done anything about it. The Williams Lake Stockyards was only one outlet where the cattle were sold. Dale simply hauled them elsewhere after that.

Finally, all the "I don't recalls" had been said, and all the files folded up and stacked neatly on their ends in the court boxes. The only rock left unturned, and the one individual who had not made an appearance, was the main spoke in the entire wheel: the banker who had started it from the beginning and got bogged right up to his axles in it at the end. Robert Erickson. It was as though he had disappeared from the face of the earth.

George Davis was not unduly concerned about this. We had submitted all our evidence about Erickson; they had to bring him in to refute the allegations. Their failure to bring him in should have been their downfall. Although they attempted many times, the bank's lawyers could not give evidence on behalf of Erickson. That was third-party testimony: hearsay.

We all went away, gratefully, and waited for the slow wheels of justice to turn. We were very optimistic. It would be three long months before the written decision of Justice Josiah Wood came down.

In the meantime, the Perry Ranch was sold to a B.C. businessman in the beef feedlot industry, a Mr. Kohler, for $1.1 million in January of 1984, of which $800,000 was paid over to the bank and the receivers got the balance.

In March of 1984, the Sullivan Pastures sold for $27,000.

In June of 1984, the Gang Ranch main headquarters was sold to High River, Alberta, rancher Melvin Nelson for $6,900,700. Within a few months, Nelson resold the Gang

Ranch, this time to a consortium of Alberta and B.C. ranchers, including John Rudiger, a cattle breeder from Calgary; ranchers Clark and Susan Borth from Vanderhoof, B.C.; Ross Adams, a buffalo rancher from Grande Prairie, Alberta; Wilbur Griffith, a Calgary businessman; and Saudi Arabian Sheik Ibraham Afandi. The sheik from Saudi Arabia later bought all the other investors out. His investment group, BSA Investors Ltd., now owned the Gang Ranch and still does at the time of this writing in 1994.

On February 8, 1985, the Crows Bar property of the Gang Ranch sold for $450,000.

Finally, the long-awaited day came. In late August 1987, Justice Wood handed down a macabre decision. He ruled in favor of the Canadian Imperial Bank of Commerce and awarded them judgment in the amount of $11,975,996.45. We were shocked. We immediately filed an appeal.

From the time the bank had foreclosed on the ranch, and all through the period that the courts had sat on the Gang Ranch controversy, the interest on the debt had kept ticking along—to the tune of more than $4 million.

Justice Wood was normally a criminal judge and based his decision squarely on the activities of Dale Alsager. He reasoned this is what had brought about the downfall of Alsager Holdings. Although he acknowledged that the rest of the family had not known of these activities, he reasoned that we "should have known." How could we have known, when everyone, including the bankers, were lying to us?

Although he did rule that the house at Bear Springs was personally owned by Denis and myself, the judgment amount against us allowed the bank to take our assets. They took the house at Bear Springs, along with the Laying R. The Canadian Imperial Bank of Commerce now had the power to take every home I had ever lived in since my birth, and Rick's, and Mom and Dad's houses and property as well.

Shortly after this decision came down, we read in the

273

Vancouver paper that Justice Josiah Wood had received an enviable position in the Supreme Court of Appeal. The article remarked on the fact that such a young judge should get such a prestigious promotion.

So far as we were concerned the legal system had failed miserably. The guilty parties walked away, the innocent ones paid the price. The one trial blamed the bank, and let Dale off the hook; the other trial blamed Dale Alsager, and let the bank off the hook. Who was going to hang from the wide oak tree for all of this? The rest of the family.

We appealed to the Appeals Court of British Columbia. Three judges presided this time. The principal issue on appeal was "whether the bank knew, or ought to have known, or suspected, that Dale was defrauding his father, brothers, sister, and brother-in-law, and should have so advised them." Although George meticulously outlined seven areas of Errors in Judgement, the main focus was that "The Learned Judge erred in finding that the bank did not participate in the fraud of Dale Alsager on the Company and its shareholders, and profited thereby, and in denying to the *appelents apendasich* of a constructive trust and the duty to account for the bank's profit from loans from which and by which Dale perpetrated the fraud on the Company."

In an appeal, no new evidence is allowed to be presented. Bob Erickson escaped again. Although one judge swung over to our side, he was outvoted by the other two. The disastrous judgment of Josiah Wood was upheld.

We had lost, all the way around. I believed we just hadn't been meant to win this one. George had given it his best shot. It just wasn't in the cards.

Even after all the facts had been brought to light, and all the court documents were open to public scrutiny, the reporters *still* could not get anything straight. We read in our local paper that Dale Alsager had to pay $12 million to the Bank of Commerce. Dale was the only one in the family who *didn't* have to pay. He had not put up any collateral

274

security. It was the rest of the family—Mom and Dad, Suzanne and Rick, Denis and I—who had to pay back the $12 million.

We were not willing to give them our properties. Not like this; it was too unfair. We appealed to politicians and the inspector general of banks. We hired Thomas McNabb & Associates from Lethbridge, Alberta, to do a full accounting. This was the first corporate trial in history in which, for some strange reason, the judge did not order that a court accounting of the debt be performed. If the bank had said that $50 million was owing, we would have had to pay it.

Incredibly, the proceeds from the sale of the Gang Ranch property and assets had not been taken into account. We went to the media and started, for the first time, to make public the gruesome details of our downfall. Thomas McNabb, after reviewing the matter and assessing the situation, concluded with his advice:

> Dale was no doubt a very intelligent individual. But regardless of how smart he was, he could never have effected the movement of funds from the Company account to his account on his own—he needed the help of the banker.
>
> Alsager Holdings Ltd. was a legal entity on its own, totally separate from Dale Alsager or for that matter, any Alsager family member. The movement of funds is similar to the movement of funds from Donald Fullerton's account (the head of C.I.B.C.) to Judy Alsager's account. You can be assured that Donald Fullerton would not tolerate that: why should the Alsager family?
>
> In short, I would look at this matter in the direction of theft charges against all that authorized the individual debits of funds from the Alsager Holdings account.

The R.C.M.P. would not lay charges of theft against Bob Erickson—nobody could really tell us why. He worked for a bank—it just wasn't done.

I came to know all the attorney generals. In January 1990, I met with then Attorney General Brian Smith in Williams Lake and placed the folio of our story right in his hands. On his way back to Vancouver, the file was lost. He claimed he was reading it on the plane and left it on the seat. I couriered another set to him immediately and confirmed with his secretary that it had arrived in the attorney general's office. One week later, I phoned the office of the attorney general to find out what had transpired. I was told that the file had "gone missing"—*again.* They never did find it.

In March 1990, I contacted Deputy Attorney General Ted Hughes, who advised, "It is not within the mandate of the Attorney General to order an accounting by Chartered Banks." I then met with Attorney General Bud Smith on May 11, 1990. The outcome of this was that he viewed it as "a civil action between private citizens and banks," but he did send me over to a Frank Quinn. I was under the assumption that an accounting was going to be commenced by this man. Frank Quinn claimed to know nothing about doing an accounting for the attorney general. Before we could get this straightened out with the attorney general, he was in the midst of a wiretap investigation and was subsequently removed from office.

Now Acting Attorney General Russell Fraser took over. We started all over again. Each time a new person came on the scene, the whole story had to be retold. When I asked Russell Fraser if he could get the file from Ted Hughes, I was informed by letter that the file appeared to be lost.

I contacted the Office of the Superintendent of Financial Institutions in Ottawa. They suggested I "seek legal counsel."

I contacted the Inspector General of Banks; they claimed that they did not become involved in actions against banks.

All these people are highly paid government officials,

either directly elected by the people or appointed by their elected representatives, to do—what? Nothing, it appears, is within their mandate or jurisdiction. Why, then, do these high-cost offices exist?

The only thing all this accomplished was to wear me out. But it did attract attention to our problem, even though no one would do anything about it. Our local MLAs, Dr. Lorne Greenaway, and later David Zirnhelt, did their best to assist us in putting some pressure on the bank. Not liking the publicity, the bank decided to settle with us.

Denis and I bought the Laying R in Alberta back from them for $100,000. With all the legal costs we had, plus the loss of the $115,000 house at Bear Springs, our losses totalled more than $250,000. That was not including the loss of the Gang Ranch and its assets, and the $30,000 cash we had invested in Idanell Korner Ranch, previous to the Gang Ranch days. We are still waiting to receive a thank-you note from the Canadian Imperial Bank of Commerce for the fine gift of the Bear Springs house that we handed to them.

Rick and Suzanne were living their own horror story in Saskatchewan, under continual bombardment from the bank. Unfortunately for the bank, Rick was usually one step ahead of them. They were no match for him in brains. He anticipated most of their moves. They threatened to come and take the elk herd away; they attempted to evict them from the house. They tried to stop an auction sale for elk Rick was having on the farm, but the auctioneer ignored their demands. Rick now hired a law firm in Saskatoon to defend the IKR. The same court cases that we had just gone through in B.C. started all over again in Saskatchewan. Rick got the local MLAs and the media involved. Receivers and bankers were afraid to go near the IKR, and eventually they decided to settle. Rick and Suzanne made a similar deal as we had with the bank, buying the IKR back from receivership, which left it in debt to the tune of

277

$350,000. IKR had borne the brunt of the legal fees and their losses were in the vicinity of $600,000, again not including the loss of the Gang.

As part and parcel of the settlement obligations, we were told we had to sign "Silence Agreements" with the bank. These were six pages of fine print, prohibiting us from ever mentioning, speaking, discussing, writing, basically even breathing. We were not to breathe a word of what had transpired on the part of the bank and the whole affair to relatives, neighbors, politicians, legal people, family, friends, reporters, basically the whole world. Throwing the paper down in disgust, I refused to sign. They claimed Denis and I would not get the settlement. I said fine. I never did sign and they went ahead with the settlement. They wanted more than anything to avoid publicity and we were being too noisy to suit them. Later on when we went after the receivers for damages, I was the only one who had not signed a Silence Agreement and was able to speak in court about the atrocities they had committed. A copy of the banks 'silence agreement' is included in the appendix so you can see their approach of trying to bury this story.

The Canadian Imperial Bank of Commerce, on the other hand, was singing all the way to the bank. The Gang Ranch and the Perry Ranch, and the other properties and assets of the ranch (timber, etc.) gleaned the bank and the bank's receivers $16.5 million, not to mention the $3-million-plus that we had repaid, prior to what I fondly refer to as the 'Great Money Diversion'. We had been a constant source of revenue for them. They took the assets of the people who bought it after us, and resold it again. The Canadian Imperial Bank of Commerce made a fortune on their dealings with the Gang Ranch.

But we learned. Boy, did we learn! We know now about lawyers and courts and banks, and the absolute futility of our legal system. It doesn't work, and people should be warned that it doesn't work before they sink their trust, their time, and their savings into it.

I hold no grudges and harbor no bitterness toward anyone. Events happen in our lives because they are *meant* to happen. I learned valuable lessons that I can pass on to my children. After standing on the top of Graveyard Mountain with the whole world at my feet, no sign of human habitation as far as the eye can see, I know that we humans are not in control here.

I feel very lucky. We saw the Gang Ranch at its best. The backcountry was free from logging roads and tourist garbage, the creeks clear and sparkling clean, the forests wild and untamed, the she-wolves free to sing their haunting praises to the sunrise.

We know it will not stay like that for long.

And if I had it to do all over again, I would do the same.

EPILOGUE

Ten years have hurried by since the events in this book. The normal turbulence of life has carried on: marriages, births, deaths, and relocations did not cease because of the upheaval of the Alsager family on the Gang Ranch:

Irene and Ted Alsager purchased a house in the town of Maidstone, Saskatchewan, and retired there. Ted, who will be eighty years old this fall of 1994, still travels the five kilometers south to the Idanell Korner Ranch to lend his assistance. In 1987, Irene and Ted Alsager were highly honored to be chosen as the Citizens of the Year for the Maidstone area.

Suzanne and Rick Alsager efficiently operate the going concern of Idanell Korner Ranch. A year after they returned to IKR from the Gang Ranch, a son, Chad Oren, was born. The two oldest boys, Lane and Jan, have now graduated from high school and assist Rick with ranching. Jan has traveled far and wide with his track and field abilities. When Lane and Jan come out to visit Shan and Dusty, the Rivard boys, they head out to their favorite stomping grounds—the Gang Ranch. Heidi is a beautiful, tall, sixteen-year-old young lady in Grade 11, and young Chad is in Grade 5.

Denis Rivard is the owner and operator of the Laying R Poultry Farm near Leduc, Alberta.

Shan Rivard graduated from Columneetza High School in Williams Lake, B.C., and now attends Malaspina College in Nanaimo, B.C. He will complete his professional chef training in August of 1994.

Buffy Rivard graduated from Columneetza High School in Williams Lake, B.C., and will attend Cranbrook College in Cranbrook, B.C., this fall, 1994. She plans to go into medicine and is enrolled in the science program.

Dusty Rivard graduates from Columneetza High School in Williams Lake in 1994. He plans to continue on with his education, possibly in the legal field, God forbid. In the meantime, his hard work on the farm at Soda Creek is much appreciated.

Lacey Rivard is sixteen years old and will enter Columneetza High School, Williams Lake, in the fall of 1994, in Grade 11. Her forte is her art—her unique, bold drawings and fine-lined carvings. Her drawn characters are strong and confident, much like those her Uncle Oren used to paint.

Judy Alsager is starting to experience an "empty nest" syndrome as the houseful of teenagers heads off to college, one by one. After the Gang Ranch upheaval, I worked for B.C. Hydro for seven years, raised four kids, and found out what life as a single parent was all about. I left Chimney Valley and eventually got a mortgage to buy a house and acreage at 150 Mile, just outside Williams Lake. In 1992, I met polka-loving happy person Richard Keep, and my singleness was no more. Richard spends a good part of his year up north in Alaska, the Yukon, and northern B.C. building drill pads for mining companies on the tops of mountains, accessible only by helicopter. He also builds bridges, and shares my love for the wilderness. Now I keep busy on the 130-acre farm on the Fraser River that we bought together. We live halfway between Williams Lake and Quesnel, near the Marguerite Ferry. I still go to court once in awhile with Gang Ranch affairs. The receiver accounts were finally settled in January of 1993, and now I am in a legal standoff with one hoodlum lawyer who was involved (at least he was supposed to be) in these proceedings. It will never end.

Donna (Alsager) and Ken Smulan still farm peacefully on K&D Farms in Wawota, Saskatchewan. Three of their children, Heather, Randy, and Greg, are all happily married, and Adrienne and Steven still attend school. The Smulans thank their lucky stars that they pulled out of the Gang Ranch deal when they did.

Dale and Betty Alsager relocated to the United States following the court trials of 1986. Their daughters Kim and Dalene are both married and living in Gibsons and Vancouver, respectively. Their son Jay is a pilot working in Dawson Creek, B.C., and their son Troy works in construction in Seattle.

Rosalie and Raymond Rosette left the Gang Ranch following the upheaval, residing for a time at the Dog Creek Reserve and now have relocated to the Canoe Creek Reserve.

Old Jimmy resides at Canoe Creek with Raymond and Rosalie. Old Jimmy is eighty years old now and, if we went to the backcountry today, I would probably still have a hard time keeping up with him. Willy and Celina Rosette and family left the Gang Ranch following the upheaval and have resided ever since on the Alkali Lake Reserve.

Francis and Adele Billy and family left the Gang Ranch following the upheaval and lived for awhile in Williams Lake, employed by the Indian Friendship Centre. They now live out west in the Chilcotin, on the Redstone Reserve.

Brian Holst left the Gang Ranch during the upheaval and worked on neighboring ranches in the following years. He is again employed by the Gang Ranch, working for the present manager, Larry Ramstead. Lonnie Jones left the Gang Ranch after his "firing" by Dale, and the last I heard from him he was at Top of the World Ranch at Fort Steele (owned by his parents) and was planning to head to the U.S. for a cowboss position on a ranch. He did return to the Gang Ranch as cowboss after the Gang Ranch trials.

Dan and Karen Patten left the Gang Ranch and relocated to Grande Prairie, Alberta, where he is employed by Ross Adams, who owns a buffalo ranch there. Karen teaches school, and they have one daughter P. J. (Patty

June), who was born on the Gang Ranch during our time there.

Stu Turton, mechanic, moved to a ranch in Water Valley, Alberta.

Bernie Radford, mechanic, and his wife, Bev, moved back to Enderby, B.C.

Lynn Dootoff, secretary, and her two sons, relocated to Kelowna, B.C.

Susan and Bill Prater divorced. Susan remarried, to Don Thouillard and they moved back east to Ontario.

Lisa Oltheimer, secretary in the Williams Lakes office, still resides in Lac La Hache with her husband.

Jacquie St. Jacques moved north to the Yukon following Oren's death. She lived alone in the bush near Beaver Creek for years, built herself a cabin, complete with outhouse, and trapped martens for a living. She now helps her partner, Gregg, run the Iskutine Lodge, specializing in guided canoe trip excursions in that beautiful northern B.C. Iskut country.

Beth and George Bryant, managers of the Perry Ranch, left the Perry Ranch in the upheaval, went back east to Ontario for a while, then returned to B.C. to Prince George. They eventually moved back to Williams Lake to become my neighbors at the 150 Mile. They bought an acreage on Likely Road and reside there today. George drives a lowbed for Double H Trucking and Beth raises her prize La Mancha dairy goats.

Vicki and Steve Andruss, and their children Leah and Owen, of the Dry Farm, moved to the United States to Coos Bay, Oregon, and ventured into the intense business of marketing mushrooms. They later moved to Hood River, Oregon, where they reside today.

Astrid and Charles Jauch, also of the Dry Farm, moved to the Okanagan with their two daughters Amy and Leah. They have gone into farming at Oliver, B.C.

Phil Gisler, the "whistling cowboy," left the Gang Ranch and cowboyed at Merritt, B.C. There he married

Ava, and they and their three children Quint, Clay, and Josie, reside in the Cherry Creek area outside of Kamloops. They still enjoy rousing times of good old-fashioned bluegrass music, with Phil on the guitar, and his talented friends on mandolins and banjoes.

Stephanie and John Schranz also reside in the Cherry Creek area outside of Kamloops. John's picture as a cowboy graced the front cover of the May 1994 issue of *B.C. Beef*, a picture taken sometime during his five and a half years as cowboss at the Ashcroft Ranch.

Hank (Henry) Krynen, who oversaw the construction of the corral system at Fosberry, bought a property and built a new house on West Fraser Road along the Fraser River, a stone's throw from our house. I could not believe my good fortune when we discovered that Hank and his wife, Julie, who nurses at the Cariboo Memorial Hospital in Williams Lake, would be our next door neighbors. We now are royally entertained by the true accounts of Hank's amazingly eventful life experiences. A seasoned and veteran cowboy, there is nobody he doesn't know, no trail he hasn't ridden, and no experience he hasn't survived.

Cowboy John Dodds lives west of Williams Lake in the Riske Creek area.

Robert Erickson is no longer employed by the Canadian Imperial Bank of Commerce. He runs a travel agency in Chilliwack, B.C.

Appendix

The following are excerpts from the silence agreement that the members of the Alsager family were forced to sign in order to be able to buy their farms back from the Canadian Imperial Bank of Commerce and the receivers. The entire agreement is twelve pages long. I'm sure many desperate people have been forced to sign similar, if not the same, documents. No one ever knows about it, for obvious reasons. I refused to sign this document—it is totally in conflict with the basic freedoms every Canadian citizen has under the Canadian Bill of Rights.

2.02 The Obligants hereby consent to and approve the accounts of Henfrey & Co. as submitted by it both in the Debenture Holder's Action and in the Saskatchewan Proceeding, and hereby abandon any previous complaints whatsoever that they have hitherto alleged or made concerning those accounts, including any complaints as to the emuneration of Henfrey & Co.

2.03 The Obligants waive the necessity, if any, of Henfrey & Co. preparing, submitting, delivering, or providing any further accountings, explanations, summaries or other documents in any way related to its actions as Receiver and Manager.

2.05 Erick Alsager and Edward Alsager hereby assume any and all of the liabilities directly related to the operations, maintenance and utilities of IKR Ltd. of Henfrey & Co. as Receiver and Manager of IKR Ltd. in any way connected with any contact made, assumed, or adopted by Henfrey & Co., or of its successors, under the agreements of which copies are annexed as Schedules "A" and "B" hereto, and Erick Alsager and Edward Alsager agree to

285

indemnify and save Henfrey & Co. and its successors harmless from all of the aforementioned liabilities.

2.06 The Obligants each hereby remise, release, and forever discharge the Bank and its employees, officers, agents, representatives, successors, and assigns of and from all manner of actions, causes of action, suits, debts, dues, accounts, bonds, covenants, contracts, claims, demands and complaints whatsoever which against the said parties they, or any of them, ever had, now has, or which any of their heirs, executors, administrators, assigns or successors hereafter can, shall or may have for or by reason of any case, matter of thing whatsoever existing up to the present time.

2.07 The Obligants each hereby remise, release, and forever discharge the Receiver, and each of them, and their employees, officers, agents, representatives, successors and assigns of and from all manner of actions, causes of action, suits, debts, dues, accounts, bonds, covenants, contracts, claims, demands and complaints whatsoever which against the said parties they, or any of them, ever had, now has, or which any of its heirs, executors, administrators, assigns or successors hereafter can, shall or may have for or by reason of any cause, matter of thing whatsoever existing up to the present time.

4.01 It is understood and agreed by each of the Obligants that it, he or she will not disclose or discuss with any person, company, or entity the terms of this agreement, except as may be strictly necessary in its, his or her dealings with financial and legal advisers and with tax authorities.

4.02 It is further understood and agreed by each of the Obligants that it, he or she will not hereafter make, circulate, publish or in any way communicate, orally or in writing, any allegation, suggestion, or complaint of any nature whatsoever respect, to any degree, any alleged dishonesty, incompetence, or negligence on the part of the Bank; its employees or agents; the Receiver, and its employees, agents, predecessors, or successors; the Obligants and their employees, agents, predecessors or successors.

5.04 It is further understood by each of the parties that all matters pertaining to AH Ltd. and IKR Ltd., the Debenture holder's Action, the Guarantor's Action, the Court of Appeal of B.C. Action CA008237 and the Saskatchewan Proceedings are to be treated with the utmost confidentiality. And further, the parties agree that it, he or she will not publish or in any way communicate the matters referred to in this clause to any party who is not a signatory to this agreement or a signatory to the agreement attached hereto as Appendix "A" and that should such publication or communication occur this agreement will become null and void and of no effect.